SAINT MAXIMUS THE CONFESSOR

Two Hundred Chapters on Theology

ST VLADIMIR'S SEMINARY PRESS
Popular Patristics Series
Number 53

The Popular Patristics Series published by St Vladimir's Seminary Press provides readable and accurate translations of a wide range of early Christian literature to a wide audience—students of Christian history to lay Christians reading for spiritual benefit. Recognized scholars in their fields provide short but comprehensive and clear introductions to the material. The texts include classics of Christian literature, thematic volumes, collections of homilies, letters on spiritual counsel, and poetical works from a variety of geographical contexts and historical backgrounds. The mission of the series is to mine the riches of the early Church and to make these treasures available to all.

Series Editor
BOGDAN BUCUR

Associate Editor
IGNATIUS GREEN

* * *

Series Editor
1999–2020
JOHN BEHR

SAINT MAXIMUS THE CONFESSOR

Two Hundred Chapters on Theology

Introduction, Translation, Notes, and Bibliography by
LUIS JOSHUA SALÉS

ST VLADIMIR'S SEMINARY PRESS
YONKERS, NEW YORK

Library of Congress Cataloging-in-Publication Data

Maximus, Confessor, Saint, approximately 580–662.

[Kephalia S' peri theologias kai tes ensarkou oikonomias tou Huiou Theou]

Two hundred chapters on theology and the incarnate economy of the Son of God / St Maximus the Confessor ; introduction, translations, notes, and bibliography by Luis Joshua Salés.

pages cm. — (Popular Patristics series, ISSN 1555–5755 ; number 53)

Original text in Greek; translation, introduction, and notes in English.

Includes bibliographical references and index.

ISBN 978-0-88141-518-6 (paper) — ISBN 978-0-88141-519-3 (electronic)

1. Theology. 2. Jesus Christ—Person and offices. 3. Incarnation. I. Salés, Luis Joshua. II. Maximus, Confessor, Saint, approximately 580–662. Kephalia S' peri theologias kai tes ensarkou oikonomias tou Huiou Theou. Greek. III. Maximus, Confessor, Saint, approximately 580–662. Kephalia S' peri theologias kai tes ensarkou oikonomias tou Huiou Theou. English. IV. Title.

BR65.M413K4 2015

230'.14—dc23

2015020250

COPYRIGHT © 2015 BY
ST VLADIMIR'S SEMINARY PRESS
575 Scarsdale Road, Yonkers, NY 10707
1-800-204-2665
www.svspress.com

ISBN 978–088141–518–6 (paper)
ISBN 978–088141–519–3 (electronic)
ISSN 1555–5755

PRINTED IN THE UNITED STATES OF AMERICA

For Ben Smith, in loving memory

Table of Contents

List of Abbreviations

Dionysius the Areopagite

C.h.	*De caelesti hierarchia* [The Celestial Hierarchies]
D.n.	*De divinis nominibus* [On the Divine Names]
Myst.	*De mystica theologia* [The Mystical Theology]

Evagrius of Pontus

Or.	*De Oratione* [Chapters on Prayer]
Cent.	*Centuriae* [The Chapters]
KG	*Kephalaia Gnostica* [The Chapters on Knowledge]
Pra.	*Praktikos* [The Man of Practice]

Gregory of Nazianzus

Or.	*Orationes* [The Orations]

Gregory of Nyssa

Anim. et res.	*De anima et resurrectione* [On the Soul and the Resurrection]
Hom. in Cant.	*Homiliae in Canticum Canticorum* [Homilies on the Song of Songs]
In Ps. 6	*In sextum Psalmum* [Commentary on the Sixth Psalm]
Virg.	*De virginitate* [On Virginity]
V. Mos.	*De vita Mosis* [On the Life of Moses]

Gregory Palamas

Cap.	*Capita physica, theologica, moralia et practica* [The One Hundred and Fifty Chapters]

Maximus the Confessor

Ac.	*Acta* [The Trial of Maximus the Confessor by Anastasius the Monk]
Ambig.	*Ambiguorum liber* [The Ambigua *or* Book of Difficulties]

Cap. theol.	*Capitum theologicorum et oeconomicorum duae centuriae* [Two Hundred Chapters on Theology]
Carit.	*Capitum de caritate quattuor centuriae* [Four Hundred Chapters on Love]
Ep.	*Epistulae* [The Letters]
Myst.	*Mystagogia* [Mystagogy]
Opusc.	*Opuscula* [Opuscules]
Qu. Dub.	*Quaestiones et Dubia* [Questions and Doubts]
Qu. Thal.	*Quaestiones ad Thalassium de scriptura* [Questions to Thalassius]

Origen of Alexandria

De princ.	*De principiis* [On First Principles]
Hom. in Gen.	*Homiliae in Genesim* [Homilies on Genesis]
Hom. in Lc.	*Homiliae in Lucam* [Homilies on Luke]
Hom. in Lev.	*Homiliae in Leviticum* [The Homilies on Leviticus]
Hom. in Num.	*Homiliae in Numeros* [The Homilies on Numbers]
Jo.	*Commentarii in evangelium Joannis* [The Commentary on John]

Philo of Alexandria

De somn.	*De somniis* [On Dreams]
De spec. leg.	*De specialibus legibus* [On Special Laws]
Leg. alleg. lib.	*Legum allegoriarum libri* [Commentary on Genesis 2 and 3]
Quis rer. div. her.	*Quis rerum divinarum heres sit* [Who is the Heir of Divine Things?]
Quod Deus sit immut.	*Quod Deus sit immutabilis* [The Unchangeableness of God]

Photius of Constantinople

Cod.	*Bibliothecae codices* [The Library]

Plato
Tim.   *Timaeus* [The Timaeus]

Plotinus
En.   *Enneades* [The Enneads]

Proclus Diadochus
In. Th.   *Institutio theologica* [The Elements of Theology]

Theophanes the Confessor
Chron.   *Theophanis chronographia* [The Chronography of
                  Theophanes the Confessor]

There is a difference in the numbering of the Psalms between the
Septuagint and the Masoretic Text; citations to the Psalms give the
LXX numbering first, then the MT sequence. The books of Samuel
and Kings are differently named and differently numbered between
the two texts; for these books, the first number is that of the MT, the
second that of the LXX.

Introduction

SAINT MAXIMUS THE CONFESSOR: HIS LIVES AND LIFE

Saint Maximus the Confessor was born around the year 580 in the middle of the reign of Constantine I Tiberius (578–582).[1] Given the scarce autobiographical details to be gleaned from his texts and the consistent factual unreliability of the two surviving biographies narrating his alleged life's events, precious little about his early days can be asserted with confidence. The first narrative (the *Syriac Life*) is commonly attributed to George of Resh'aina (d. ca. 680), who would have written it contemporaneously in Syriac.[2] It is primarily a defamatory biography invoking every cherished trope of infamy, including Maximus' unbecoming birth in Hesfin, Palestine, the adulterous offspring of a Samaritan and a Persian slave girl's high-run passions, orphaned, before the meaningful age of ten, and heretically brainwashed in no less than an Origenist monastery. Michael Exaboulites (10th c.), a Studite monk, wrote the second biography (the *Greek Life*). While it is substantially kinder than Resh'aina's and most of the later events in Maximus' life are accurate, the composer clearly had no information about the Confessor's birth and early years and considered it wise—if he was to say anything about the legendary monk's birth and upbringing—to fill his gaps in knowledge with the particularities of another saint in stature at

---

[1] When Maximus stood trial at Constantinople in 655 he noted he was 75 years of age; *Ac.*, PG 90.128C.

[2] Brock, Sebastian P., ed., *An Early Syriac Life of Maximus the Confessor*. In *Analecta Bollandiana*, 91 (1973), pp. 299–346.

least approximating the Confessor, for which Theodore the Studite seemed the logical choice.

But in their specific details both accounts cannot be trusted simply. As a result, Maximus' early life is often conjectured on the basis of a single particularly noteworthy achievement of his young adulthood—the first real known fact about his life accepted by contemporary scholarship. At thirty years of age he was appointed head of the imperial chancellery (*protoasekretis*) by the recently-crowned emperor Heraclius (r. 610–641).[3] The age of his appointment was as unusual as the particular political circumstances under which he assumed the position. Therefore, the possibilities available to the young Maximus were few and aid in sketching the following tentative scenario of his early life.

Following his murder of Emperor Maurice (r. 582–602), Phocas (r. 602–610) systematically annihilated key members of the Byzantine aristocracy with such cruelty, determination, and ferocity that the *deme*, or party, of the "Greens," who had initially aided him in Maurice's demise, turned on him, becoming so bold as to call him a drunkard and madman at a public horse race.[4] In response to what was doubtless an accurate assessment of his character, Phocas not only banned every member of the party of the Greens from holding any political or bureaucratic office, but left it to the trusty brutish nature of his prefect Kosmas to decapitate, mutilate, or tie up in a sack and cast in the sea those even suspected of involvement in political intrigues.[5]

At least half of the Byzantine aristocracy despised the man, not to mention *hoi polloi*, who well-nigh considered him Caligula reborn. His rule endured solely by the ambivalent support of the "Blues."[6] If Maximus held any political post under Phocas, the record

[3]Cf. Lackner, W. "Der Amtstitel Maximus des Bekenners." *Jahrbuch der Österreichischen Byzantinistik* 20, pp. 63–65 and Maximus' *Ep.* 12, PG 91.505B.

[4]Cf. Theophanes the Confessor, *Chron.*, p. 296.

[5]Cf. Theophanes the Confessor, *Chron.*, pp. 297–298.

[6]For further details about these events see Ostrogorsky, *History of the Byzantine State*, 83–85, and some of the relevant sources for which I am indebted and grateful

of his service—like everything else from that terror-stricken time—has not survived. It is, however, altogether unlikely that Maximus served under Phocas at all, since it would be incomprehensible that Heraclius would have seen fit to reward him for his service to the madman with promotion to one of the most prestigious and powerful positions in the Capital. It is more reasonable to take Maximus for a member of the Constantinopolitan aristocracy, in all likelihood connected with the Greens, and already enjoying a reputation for political refinement of such distinction that he would be the first logical choice to fill the recently vacated office of first secretary of the Empire, a position prestigious enough that several Patriarchs and the Emperor Anastasius II (r. 713–715) were drawn directly from it.

Moreover, numerous of his surviving letters are addressed to figures of considerable position with a tone of familiarity that belies more than the simple acquaintance of one who held the above-named office for a mere three years. They ring with the comfortable voice of the *parrhesia* that comes with the confident establishment of rank, the type that can utter tongue-in-cheek self-deprecation and walk away internally unscathed. His letters were placed in the illustrious hands of figures like Peter, the *strategos* (the supreme military and civil leader of the newly formed regional "themes") of Numidia; George,[7] the *eparch* (prefect) of Alexandria (who in time would make a failed claim to the throne);[8] a certain Constantine the *sakellarios* (secretary of the imperial treasury);[9] and John the *koubikoularios* (imperial chamberlain).[10]

If his ease of maneuvering in the innermost Byzantine aristocratic and political circles is insufficient to establish the man's birth

---

to him, Kulakovskij, J. "K kritike izvestij Feofana o poslednem gode pravlenija Foki," VV 21, (1914); Bury, *Later Roman Empire* II, p. 204ff; Pareti, "Verdi e azzurri ai tempi di Foca," *Studi Italiani di Filologia Classica* 19 (1912); Levčenko, M. "Venety i prasiny v Vizantii v V–VII vv," VV 26 (1947), 177ff.

[7]*Ep.* 12–14.
[8]*Ep.* 1.
[9]*Ep.* 24.
[10]*Ep.* 2–4, 10, 27.

into the higher echelons of Byzantine society, his astonishing knowledge of philosophy, mathematics, astronomy, natural sciences, classical literature, and patristic writings can leave precious little room to doubt that from childhood on he enjoyed an incomparably elite education to be had at that time solely within capitaline walls. The breadth of his knowledge possibly even indicates the famed educational curriculum of the University of Constantinople or direct and private tutoring by one of its renowned faculty; any of these options was for those alone whose financial roots ranged far through and deep under the venerable city mausoleums. If there is any gap in his education to be found, a few phrases in his writings disclose it, in which he refers to himself as "unschooled in the rules of style and inexperienced in their practical exercise."[11] The monk's statement is not the pretense of false humility. By Byzantine stylistic standards the majority of his prose would have been considered turgid or, in his own words, "rough-hewn phrases."[12]

The Confessor's power lies elsewhere, most especially in his exemplary precision with philosophical terminology and his consistent universal vision. Adam Cooper captures this aspect well by speaking of Maximus' "ability to contain the whole of his immense vision within each of its parts."[13] Since his time, his natural genius for coordinating a cacophonous maelstrom of opposing voices into a unified, gentle, and harmonious stream has only seen equivalent analogues in Saint Thomas Aquinas' cathedral-like *Summae*, John Donne's metaphysical conceits, and Johann Sebastian Bach's fugues. Perhaps the necessary cleverness required in politics to reconcile diverging extremes was good training for the young Maximus' upcoming prominence on the ecclesiastical, theological, and philosophical fronts.

Maximus left imperial service three years after his appointment and became a monk at a monastery in Chrysopolis (modern day

[11] *Ambig.* prol., DOML 28, p. 67. Also see *Myst.*, PG 90.660B.
[12] *Ambig.* prol, p. 67.
[13] Cooper, Adam. *Holy Flesh, Wholly Deified*, p. 15.

Üsküdar, Turkey), on the Anatolian (eastern) side of the Bosporus. It is not likely he would have considered his "death to the world" at the age of Christ's death insignificant, especially given his fascination with numerology.[14] Around 624 he transferred to the monastery of St. George in Cyzicus by the Sea of Marmara (modern day Erdek, Turkey). It seems it was there that he met the regional archbishop, John, with whom he discussed numerous difficult texts of Gregory of Nazianzus; their discussions would later form the basis of his most important work, the *Ambigua to John* (or *Earlier Ambigua*). His time at Cyzicus was highly productive, and it resulted in several notable works; among these are the *Questions and Doubts*, *Four Hundred Chapters on Love*, and *On the Ascetical Life*.[15]

In the meantime, the Byzantine-Sassanid War (602–628), begun by Phocas' deranged genius, raged on. In the early summer of 626 a substantial Persian force under Shahrbaraz slipped past the main Byzantine offensive led by Heraclius himself and made for Anatolia. Maximus, along with a considerable part of the community, fled the area. The monk spent the next few years wandering through Crete and Cyprus in the uncertainty of exile, but eventually he landed in Carthage around 628–630. Between this time and 633 he produced his greatest works, most notably the *Ambigua to John*, the *Questions to Thalassius*, the *Commentary on the Lord's Prayer*, the *Mystagogy*, and the present work, the *Two Hundred Chapters on Theology*.

Within the year the Monenergistic controversy broke out in full force,[16] shattering any hope Maximus had ever harbored for a life of quietude and the prolonged exercise of contemplation, for which he had likely resigned his imperial post.[17] In an effort to reconcile Chalcedonians and non-Chalcedonians, particularly in the problematic

---

[14]Cf. e.g., *Cap. theol.* 1.79 below and *Myst.* 5.

[15]See Sherwood, *An Annotated Date-List*, p. 59.

[16]The outbreak was not, as some perhaps might think, unprecedented, since as early as 617 Patriarch Sergius of Constantinople had already requested George Arsas to send him patristic florilegia in support of the one energy in Christ. See Sherwood, *An Annotated Date-List*, p. 9.

[17]Cf. *Ep.* 12, PG 91.505B.

region of Egypt, Cyrus of Phasis had been appointed in 631 as the Chalcedonian Patriarch of Alexandria and entrusted with religious reconciliation. By 633 he had produced a formula of agreement in nine headings, surviving in its entirety and quoted in full at the Sixth Ecumenical Council (less than favorably), whereby Chalcedonians and non-Chalcedonians were to be unified under Imperial orthodoxy by confessing "one activity in Christ." The first resistance came that same year, as Maximus' dear friend, Sophronius, an elderly monk who commanded noteworthy respect in every circle and who was elevated to the Jerusalem Patriarchate a year later, declared Cyrus' formula heretical.

When Cyrus disregarded him, Sophronius traveled to Constantinople and appealed to the Patriach Sergius in person. In the fall of 633 the Constantinopolitan Patriarch issued a *psephos*, strictly forbidding mention of either one or two energies (or activities) in Christ's person. Initially Maximus' approval of the *psephos* was qualified inasmuch as it halted Monenergistic advances,[18] but almost immediately thereafter he produced one of his most subtle, influential, and compelling antirrhetics, the *Ambigua to Thomas* (or the *Later Ambigua*), consisting in an epistolary prologue and five difficulties "deproblematized" at varying lengths. It is the last *ambiguum* that crowns the achievement: an extensive exegesis of Saint Dionysius the Areopagite's fourth *Epistle to Gaius*, quoted seriatim with theological elucidations, climaxing in an orthodox exposition of Christ's "*theandric* energy" in what is nothing less than an exemplary piece of writing of exceptional genius.

Patriarch Sergius wrote to Pope Honorius I explaining the *psephos* and its relative success, receiving a congratulatory epistle from the Roman See in return, which appended the most unfortunate concluding remark, speaking of the "one will of our Lord Jesus Christ." It was this phrase that was embedded in a further imperial edict of union published and circulated in 638, known as the *ekthesis*. To Sophronius and Maximus the idea of a single will (Monothelitism)

---

[18]*Ep.* 19, PG 91.593A.

in Christ seemed a natural yet untenable result of holding a single nature (Monophysitism) and a single activity (Monenergism) in Christ. The two original promoters of the *ekthesis*, Sergius and Honorius, both died in the fall of the same year and their successors, Pyrrhus and John IV respectively, were hesitant about accepting the *ekthesis*, albeit Pyrrhus eventually "came round" and saw things the Emperor's way. Sophronius had also died (December 9th) soon after ceding Jerusalem to the newly-emerging Islamic power in the south. The intellectual burden of championing the cause against the *ekthesis* fell to Maximus, who heard about it in 640. The successive Roman bishops were openly hostile to the *ekthesis*, including John IV, his successor Theodore, and especially Pope Martin I after him.

In 645 many enjoyed the privilege of witnessing the most famed dispute of the Monothelite controversy when Maximus, at the mature age of 65, took on Pyrrhus (now deposed from the Constantinopolitan bishopric) in an open debate about the "one will" of Christ. The Confessor's unwavering position held in that *Disputation* and elsewhere is that because activity and will belong to the level of nature, not person, Christ must be affirmed to have two energies and two wills if indeed he has two natures. Otherwise, he would be incomplete God and incomplete human, lacking what is proper to each,[19] and thereby falling short of the Chalcedonian givens.

The following year Maximus sailed to Rome to join ranks with the Latins, who had become a stronghold against the official imperial decrees they considered heretical. It is likely that while in Rome he wrote the *Opuscules* 1–3, each of them strongly tinged with the problematic of his time and refuting at length some of the fundamental aspects of the Monothelite axioms. The new emperor Constans II attempted a measure similar to Sergius' *psephos* and issued a *typos* to Pope Theodore, who, however, died before receiving it. He was succeeded by a zealous and uncompromising man, Pope Martin I, who in October of 649 convoked a Lateran Council attended by 105 bishops, mostly from North Africa and Italy. The

[19]Cf. *Opusc.* 7, PG 91.73CD.

Council proceeded against the Monenergistic and Monothelite heresies, condemning the *ekthesis* and the *typos*. Although the members were careful not to condemn the previous and present emperor, they nevertheless consigned Sergius, Cyrus, Pyrrhus, and then-ruling Constantinopolitan Patriarch Paul to a scathing *psogos* riddled with accusations of heresy. One of the most distinctive phrases from the Council is likely by Maximus' own mind, holding that Christ "wills and acts out our salvation."[20]

Constans II viewed the Lateran Council of 649 as an act not only of religious, but also of political, rebellion and ordered the exarch of Ravenna, Olympius, to arrest the Pope and take him to Constantinople to stand trial for treason and sedition. Olympius was himself ill-disposed to the Emperor and had been machinating plans for separation from the Eastern *themata* for some time. When he faced formidable popular resistance to Martin's arrest, he disregarded the imperial injunction and departed to Sicily. In 652, after Olympius' death, the new (and certainly more loyal) exarch Theodore Kalliopas arrested the Pope and escorted him to Constantinople, where he was found guilty of treason and complicity in Olympius' schemes. The enfeebled Pope was deposed, treated brutally, and exiled to the Crimean region, where he died in 655.

The same year Maximus stood trial at Constantinople in May. When the cross-examination was unable to implicate the monk in political intrigues, they attempted to condemn him in matters religious. His defense proved not only his staggering natural intellect, but his thorough understanding of the internal politics of the Byzantine court system. Maximus was exiled to Byzia (Thrace) "to cool his heels," as it were, and make him realize his theological position could severely endanger his bodily well-being. A year later, and after having held an open dispute there, the unwavering monk was brought back to be offered an opportunity to accept Constans' *typos*, which proved unsuccessful. Like most notable Church fathers, he was exiled a second time, this time to Perberis (Thrace) for six

---

[20]Cf. θελητικὸν καὶ ἐνεργητικὸν τῆς ἡμῶν σωτηρίας. *Op.* 28, PG 90.320C.

years. In 662 the frail monk, at the advanced age of 82, was made to stand trial at Constantinople again, where, judged by a Monothelite council, he was found guilty of heresy and political treason. As was characteristic of Byzantine law, the sentence for such crimes was severe. The Confessor's tongue and right hand were mutilated before he was exiled to Lazika, near the Black Sea, where he arrived on June 8th, was kept in the military prison of the fortress Schemarion, and died from his wounds a scarce two months later, on August 13th, 662. His feast is celebrated twice in the year, on January 21st for the translation of his relics and on August 13th, the day of his death, or, as he would have more likely interpreted it, his ability to experience in his whole being through blessed passivity the fullness of the divine energy.[21]

The Two Hundred Chapters on Theology:
The Text

The Greek Edition

The present text has come down to us under the full name *Two Hundred Chapters on Theology and the Incarnate Economy of the Son of God*, although it is likely the original title the Confessor gave it was expanded, as was frequently done in later Byzantine manuscript traditions. Although numerous works have long been honored by being mistakenly attributed to the Confessor, the authenticity of these *Chapters* is disputed by no recent or contemporary Maximian scholar. A critical edition is not yet available for this particular work.[22] This is only a working edition, the result of a comparison of

---

[21]Cf. *Ambig.* 7.12.

[22]The text itself, and especially the genre, tends not to treat critical editors kindly because of the frequency with which altogether different chapters appear in the manuscripts or, what is equally common, the ordering of the chapters might be significantly different. Moreover, the aphoristic and relatively popular nature of the "chapters genre," was accompanied by immense number of copies, making the direct

three prior editions (Combefis: 1675, Migne: 1860s, and a 1992 Thessaloniki reproduction of Migne's text; Migne's column numbering is preserved in the present work).

The "Chapters" Genre

Much can be said about the generic precedents of and literary forms related to the style of composition known as "chapters" (*kephalaia*),[23] but when the dust blown off the ancient tomes settles, it is the form of Evagrius of Pontus that emerges from the cloud as the man responsible for the distinctive features of the genre. A "chapter" quite literally means a "heading" and tends to be a short aphoristic phrase with a single theme for facility of memorization[24] and recitation. They tend to be organized by "decades" and sometimes by "centuries," although the freedom with which authors of the genre employed the numeration discourages any sweeping generalization. The decades and centuries do not even necessarily have to consist in sets of tens and hundreds, as Evagrius' own *Gnostic Chapters* evidences by falling a decade short in each of the six centuries for a total of 540 chapters. Moreover, the number of chapters can be taken from a numerical figure in Scripture or elsewhere and thereby keep conceptual association with it for stated or implied purposes. Evagrius, for example, uses the number 33 to echo the Savior's earthly years, or 153 to parallel the number of fish caught by Peter at Jesus' command. Caution, however, must be exercised when

and relevant witnesses, in what is an editor's bitter-sweet dream and nightmare, an unwieldy number of texts. Perhaps this is why the last person to promise a critical edition, F. Skutella, swerved away from it upon consideration of the evidence; nearly a century has passed since then. Cf. von Balthasar, *Kosmische Liturgie* (henceforth KL), p. 487.

[23]I wish to thank Joel Kalvesmaki for providing me with exemplary pieces of scholarship on the chapters genre that he compiled.

[24]See, for example, Maximus' *Carit.*, prol.: "I went through the holy fathers' phrases and picked out from them the sense contributing to my subject matter, gathering many things into a few words by way of summary for facility of memorization . . ."

approaching numerological meaning, since it is a two-edged sword: sometimes number is of the uttermost significance and at others it is entirely inconsequential; there is no hard, fast, and universal rule to determine which it might be.

By Maximus' time, writing in the genre of chapters was a way of situating oneself squarely within the logical and discursive apparatus of Evagrian spirituality, while retaining personal freedom to infuse the style with one's own idiosyncrasies and, perhaps, considerably different spiritual axioms. In some cases an author could employ the genre to indicate continuity with Evagrius by associating himself with the man's considerable spiritual heritage through the adoption of the same fundamental principles. In others, the composition was less laudatory and more corrective; by establishing a different spiritual axiom, a writer could hope to make the whole of the organic system converge around a different goal while losing none of its inbuilt vital force. In this way one could preserve the inherent worth of the genre and alter its course while not appearing to be an openly hostile adversary. Maximus decidedly belongs to the second category, of which the *Chapters on Love*, a "determined rewriting of nearly one hundred passages" from Evagrius' pen,[25] is a fine exemplar.

Only two works written in the "chapters" genre are indisputably by the Confessor's hand, the *Chapters on Love* and the *Chapters on Theology*. The *Chapters on Love* is the lengthier of the two by some six thousand words, but averages over twenty words less than its later counterpart. Both compositions—like any writing in the genre—are eclectic, dealing with wide-ranging topics often remotely organized around a unifying theme, to which each chapter contributes in a way appropriate to its conceptual content. Maximus himself rarely respects a thematic unit for an entire decade, although there are some noteworthy exceptions like the *Chapters on Theology* 1.1–1.10 and 1.50–1.60. As is characteristic of his work on the whole, certain topical threads are dropped at one point, only to be picked up at another, eventually weaving a complex tapestry, the logic

[25]Constas, DOML 28, p. viii.

and imagistic representation of which often remain accessible to Maximus' impenetrable intellect alone. If, however, anything can be asserted with any degree of confidence about the Confessor's composition in this form, it is that not a single chapter or word is out of its proper order.

The Date and Context of the Work

The date of the composition of the work can be pinpointed to the years after Maximus arrived in Carthage between 628 and 630, yet prior to the outbreak of the Monenergistic controversy in 633. At most, the window is of some five years, but there are compelling reasons internal to the text, impossible to be rehearsed at length and in detail here, to hold that the Confessor wrote it almost immediately before Monenergism appeared on the horizon, but after his successful conclusion of other key works, thereby narrowing the time frame to perhaps 632 and in no way later than the summer of 633. This brief window casts substantial light on the internal logic of the work as well as the semantic range of its lexical contents, since it happens to coincide with the monk's second and vastly most productive episode, adorned by his two masterpieces, the *Ambigua to John* and the *Questions to Thalassius*, and complemented by his two liturgical works, the *Mystagogy* and the *Commentary on the Lord's Prayer*.

The *Ambigua to John* is commonly held to have been finished by 630, and moving it past that year would summarily outrun the evidence. The *Questions to Thalassius* continues many of the *Ambigua's* central themes, particularly the cosmological centricity of the person of Jesus Christ, the relationship between virtue and the hominization of God and the deification of the human, and the attempt to make one's life align with God's *logos* (idea) of oneself. In the ninth century, Photius identified the striking similarity between the *Questions to Thalassius* and the *Chapters on Theology* in order to establish the authenticity of the latter.[26] In the twentieth century,

[26]*Cod.* 194, PG 103.651.

von Balthasar added that he considers the *Chapters on Theology* to be dependent on the *Questions to Thalassius*, and there is no self-evident reason to think otherwise.[27]

There is also compelling evidence to believe that Maximus had previously adapted the *erotapokriseis* (questions-answers) genre to the *kephalaia* (chapters) genre, during his first episode of theological production at Cyzicus. There, numerous themes first exposited by way of responses in the *Questions and Doubts* see a stylistic reframing into the *Chapters on Love*. While the two genres are loosely related, the impress each specific genre is intended to have on the reader is notably different. The questions-answers method recognizes explicitly the difficulty of a text and attempts to resolve the ambiguity. The chapters, while occasionally—albeit rarely—implying that a term or concept might be disputed,[28] try to reenact a very different scenario for the reader. The reader is automatically the student listening to wise sayings of an elder, or, perhaps even a pilgrim seeking out the renowned ascetic and begging for "a word." This restructuring transposes what had previously been a matter of dispute into an altogether different referential modality. Rather than inviting him to questioning and further examination of an issue, the codification into the chapters genre presupposes the findings already covered in the question-answer genre in order to offer an indisputable pearl of wisdom by force of the figure's inherent authority. And this is manifest if we consider that the chapters genre rarely justifies its assertions or elucidates an argument at length.

On the basis of the foregoing it might be suggested that the *Chapters on Theology* is a development of numerous threads largely begun in the *Ambigua to John* and made starkly explicit in the *Questions to Thalassius*. The correlation, however, goes further than mere similarity of content, as Photius properly identified, or even dependence, as von Balthasar rightly added. Rather, it seems that an idea latent throughout all of the works of the Confessor (the ὅσον

[27]Von Balthasar, *KL*, pp. 487–488.
[28]E.g., *Cap. theol.* 2.88–90.

. . . τοσοῦτον [hoson tosouton] or "as much as . . . so much" often also called the *tantum . . . quantum* principle)[29] finally crowned in the twenty-second question to Thalassius and gives us an entry point to reading the *Chapters on Theology*.

This question is an exposition of cosmic dimensions of his ὅσον . . . τοσοῦτον principle expressed previously in other works only in sketch form.[30] The twenty-second question to Thalassius is a relatively brief question attempting to elucidate the meaning of 1 Cor 10:11 by asking "If in the upcoming ages God will show us his wealth, how is it that we have [already] encountered the end of the ages?"[31] Maximus responds by dividing the ages in two, one leading to God's incarnation, one to human deification.[32] While there is a spatio-temporal aspect to each of these ages, the Confessor would not have reduced them merely to such a limited scope. Rather, the two ages can also refer to a single, unifying movement of divine condescension and human exaltation whereby the human experience of the divine and the divine experience of the human interweave and transcend the fabric of space and time.

Now, if we can hold that the Confessor had already written one set of centuries (*On Love*) drawing on conclusions arrived at through an *erotapokriseis* (*Questions and Doubts*), and add the close proximity of the composition of the *Questions to Thalassius* and the *Chapters on Theology* to each other (as also the chronological priority of the former), then it does indeed appear that the *erotapokriseis Questions to Thalassius* belongs together with the *Chapters on Theology*. Here the "two age" dynamic functions as the generally structuring principle of the *Chapters on Theology*. By taking a key

[29]Cf. Von Balthasar, *KL*, p. 277, Thunberg, *Microcosm and Mediator*, p. 127, and for elucidation, Larchet, *La divinisation de l'homme*, 376–382.

[30]The principle, of course, is not unique to Maximus, who takes it over from his dearly beloved Gregory of Nazianzus, who had already established the framework in the *Third Theological Oration* (*Or.* 29.19, SC 250, p. 218.7–8). The Confessor uses it repeatedly, e.g., *Ambig.* 3.5 (quoting Gregory directly), *Amb Io* 10.9, 60.4.

[31]Εἰ ἐν τοῖς αἰῶσι τοῖς ἐπερχομένοις δείξει τὸν πλοῦτον αὐτοῦ ὁ θεός, πῶς εἰς ἡμᾶς τὰ τέλη τῶν αἰώνων κατήντησεν; *Thal.* 22, SC 529, p. 262.2–4.

[32]*Qu. Thal.* 22, SC 529, p. 262.13–16.

feature and making it the operative spiritual axiom around which all other particles of the centuries' cosmos gravitate and by the power of which they derive their cohesion, the Confessor not only draws out the conclusions of *Thalassius*, but also creates space for a truth previously established in the discursive work to provide a meditative dynamic well-suited to the centuries genre. The "two age" principle divides the work into two centuries. The perfection of the ages is, in turn, mirrored in the completeness of the centuries, both consisting in exactly one hundred chapters, as opposed to Evagrius' six centuries of ninety chapters.[33] As mentioned earlier and as will be seen in this work, Maximus attached deep meaning to numerology. While there is no prologue or dedication at the outset of this treatise, Maximus previously had explicitly stated the significance of the number four in the composition of his *Chapters on Love*.[34] It would seem most implausible to argue that a man deeply invested in numerology would have written a work in two centuries, and then consider the number altogether inconsequential.

Moreover, beyond the fact that this work is divided into two centuries, the movement within each century reflects the "two age" dynamic relatively well. As was brought up in passing above, the "ages" do not refer exclusively, nor even primarily, to a linear spatio-temporal distension toward an end, but rather to a logical-categorical dimension of relation that would seek to describe how divine incarnation and human deification are a single magnetic attraction consisting of two ontologically different poles. God's hominization just is humanity's deification. Humanity's deification just is God's hominization. As such, the two-age dynamic in the *Chapters on Theology* is a representation of an aspect in divine-human relations that exceeds the four spatio-temporal dimensions. It is an impressive cosmic vision attempting to portray the paradox of God's hiddenness in his revelation and his revelation in his hiddenness. The Logos of God is seen most clearly where he remains most hidden.

[33]*Or.*
[34]*Carit.* prol.

And when he is most clearly apprehended he escapes the mind's eye. The *Chapters*, thus, are an intricate quest to find God in all things and all things in God. The Logos of God appears everywhere in the treatise, and nowhere; the virtues reveal him, the vices conceal him; the Logos is everywhere seen as invisible.

The foregoing should not, however, be taken to signify the irrelevance of the space-time distention, since there are certain indicators in the text that the first century corresponds to the age for God to be made human and the second to the age for humans to be made God, although both contain elements embodying the sense of the Gospel's words, that the "kingdom of God is [already] in you."[35] We do not find anywhere in the first century, for example, any overt Trinitarian passage, but we see a good many partial foreshadowings, glimpses, as it were. In fact, the first decade of the first century is very much an assertion of God's ineradicable distance and otherness from humans, denying even the category of relation in 1.7 as an applicable term between God and humanity. The radically apophatic opening, however, also sets up the need for and beginning of divine self-disclosure through the Incarnation. The second century, in turn, opens not only with the most extensive chapter in the entire treatise, but a chapter stating at length the Confessor's Trinitarian theology made possible solely on account of the Logos' embodiment in the first century.

Yet, Maximus is aware of the real metaphysical tension inhering in the fact that those who lived before the chronological advent of the Logos of God can themselves still be deified by participation in an atemporal reality not yet brought to term chronologically.[36] This is perhaps why we encounter a noticeably larger number of Old Testament references in the first century and many of those presented in the second century are seen in a very self-aware backward-looking modality. Yet it is equally true that the first century contains extensive sections on divine condescension and human deification, such

[35]Lk 17:21.
[36]Cf. 2.28–29.

as the extended section between 1.50 and 1.60. Many of these are oriented around the way in which virtue functions as a catalytic power to make of God a human through human deification. This is, as a matter of fact, one of the scriptural tropes Maximus often invokes[37] by referring to humans becoming the "dwelling place of God"[38] or, as he concludes his work, the dwelling place of the Logos.[39]

THE TWO HUNDRED CHAPTERS ON THEOLOGY: GUIDING IDEAS

While the full extent of each and every one of the dynamics at play in the work cannot be rehearsed in this brief introduction; a few have been provided below.

Radical Divine Transcendence and Limitation of Creation

This theme opens the *Chapters* and remains a constant throughout. Maximus resorts to numerous famed Aristotelian divisions and categories, including the recurrent triad of substance-potentiality-actuality and several of the categories, but especially the fourth (relation),[40] in order to assert the radical otherness and world transcendence of the divine. This idea in many ways functions as the best point of departure for numerous other themes, but particularly those which attempt to explain the logic behind the transcendent God and his incarnation as a concealed self-disclosure in the person of Jesus Christ.[41]

[37] 1.12, 2.5, 2.21, 2.71, 2.78.
[38] Eph 2:22.
[39] 2.100.
[40] E.g., 1.7 and 1.68
[41] See 1.1–1.10, 1.49–1.50, 1.56, 1.68, 1.69–1.70, 1.79, 1.81–1.84, 2.10, 2.60, 2.80, 2.85–2.86, 2.91.

*Cosmos as Veil of God: Apprehension of God through Knowing the
Logoi and Unknowing*

Taking over one of Dionysius' favorite tropes, the Confessor reworks
the Areopagite's content into a complex universal vision that attempts
to experience God through the *via negativa* and *via positiva*, though
he clearly thinks more of the former. Saint Maximus often discourages "apprehending" the Logos literally, since it is often only a veil
that one has clutched, not the Word himself (e.g., 1.62, 2.47, 2.60,
2.73). He acknowledges, however, that it is often necessary to begin
somewhere and thus concedes that for some it is best to begin with
parables and stories to get some sense about the Word of God (see
2.60). In other cases, he invokes the recurrent theme of experiencing God in a way appropriate to the one experiencing him (1.100,
2.27, and 2.56). But the emphasis decidedly falls on the Dionysian
sense of knowing God beyond mind by knowing nothing,[42] (see
especially 1.43, 2.8, 2.39, and 2.46) since, as the following idea covers,
God cannot be known by any thought, since thought is compound
and God simple.[43]

Uncreated-Created Distinction: Divine Simplicity, Cosmic Plurality

One of the centerpieces of the Confessor's *Chapters* is the juxta-
position of divine simplicity and cosmic plurality. Any being is
inherently manifold, even including the cognitive capacities, which
are by nature at least a duality, as explained in 1.82 and 1.83. This is
why Maximus furthers the Dionysian tradition of "unknowing" as
a way to experience the divine, since it is solely by progress in the
cultivation of passivity in the noetic faculties that one can ultimately
render oneself passive to the divine. This theme develops the radical

[42]*Myst.* 1.3.
[43]See 1.17, 1.21–1.22, 1.32, 1.54–1.56, 1.59, 1.61–1.63, 1.65–1.67, 1.70, 1.78–1.80, 1.82–
1.85, 1.88, 1.97, 2.4, 2.8–2.10, 2.13, 2.16–2.18, 2.23, 2.27–2.29, 2.33–2.34, 2.36, 2.39, 2.41,
2.43, 2.45–2.46, 2.50–2.51, 2.59, 2.61, 2.74–2.76, 2.80, 2.82, 2.98–2.100.

transcendence of the divine mentioned above by adding a qualified sense in which it is possible to experience it.[44]

Cosmic Sabbath: Mystical Contemplations of Scripture and the Practical and Contemplative Life

Maximus continues the theme of the passivity of the human by expounding at great length, particularly in the first century, a mystical contemplation of the Sabbath. The Sabbath has numerous meanings for the monk, but includes primarily the conclusion of virtuous deeds, rendering oneself fully passive to the divine, ceasing from one's natural energies or activities, coming to rest in God as the final end of every being, and the relation the practical and contemplative lives have to all of the foregoing. The "intermediate state"[45] as Maximus often refers to it, is the period that marks all activities of beings, but it is the aim of this stage to cultivate, through the practical and contemplative life, the dispositions that ultimately enable one to come to full rest by having the same activity as God, wherein one's natural energies come to a halt, as expressed in 1.43 and 1.47, and are moved solely by the divine power.

A substantial part of this theme develops a very particular method of scriptural interpretation that never shies away from finding numerous levels of meaning in the text. The Confessor often terms this a "spiritual"[46] sense of Scripture, drawing on the treasury of Alexandrian hermeneutics. It is the literal level that kills the Logos of God, depriving him of his vital force and underlying spiritual significance. It is the spiritual contemplation of a text that elevates the human beyond the mere "flesh" of the text, to the divine rationale or principle undergirding it. It is not, however, only the Scripture that is liable to spiritual interpretation, but everything in the universe.[47]

---

[44]See 1.82–1.83, 2.2–2.5, 1.67, 1.69, 1.82–1.83, 1.85, 2.1–2.5, 2.16, 2.18, 2.20, 2.22, 2.71, 2.73, 2.81–2.82.

[45]Cf. 1.2–1.5.

[46]E.g., 1.98, 2.14–2.15.

[47]See 1.35–1.70, 1.71, 1.72, 1.79, 1.89, 1.90–1.97, 1.99, 1.100, 2.5, 2.6, 2.14, 2.31, 2.32,

Transformation and Presence: Seeing the Logos

Saint Maximus expands the "spiritual" vision of the human to encompass the totality of creation, where the Word of God can often be seen by those who have the ability to witness his transformation.[48] The "gnostic" is the human who is able to transcend the merely fleshly level of the cosmos, seeing in all things the hidden wisdom of God. Part of the Confessor's genius in this particular set of propositions is that the penetrating theological vision that enables the human to see God in all things is the same movement whereby they reflect to others that which they see, as argued in 1.79. Such contemplations allow the human to transcend all things after God[49] by seeing the Logos of God within them.[50]

Asceticism and Ascent: Virtues and Vices, Similarity and Dissimilarity to God

This is by far the most dominant idea in the *Chapters*, and thus Maximus stands squarely in the ascetic tradition that attempted to provide a coherent and rather comprehensive elucidation of the virtues, both as character states taking place in the human, cultivated by the practical life, and as participation in divine principles of goodness whereby the human was transformed into God by grace. The virtues were always of great importance to Maximus, who elsewhere had called Jesus Christ their very substance.[51] The virtues are that principle by the power of which humans are assimilated to the divine simplicity, since the virtues cannot be at odds with one another, given that their very substance is divine, thus transforming the mind into a unified center of action having no other *operative* powers (i.e., the passions) to draw the human away from divine contemplation.

2.42, 2.53, 2.62, 2.63, 2.64, 2.65, 2.67, 2.68, 2.69, 2.70, 2.80, 2.89, 2.90, 2.91, 2.96.
[48]Cf. 2.41.
[49]Cf. 1.70.
[50]See 1.70, 1.79, 2.13–2.15, 2.37–2.47, 2.57–2.58, 2.60, 2.73–2.74, 2.76, 2.82.
[51]*Ambig.* 7.22.

The virtues thus aid in that character state the Confessor termed "dispassion," which is not apathy or lack of emotion, but rather the absence of contrary forces at work in the human mind to divide it on the level of mode of existence. This theme would be of crucial import later on in the Monothelitic controversy, since Maximus' fundamental understanding of the human will vis-à-vis its psychological capacities relied ultimately on a precise grasp of what constitutes human nature and what does not. He could argue for the Savior's dispassion, for example, by clarifying that the state of dispassion is not an unqualified annihilation of the human emotive ability, but, rather, its operation in line with the parameters of virtue. To operate in line with virtue is therefore an imitation of Christ by "putting on the mind of Christ"[52] and as such a participation in the divine.

In the foregoing we can appreciate one of the most distinctive features of Maximus' aretology, namely, the fact that it has two foci. On the one hand, the Confessor is a true advocate of the ascetical tradition that attempted through introspection to analyze and grasp the innermost workings of the human soul in respect of the virtues and vices. On the other hand we can see the monk's curious, yet consistent, ability to see the ripple effects of a single human's underlying character state or disposition in cosmic proportion. For him there was no clear dividing line between ethics and metaphysics, since the former was simply the working out of the latter.[53]

Deification and the Principle of Reciprocity

Like most of Maximus' works, the *Chapters on Theology* provides a vision of deification of substantial complexity. Developing themes already seen in the *Ambigua to John* and the *Questions to Thalassius*,

[52]Cf. 2.83.

[53]See 1.11, 1.13–1.16, 1.18–1.20, 1.23–1.30, 1.33, 1.52–1.53, 1.55, 1.57–1.59, 1.61, 1.64–1.65, 1.72–1.78, 1.80–1.81, 1.85–1.88, 1.94–1.100, 2.6–2.9, 2.11–2.12, 2.16–2.18, 2.21, 2.26, 2.28–2.29, 2.31–2.34, 2.37–2.38, 2.40, 2.43–2.44, 2.48–2.49, 2.51, 2.53, 2.55, 2.58, 2.65–2.68, 2.70, 2.72, 2.74, 2.77–2.79, 2.83–2.84, 2.87–2.88, 2.94–2.95, 2.97–2.98, 2.100.

the *Chapters on Theology* is perhaps distinguished by the intricacy with which it interweaves scriptural hermeneutics, the natural energies of humans, the Aristotelian metaphysical divisions of nature, and deification. Although not unique to the *Chapters on Theology*, the idea of human passivity to the divine reaches a climax here not paralleled by any other of the saint's works. Almost an entire third[54] of the first century is set up as a contemplation of deification vis-à-vis the Sabbath in its multiform variety. The cosmic Sabbath enacted through the human being seems to be an expansion on *Ambiguum* 41, which discourses at considerable length about the cosmic dimensions of the human being (ἄνθρωπος—*anthrōpos*) and his actions in universal perspective. As such, many passages concerning deification also show a highly sophisticated understanding of the principle of reciprocity (ὅσον . . . τοσοῦτον), mentioned above, and similar formulas.[55] Perhaps one of the most interesting elements of the Confessor's language with respect to deification is the consistency with which he uses the aorist tense for human actions that align with God's will. It is not unlikely the Confessor attempts to yoke virtuous human actions with a divine quality by using the tense of simplicity and boundlessness (ἀόριστος) with which he had described God toward the very beginning of the work in 1.2. In this way, humans also rest with God on the Sabbath.[56] One of the finest examples of Maximian genius in this respect can be found in 1.54.[57]

The Dwelling Place of God

Finally, one of the key themes—the one with which the Confessor chooses to close the work—is the multi-level interpretation whereby humans are said to be the "dwelling place of God."[58] The idea is an

[54] 1.35–1.70.
[55] E.g., 2.23, 2.36, etc.
[56] 1.57.
[57] See 1.31, 1.47, 1.54, 1.60, 1.61, 2.7, 2.21, 2.23, 2.24, 2.25, 2.27, 2.30, 2.31, 2.36, 2.37, 2.76, 2.82, 2.88.
[58] See Eph 2:22.

expansion on deification by clarifying what it means that humans are the body of Christ, the temple of the Spirit, etc. If it is correct to take the "two-age" dynamic derived from *Questions to Thalassius* 22 as the structuring principle of the *Chapters of Theology*, then it makes good sense that the monk would develop the idea of the "dwelling place of God" rather substantially.

There are two general senses in which the monk expounds on the theme of the divine dwelling in the earthly. The more evident of the two is the Incarnation of the Logos of God in the person of Jesus Christ, which brings about the eternal plan of God the Father and accomplishes the salvation of humanity. But there is a different sense in which the Word of God comes to dwell in the earthly, namely, through the viaticum of virtuous humans. We see here an expansion of another theme from the *Ambiguum* 7.23 and the *Questions to Thalassius* 22, that God wills to be incarnate in all things, and is so in the worthy.[59] Perhaps it was fortuitous that Maximus had such a highly sophisticated understanding of the relationship between divine and human energies, where the two are able to coexist with each other without requiring the other's annihilation, since it was precisely this that formed the center of the Monenergistic controversy looming large on the horizon even as Maximus concluded this treatise.[60]

SOURCES AND APPROPRIATIONS

As indicated in the section concerning the Confessor's life, Saint Maximus had enjoyed an unparalleled education in nearly every possible field and it is therefore often difficult to pinpoint the exact sources from which he may be drawing. Did he know Origen's and Evagrius' writings first-hand or had he only come across excerpts being quoted in the aftermath of the anathematization of their writ-

[59]Cf. Larchet, *La divinisation de l'homme*, p. 661.
[60]See 1.12, 2.21, 2.27, 2.28, 2.35, 2.36, 2.47, 2.71, 2.78, 2.80, 2.84, 2.88, 2.91, 2.92, 2.94, 2.95, 2.97, 2.100.

ings? Had his knowledge of Philo of Alexandria come to him through a watered-down transmission of some of his key ideas? Some of these questions are difficult to address and many more insinuate themselves in respect of the man's work. Von Balthasar concluded on the basis of his source analysis[61] that the Confessor had in fact read all of these authors directly, and I am inclined to agree with him to some considerable extent.[62] The non-problematic sources, of course, he would have learned, like any other good aristocratic Byzantine boy, from youth. That would have included the writings of the great Cappadocians, Clement of Alexandria, Athanasius of Alexandria, and many others. Yet, it is clear in this work that Maximus has drawn distinctive ideas from only a handful of characters and has appropriated them into his own universal vision.

Maximus employs the writings of Dionysius,[63] Gregory of Nyssa,[64] Origen,[65] Philo,[66] and Evagrius[67] in numerous and fascinatingly interconnected ways. He had a remarkable ability for coordinating the wisest thoughts and most functional systems of all of these, whether cosmic, exegetical, spiritual, eschatological, etc. and to bring them under the compelling power of his own cosmic perspective. Thus, he is able to take the radical divine transcendence encountered in Dionysius, and particularly his concept of "unknowing," and somehow yoke it into a functional team with Philo's and Origen's scriptural-exegetical methods in order to develop a Sabbath of cosmic proportions, where the human stands as the mediating center between extremes.[68]

He also revisits many other themes covered in some of his previous works. The common Byzantine trope of Pharaoh's heart being

[61]*KL*, pp. 482–643. There is no English translation of this section of the book.
[62]*KL*, p. 506.
[63]See 1.2, 1.4, 1.5, 1.6, 1.43, 1.47, 1.50, 1.82, 2.1, 2.3, 2.39.
[64]See 1.12, 1.85, 1.88, 1.99, 1.100, 2.5, 2.56, 2.80, 2.86.
[65]See 1.12, 1.34, 1.36, 1.65, 1.89, 1.92, 2.18, 2.20, 2.22, 2.37, 2.43, 2.56, 2.64, 2.85, 2.86, 2.88.
[66]See 1.12, 1.17, 1.22, 1.36, 1.88.
[67]See 1.35, 1.40, 1.51, 1.59, 1.72, 1.78, 2.2, 2.9, 2.68, 2.90.
[68]Cf. *Ambig.* 41.

hardened by God as a matter of free will sees the Confessor's own articulation in a passage (1.12) drawing from what Philo, Origen, and the Nyssen did with it. At the same time, the text is not concerned with the "depoisoning" (in von Balthasar's memorable phrase)[69] of Evagrian spirituality, a deed achieved in the *Chapters on Love*, but it is more at ease in incorporating some of Evagrius' most beautiful insights. When we step back from the work as a whole and attempt to take in what the Confessor did in a mere two hundred chapters, there is little doubt that his accomplishment was the refined product of a man at the zenith of his career, a man able to take the very best of every theologian, philosopher, and master of spirituality into the comprehensive scope of his universal vision, and make the voices of those whom history and politics called sworn adversaries ring together in an incomprehensible but shudderingly beautiful harmony.

Notes on the Translation

The English text presented here is not exactly a translation, since the language of the Confessor relies on a constant multivalent dimension that cannot be captured by any rendition in English (or any other language, for that matter). To translate a Maximian sentence with a single phrase is like asking a light technician to show all of the images of a Denis Ditinyuk painting (elaborated with paints that appear or disappear based on the light spectrum) using a single-spectrum light bulb.[70] In consequence, I have supplemented the text with footnotes at places where I considered that something would have been irremediably lost in the translation. I have attempted to make this text as accessible as is reasonable for a man of the writing style and depth of Maximus. While readability and consistency are the ultimately desirable ends of any translation, they are not always possible without being unfaithful to the underlying Greek. Since

[69]*KL*, p. 506.
[70]See https://www.youtube.com/watch?v=wy_VzYSQ3gQ [accessed May 27, 2015].

Maximus made up a number of words in the text, I have taken similar liberties, so the reader should not be surprised by the presence of certain English words that might not be found in dictionaries. There are, moreover, several distinctive terms I have rendered in particular ways, as follows.

The term ἄναρχος (*anarkhos*)[71] I have consistently rendered as "without first principle," but not without some remorse. The term is inherently philosophical, consisting merely of the denial of an ἀρχή (*arkhē*), a first principle. But a "first principle" also means "beginning" and "origin" simultaneously and, as such, conveys numerous aspects that cannot all be conjured up in English by a single term.

The term δύναμις (*dynamis*)[72] I have rendered in numerous ways, since it can have different context-based meanings. The four general renditions I have employed are "power," "potentiality," "capacity," and "faculty." This term functions to indicate vital force and its connatural abilities,[73] potentiality in opposition to actuality within a clearly Aristotelian framework,[74] as inherent capacities the soul or body have,[75] and similarly, but not exactly identically to the foregoing, to designate faculties able to carry out certain tasks.[76]

The term πῶς (*pōs*), meaning most basically "how," was by Maximus' time a manner of qualifying any kind of assertion. Thus, it seemed most appropriate to me to render the term as "qualified" when used in that particular way.[77]

The infinitive verb εἶναι (*einai*) can also have a non-verbal function (which Maximus consistently uses), meaning "being," that is, anything that *is* in any sense of the word. This includes everything and anything apart from God (and evil, which is a

[71]E.g., 1.1, 1.5, 1.69, 2.1.
[72]E.g. 1.1, 1.3, 1.4, 1.15, 1.33, 1.49, 1.66, 1.81, 1.82, 1.92, 1.98, 1.100, 2.1, 2.15, 2.18, 2.27, 2.34, 2.38, 2.42, 2.67, 2.77, 2.83, etc.
[73]E.g., 1.1.
[74]E.g., 1.3, 1.4.
[75]E.g., 1.82, 1.100.
[76]E.g., 2.83.
[77]E.g. 1.4.

privation of being). I have had to translate the term as either "being" or "existence," depending on what aspect the Confessor might be highlighting.[78]

One particular oddity that needs explanation is my curious rendering of the term φυσικῶς (*physikōs*), an adverb, through an adverbial phrase, instead of simply the typically corresponding adverb. I have often translated φυσικῶς as "in nature," rather than "naturally" for several reasons, but the most important is that the Confessor institutes a dynamic in this treatise between the God-given nature that corresponds with a being and the supernatural grace of deification, whereby the natural characteristics are sublimated. While "naturally" would largely be correct, there are some cases where it is clear the Confessor means by φυσικῶς something that is particular to the sphere of nature; for this "sphere" I have considered the locative preposition "in" to be an appropriate rendition not adequately grasped by the English adverb.

Based on long-standing tradition, I have rendered the term οὐσία (*ousia*) as "substance." There is no real word in English that conveys both the dynamic sense of οὐσία as "being" and also as a reality from which principles and concepts can be derived or abstracted for the purposes of analysis.

The term ἐνέργεια (*energeia*) can have numerous meanings in this text. Some are clear references to the Aristotelian triad of substance-potentiality-actuality, whereas others refer to activities or operations proper to a human, yet not easily rendered by "operation" or "activity." The context has had to dictate the translation of this term. Thus: "actuality" at 1.2, "activity" at 1.46, "accomplishment" at 1.57, "performance" at 1.90 and 2.9, "commission" at 1.95, and "perpetration" in 2.67.

Without a doubt the most difficult term to translate is the word λόγος (*logos*). The term can often refer to the Word of God, to reason, to a discourse, to an argument, etc. Maximus, however, has a famed doctrine of the "logoi" of creation. When it is clear or mostly

[78]Cf. 1.1

certain that he is using the word in this way, I have simply transliter-
ated the Greek into *logos* or *logoi*. Other uses are context-based, such
as "rationality" at 1.13, "Scripture" at 1.23, "phrase" in 1.25, "principle"
in 1.78, "public discourse" in 1.83, "voice" at 1.95, "rationale" in 2.16,
"reason" at 2.21, "sense" in 2.74, and "treatise" at 2.85.

The term πότε (*pote*) can have various meanings, but only one
of them, which I translate as "when," needs explanation here. In 1.1
and 1.5 the term seems to be a direct reference to Aristotle's sixth
category. It is not entirely correct to render the term as "temporal"
or "when," since these terms convey a rather different understanding
in contemporary minds than the Confessor (and Aristotle) meant by
them, but there are no better terms. The category of "when," refers
not to time or temporality proper, but rather to the nature of the
relationship of a being to this category. As such, the reader should
be advised that the idea of "temporal" expresses a being's relation to
an existential category, not simply an abstract idea.

One of the translations most likely to be contested is my translation of αἰών (*aiōn*) as "eternity" in a few places, like 1.5. This
"eternity" is not to be confused with God's radically transcendent
eternity. The term αἰών is built from ἀεί and ὄν, that is, "ever-being"
and in Maximus particularly it refers to a non-diastemic, non-dis-
tended reality into which beings can be admitted. It preserves their
distinctive particularities or natural limitations in what might—not
without some hesitation—be called an "ideal" way grounded in the
divine will.[79]

Finally, a word on two unusual constructions:

Goods: I have preferred to translate ἀγαθά (*agatha*) and its
plural derivatives as "goods" over the perhaps more common rendering "good things." The reason is that "things" may give the false
impression that these "good things" are, indeed, "things," which

---

[79]See Constas, DOML 28, p. 488, note 52: "The age (*aion*) is the 'eternity' of created beings, a transcendent dimension that is distinguished from the eternity that is
proper to God alone. It is an intermediate state between divine eternity and ordinary
time, being a kind of synthesis of the two, enabling the divinized creature to exist in
divine infinity without obliterating the limits proper to created beings."

they are not. Rather, they are a pluralization of the ancient Greek concept of "the Good" that becomes in some sense manifold in its self-disclosure in the universe. But the "goods" are not *any thing* in the universe; rather, *every thing* in the universe owes both the fact of its existence and the manner of its subsistence to these "goods," but nothing in the universe *is* these goods. Rather, all that is is what it is and is as it is by its analogical manner of participation in them. The forms of the goods are self-subsisting (cf. 2.17) and preexist in God (cf. 2.90), already being before all time (cf. 1.48–1.50). It is altogether likely that the goods are nearly interchangeable with Maximos' understanding of the *logoi*.

Contemplations: The noun "contemplation" is rarely encountered in the plural in English, perhaps because an unwritten assumption of early Platonic and late scholastic thought holds that contemplation is of a singular nature and indistinct. While this latter especially might have formed the logical basis for the common linguistic exclusion of "contemplations" in English, it would be fundamentally misleading to Maximus' thought always to render contemplation in the singular, since he clearly understands it as a varying activity, practice, or event. This is to say that there is no one "set" form of contemplation nor a single contemplation by reference to which all others are determined. Rather, as Maximus beautifully says: "'The house of God' is the knowledge consisting in many and diverse contemplations, in accordance with which God, indwelling the soul, fills up the cup of wisdom" (2.78). He also refers to different contemplations, such as ethical, natural, and theological contemplations (2.79). But different contemplations may also be a reference to the numerous ways in which humans experience God differently, even depending on their own stage in the spiritual life (cf. 1.17–1.18, 1.70, 1.83, and especially 2.20).

Luis Joshua Salés
New York, NY
August 13th, 2014
Feast of Saint Maximus the Confessor

[PG 90.1084] ΕΚΑΤΟΝΤΑΣ α'

1 Εἷς Θεός, ἄναρχος, ἀκατάληπτος, ὅλην ἔχων τοῦ εἶναι τὴν δύναμιν διόλου· τὴν πότε καὶ πῶς εἶναι παντάπασιν ἀπωθούμενος ἔννοιαν, ὡς πᾶσιν ἄβατος καὶ μηδενὶ τῶν ὄντων ἐκ φυσικῆς ἐμφάσεως διεγνωσμένος.

2 Ὁ Θεὸς οὐκ ἔστι δι᾽ ἑαυτόν, ὡς ἡμᾶς εἰδέναι δυνατόν, οὔτε ἀρχή, οὔτε μεσότης, οὔτε τέλος, οὔτε τι τὸ σύνολον ἕτερον τῶν τοῖς μετ᾽ αὐτὸν φυσικῶς ἐνθεωρουμένων· ἀόριστος γάρ ἐστι καὶ ἀκίνητος καὶ ἄπειρος ὡς πάσης οὐσίας καὶ δυνάμεως καὶ ἐνεργείας ὑπερέκεινα ἀπείρως ὤν.

3 Πᾶσα οὐσία τὸν ἑαυτῆς ὅρον ἑαυτῇ συνεισάγουσα, ἀρχὴ πέφυκεν εἶναι τῆς ἐπιθεωρουμένης αὐτῇ κατὰ δύναμιν κινήσεως. Πᾶσα δὲ φυσικὲ πρὸς ἐνέργειαν κίνησις, τῆς μέν οὐσίας μετεπινοουμένη, προεπινοουμένη δὲ τῆς ἐνεργείας, μεσότης ἐστίν ὡς ἀμφοῖν κατὰ τὸ μέσον φυσικῶς διειλημμένη. Καὶ πᾶσα ἐνέργεια, τῷ κατ᾽ αὐτὴν

First Century

1.1   God is one, without first principle, incomprehensible, throughout being the total potentiality of being; he excludes absolutely the concept of temporal or qualified existence,[1] since <he is> inaccessible to everyone and not discernible to any being as a result of natural reflection.

1.2   God is not in himself—inasmuch as is possible for us to know[2]—a first principle, nor an intermediate state, nor an end, nor any other of those concepts that are in nature observed in what is after him, for he is indefinite, immobile, and infinite,[3] since he is infinitely beyond substance, potentiality, and actuality.[4]

1.3   Each substance, including its own definition in itself, is a first principle by nature productive of the movement discerned in potentiality in it. Each natural motion toward actuality, conceptualized as after substance, yet prior to actuality, is an intermediate state, since in nature it divides both as that which mediates between them. And

---

[1]See *Ambig.* 10.91–92, particularly n. 68.

[2]These words and the following are distinctive echoes of Dionysius the Areopagite's *Myst.* 5.

[3]These three negations are negations of the distinctive properties of substance, potentiality, and actuality. Substance must be defined, potentiality realized through motion, and actuality accomplished by finitude.

[4]Substance (οὐσία), potentiality (δύναμις), and actuality (ἐνέργεια) form a famous and paradigmatic Aristotelian threefold metaphysical division of nature (φύσις) elucidated in book 9 of Aristotle's *Metaphysics* and traditionally corresponding with the first principle, beginning, or origin (ἀρχή), the intermediate state (μεσότης), and the end (τέλος), although Maximus will play with their relationship in significant ways, particularly in 1.4 and 1.50–60, as well as clarifying his position in this regard in *Ambig.* 20.2 and *Opusc.* 1, PG 91.33B, this latter work many years after the composition of this present treatise.

λόγῳ φυσικῶς περιγραφομένη, τέλος ἐστὶ τῆς πρὸ αὐτῆς κατ᾽ ἐπίνοιαν οὐσιώδους κινήσεως.

4 Οὐκ ἔστιν ὁ Θεὸς οὐσία, κατὰ τὴν ἁπλῶς ἢ πῶς λεγομένην οὐσίαν, ἵνα καὶ ἀρχὴ· οὔτε δύναμις κατὰ τὴν ἁπλῶς ἢ πῶς λεγομένην δύναμιν, ἵνα καὶ μεσότης· οὔτε ἐνέργεια, κατὰ τὴν ἁπλῶς ἢ πῶς λεγομένην ἐνέργειαν, ἵνα καὶ τέλος ἐστὶ τῆς κατὰ δύναμιν προεπινοουμένης οὐσιώδους κινήσεως. Ἀλλ᾽ οὐσιοποιὸς καὶ ὑπερούσιος ὀντότης, καὶ δυναμοποιός καὶ ὑπερδύναμος ἵδρυσις, καὶ πάσης ἐνεργείας δραστικὴ καὶ ἀτελεύτητος ἕξις· καί, συντόμως εἰπεῖν, πάσης οὐσίας καὶ δυνάμεως καὶ ἐνεργείας, ἀρχῆς τε καὶ μεσότητος καί τέλους ποιητική.

5 [1085] Ἡ ἀρχὴ καὶ ἡ μεσότης καὶ τὸ τέλος τῶν χρόνῳ διαιρετῶν εἰσι γνωρίσματα—εἴποι δ᾽ ἄν τις ἀληθεύων καὶ τῶν ἐν αἰῶνι συνορωμένων. Ὁ μὲν γὰρ χρόνος, μετρουμένην ἔχων τὴν κίνησιν, ἀριθμῷ περιγράφεται· ὁ αἰών δέ, συνεπινοουμένην ἔχων τῇ ὑπάρξει

each actuality, in nature circumscribed by its corresponding *logos*, is the end of the substantializing movement conceptually prior to it.

1.4   God is neither a substance, meant as unqualified or qualified substance, and therefore not a first principle; nor a potentiality, meant as unqualified or qualified potentiality, and therefore not an intermediate state; nor an actuality, meant as unqualified or qualified actuality, and therefore not the end of the substantializing motion that is conceived prior in terms of potentiality.[5] He is, however, a substance-causing reality while beyond substance, a potentiality-causing ground while beyond potentiality, and the effecting and unending state of each actuality; so, to speak concisely, he is causative of each substance, potentiality, and actuality, also of each first principle, intermediate state, and end.[6]

1.5   The first principle, the intermediate state, and the end are identifying marks of things divided by time—and one could add, speaking truly, even of things seen as a unity in eternity.[7] For time, which is measured motion,[8] is circumscribed by number, whereas eternity, possessing the category of "when"[9] as conceptualized together with

[5]Maximus here qualifies only what he means by "end" in order to indicate that the actuality of human potentialities is not divine, but he breaks the traditional correspondence between the two terms, by his qualification indicating a difference between the natural realization of human potentialities and laying the ground for supernatural deification, the ultimate human end beyond any natural actualization of potentialities. See *Ambig.* 10.42–49. Gregory Palamas expounds on this particular point in *Tri* 3.1.31.

[6]The parallel to Dionysius the Areopagite's *D.n.* 5.5 is striking.

[7]Maximus' position is distinctive. He is referring to a very particular understanding of the *aeon* as "eternal being" (ἀεὶ ὄν), which is a dimension that transcends the present human condition but is also not identical with the eternity commonly ascribed to God. The natural limits of humanity are preserved, while permitting them to endure without the diastemic nature of time. See Dionysius the Areopagite, *D.n.* 5.10.

[8]This was one of the most basic definitions of time. See Plato, *Tim.* 38a–c; Aristotle, *Phys.* 218b21–222a9; Plotinus *En.* 3.7.2, LCL 442, p. 298; Dionysius the Areopagite, *D.n.* 10.3, PTS 33, pp. 214–216; and Maximus *Ambig.* 10.73 and *Qu. Thal.* 65, CCSG 22, p. 285.532ff.

[9]Maximus is using Aristotle's sixth category, or predicate, *Cat.* 4, 1b26, as

τὴν πότε κατηγορίαν, πάσχει διάστασιν, ὡς ἀρχὴν τοῦ εἶναι λαβών. Εἰ δὲ χρόνος καὶ αἰών οὐκ ἄναρχα, πολλῷ μᾶλλον τὰ ἐν τούτοις περιεχόμενα.

6 Εἷς καὶ μόνος κατὰ φύσιν ἀεὶ κυρίως ἐστὶν ὁ Θεός, ὅλον τὸ κυρίως εἶναι κατὰ πάντα τρόπον ἑαυτῷ περικλείων ὡς καὶ αὐτοῦ τοῦ εἶναι κυρίως ὑπέρτερος. Εἰ δὲ τοῦτο, οὐδαμῶς οὐδὲν οὐδαμοῦ τῶν εἶναι λεγομένων τὸ σύνολον ἔχει τὸ κυρίως εἶναι. Οὐκοῦν οὐδὲν αὐτῷ τὸ παράπαν ἐξ ἀϊδίου συνθεωρεῖται κατ᾽ οὐσίαν διάφορον, οὐκ αἰών, οὐ χρόνος, οὐδέ τι τῶν τούτοις ἐνδιαιτωμένων. Οὐ γὰρ συμβαίνουσιν ἀλλήλοις πώποτε τὸ κυρίως εἶναι καὶ οὐ κυρίως.

7 Ἀρχὴ πᾶσα καὶ μεσότης καὶ τέλος, εἰς ἅπαν τὴν σχετικὴν δι᾽ ὅλου κατηγορίαν οὐκ ἤρνηται· Θεὸς δέ, καθόλου πάσης σχέσεως ὑπάρχων ἀπειράκις ἀπείρως ἀνώτερος, οὔτε ἀρχή, οὔτε μεσότης, οὔτε τέλος εἰκότως ἐστίν, οὐδέ τι τὸ σύνολον ἕτερον τῶν οἷς ἐνθεωρεῖσθαι κατὰ τὴν σχέσιν ἢ τοῦ πρός τι δύναται κατηγορίαν.

8 Πάντα τὰ ὄντα νοούμενα λέγεται τῶν ἐπ᾽ αὐτὰ γνώσεων ἐναποδείκτους ἔχοντα τὰς ἀρχάς· ὁ δὲ Θεὸς οὐ νοούμενος ὀνομάζεται, ἀλλ᾽ ἐκ τῶν νοουμένων μόνον εἶναι πιστεύεται· διόπερ οὐδὲν τῶν νοουμένων αὐτῷ καθ᾽ ὁτιοῦν παραβάλλεται.

its existence, undergoes distension, since it presupposes a first principle of being. And if time and eternity are not without first principle, all the more the things contained within them.

1.6   God is in the proper sense always by nature one and unique, encompassing in himself in every way the totality of what being is in the proper sense, since indeed he is in the proper sense beyond being itself. And if so, in no way anywhere does anything of which being is predicated have being in the proper sense. Consequently, nothing at all different in substance can simultaneously be contemplated with him coevally, neither eternity, nor time, nor any of those things living within these.[10] For what being is in the proper sense and what is not being in the proper sense do not ever coincide with each other.[11]

1.7   No first principle, intermediate state, and end is absolutely precluded from every relational category; God, however, incomprehensibly being infinitely above absolutely every relation, is evidently neither first principle, nor intermediate state, nor end, nor altogether anything else of those things in which the category of "toward something"[12] can be envisioned as corresponding with the category of relation.

1.8   All beings possessing the identifying first principles that demonstrate what is known about them are called "intelligible"; God, however, is not termed intelligible, but is only believed to be on the basis of intelligible things; therefore, none of the intelligible things in any way is to be compared with him.

necessarily applying to anything with substantive existence, whether subject to the diachronic nature of the present time or not. God is beyond any application of any of the categories, given that the first category and precondition of all others, "substance," has already been denied of him in 1.1 (anything that has an ἀρχή is logically also a substance), 1.2, and 1.4. Cf. *Amb Io* 7.12, 10.59, 73.

[10]Cf. Dionysius the Areopagite, *DN* 5.10.

[11]Cf. *Ambig.* 36.2 and 41.5–11.

[12]The fourth category of Aristotle. *Cat.* 4, 1b27.

9 Αἱ τῶν ὄντων γνώσεις συνηρτημένους φυσικῶς ἔχουσι
πρὸς ἀπόδειξιν τοὺς οἰκείους λόγους οἷς περιγραφήν φυσικῶς
ὑπομένουσιν· ὁ δὲ Θεὸς διὰ τῶν ἐν τοῖς οὖσι λόγων εἶναι μόνον
πιστεύεται, πάσης ἀποδείξεως βασιμώτερον, τοῖς εὐσεβέσι τὴν ὅτι
κυρίως ἐστὶν ὁμολογίαν καὶ πίστιν διδούς. Πίστις γάρ ἐστι γνῶσις,
ἀληθής ἀναποδείκτους ἔχουσα τὰς ἀρχάς, ὡς τῶν ὑπὲρ νοῦν καὶ
λόγον ὑπάρχουσα πραγμάτων ὑπόστασις.

10 Ἀρχὴ τῶν ὄντων καὶ μεσότης καὶ τέλος ἐστὶν [1088] ὁ Θεὸς
ὡς ἐνεργῶν, ἀλλ᾽ οὐ πάσχων, ὥσπερ καὶ τὰ ἄλλα πάντα οἷς παρ᾽
ἡμῶν ὀνομάζεται. Ἀρχὴ γάρ ἐστιν ὡς δημιουργὸς καὶ μεσότης ὡς
προνοητὴς καὶ τέλος ὡς περιγραφή. Ἐξ αὐτοῦ γάρ, φησί, καὶ δι᾽
αὐτοῦ καὶ εἰς αὐτὸν τὰ πάντα.

11 Οὐκ ἔστι ψυχὴ λογικὴ κατ᾽ οὐσίαν ψυχῆς λογικῆς τιμιωτέρα.
Πᾶσαν γὰρ ψυχὴν κατ᾽ εἰκόνα ἑαυτοῦ δημιουργῶν, ὡς ἀγαθὸς ὁ
Θεός, αὐτοκίνητον εἰς τὸ εἶναι παράγει· ἑκάστη δὲ κατὰ πρόθεσιν
ἢ τὴν τιμὴν ἐπιλέγεται, ἢ τὴν ἀτιμίαν ἑκοῦσα διὰ τῶν ἔργων
προσίεται.

12 Ὁ Θεός ἥλιός ἐστι δικαιοσύνης, ὡς γέγραπται, πᾶσιν ἁπλῶς τὰς
ἀκτῖνας ἐπιλάμπων τῆς ἀγαθότητος· ἡ δὲ ψυχὴ ἢ κηρὸς ὡς φιλόθεος, ἢ πηλὸς ὡς φιλόϋλος κατὰ τὴν γνώμην γίνεσθαι πέφυκεν.
Ὥσπερ οὖν ὁ πηλὸς κατὰ φύσιν ἡλίῳ ξηραίνεται, ὁ δὲ κηρός φυσικῶς
ἁπαλύνεται, οὕτω καὶ πᾶσα ψυχὴ φιλόϋλος καὶ φιλόκοσμος ἀπὸ
Θεοῦ νουθετουμένη, καί ὡς πηλὸς κατὰ τὴν γνώμην ἀντιτυποῦσα,
σκληρύνεται· καὶ ἑαυτὴν ὠθεῖ κατὰ τὸν Φαραὼ πρὸς ἀπώλειαν.

1.9   What is known of beings naturally includes the interwoven intrinsic *logoi* as what make it demonstrable, by which it naturally admits of circumscription; but God is only believed to be through the *logoi* in beings, since it is more certain than any demonstration, giving to the pious the assent and faith that he is in the proper sense. For faith is true knowledge, having indemonstrable first principles, since it is the foundation of realities subsisting beyond mind and reckoning.[13]

1.10   God is the first principle, intermediate state, and end of beings—insofar as he is active, but not passive—just as all the other terms by which he is named among us. So, he is first principle as creator, intermediate state as provider, and end as circumscription. Since 'From him,' it says, 'and through him, and unto him are all things.'[14]

1.11   A rational soul is not in substance more valuable than another rational soul, for God, fashioning each soul according to his image given that he is good, brings it into being as self-moved; but each one, according to its inclination, is either declared honorable or willfully takes on dishonor through its deeds.[15]

1.12   God is the sun of righteousness, as is written,[16] shining his rays of goodness simply on everyone; but the soul by its natural capacity becomes in character either wax when God-loving or clay when matter-loving. Consequently, just as clay by nature is dried by the sun, yet wax is naturally softened, so also every matter-loving and world-loving soul, being admonished by God yet molding itself in character after clay, is hardened; and it thrusts itself, like Pharaoh,[17]

[13]Heb 11:1.
[14]Rom 11:36.
[15]Cf. *Ambig.* 37.10.
[16]Cf. Mal 4:2.
[17]Cf. Ex 7:13. Maximus is here operating in a long tradition that exegeted the passage of Pharaoh as a problem involving free will; the image of wax and mud is already

Πᾶσα δὲ φιλόθεος, ὡς κηρὸς ἀπαλύνεται καὶ τοὺς τῶν θείων τύπους καὶ χαρακτῆρας εἰσδεχομένη, γίνεται Θεοῦ κατοικητήριον ἐν πνεύματι.

13 Ὁ τόν νοῦν ταῖς θείαις καταστράψας νοήσεσιν καὶ τὸν λόγον ἐθίσας θείοις ὕμνοις ἀπαύστως γεραίρειν τὸν Κτίσαντα, καὶ ταῖς ἀκηράτοις φαντασίαις καθαγιάσας τὴν αἴσθησιν· οὗτος τῷ φυσικῷ κατ᾽ εἰκόνα καλῷ προσέθηκε τὸ καθ᾽ ὁμοίωσιν γνωμικὸν ἀγαθόν.

14 Φυλάττει τις τῷ Θεῷ τὴν ψυχὴν ἀκηλίδωτον εἰ τὴν μὲν διάνοιαν περὶ μόνου Θεοῦ καὶ τῶν αὐτοῦ ἀρετῶν διανοεῖσθαι βιάσαιτο, τὸν δὲ λόγον ὀρθὸν ἑρμηνέα καὶ ἐξηγητὴν τῶν αὐτῶν ἀρετῶν καταστήσειε, καὶ τὴν αἴσθησιν εὐσεβῶς τὸν ὁρατὸν κόσμον, καὶ τὰ ἐν αὐτῷ πάντα, φαντάζεσθαι διδάξειε τὴν τῶν ἐν αὐτοῖς λόγων μεγαλειότητα τῇ ψυχῇ διαγγέλλουσαν.

15 Ὁ, τῆς πικρᾶς δουλείας τῶν τυραννούντων δαιμόνων ἐλευθερώσας ἡμᾶς, Θεός φιλάνθρωπον θεοσεβείας ἡμῖν ζυγὸν ἐδωρήσατο τὴν ταπεινοφροσύνην, δι᾽ ἧς πᾶσα μὲν διαβολικὴ δαμάζεται δύναμις, [1089] πᾶν δὲ τοῖς ἑλομένοις αὐτὴν ἀγαθὸν δημιουργεῖται καὶ ἀραδιούργητον διαφυλάττεται.

16 Ὁ πιστεύων, φοβεῖται· ὁ δὲ φοβούμενος, ταπεινοῦται· ὁ δὲ ταπεινούμενος, πραΰνεται, τὴν τῶν παρὰ φύσιν τοῦ θυμοῦ καὶ τῆς ἐπιθυμίας κινημάτων ἀνενέργητον ἕξιν λαβών· ὁ δὲ πραῢς, τηρεῖ

toward destruction. But every God-loving soul is softened as wax, and letting in both the impressions and characteristics of divine traits, it becomes "by the Spirit the dwelling place of God."[18]

1.13 He who has dazzled the intellect with divine thoughts, and has accustomed his rationality unceasingly to celebrate the creator with divine hymns, and has hallowed his sensory perception with unadulterated mental representations—such a one has added to the natural beauty in accordance with the image, the deliberate good in accordance with the likeness.[19]

1.14 One keeps his soul impeccable for God if he constrains his thought around God alone and keeps his virtues in mind, if he establishes his reason as an accurate interpreter and elucidator of these same virtues, and if he teaches sensory perception to represent in a sacred way the visible world and all things within it, so that it declares to the soul the magnificence of the *logoi* within them.[20]

1.15 God, having liberated us from the bitter slavery of the tyrannical demons, has gifted us the humane yoke of divine service,[21] namely, humility, through which every diabolical power is subdued and through which, for those choosing it, every good is brought about and is carefully kept inviolate.

1.16 He who believes, fears; he who fears, grows humble; he who is humble, grows gentle, having acquired a character state that is not made active by the movements of anger and desire that are against nature; and he who is gentle, observes the commandments; and he who observes the commandments, is purified; and he who has

present in Philo *Quis rer. div. her.* 181. Origen repeats the theme in the *De princ.* 3.1.11. Gregory of Nyssa also reiterates the theme in *V. Mos.* 2.73–88.

[18]Eph 2:22.
[19]Cf. *Carit.* 3.25 and *Myst.* 24.
[20]Cf. *Myst.* 2.
[21]Cf. Mt 11:30.

τὰς ἐντολάς· ὁ δὲ τηρῶν τὰς ἐντολάς, καθαίρεται· ὁ δὲ καθαρθείς, ἐλλάμπεται· ὁ δὲ ἐλλαμφθείς, ἐν τῷ ταμιείῳ τῶν μυστηρίων ἀξιοῦται τῷ νυμφίῳ Λόγῳ συγκοιτασθῆναι.

17 Ὥσπερ γεωργός, ὑπὲρ τοῦ τι τῶν ἀγρίων μεταφυτεῦσαι δένδρων ἐπιτήδειον σκοπῶν χωρίον, ἀνελπίστῳ θησαυρῷ περιπίπτει, οὕτω καὶ πᾶς ἀσκητής, ταπεινόφρων καὶ ἄπλαστος καὶ λεῖος κατὰ ψυχὴν τῆς ὑλικῆς δασύτητος—κατὰ τὸν μακαριώτατον Ἰακώβ, ὑπὸ τοῦ Πατρὸς ἐρωτώμενος τῆς ἐπιστήμης τὸν τρόπον· Τί τοῦτο ὃ ταχὺ εὗρες, τέκνον; ἀποκρίνεται λέγων· Ὁ παρέδωκε Κύριος ὁ Θεὸς ἐναντίον μου. Ὅταν γὰρ ἡμῖν ὁ Θεὸς παραδῷ τῆς ἰδίας σοφίας τὰ σοφὰ θεωρήματα καμάτου χωρίς, οὐ προσδοκήσασι, θησαυρὸν ἐξαίφνης πνευματικὸν εὑρηκέναι νομίσωμεν. Γεωργὸς γὰρ πνευματικός ἐστιν ὁ δόκιμος ἀσκητής, τὴν πρὸς αἴσθησιν τῶν ὁρατῶν θεωρίαν—ὡς ἄγριον δένδρον—πρὸς τὴν τῶν νοητῶν χώραν μεταφυτεύων καί θησαυρὸν εὑρίσκων, τὴν κατὰ χάριν τῆς ἐν τοῖς οὖσι σοφίας φανέρωσιν.

18 Ἄφνω προσπεσοῦσα γνῶσις θείων θεωρημάτων τῷ ἀσκητῇ, μὴ προσδοκήσαντι διὰ τὴν ταπείνωσιν, κατακλᾷ τὸν λογισμὸν τοῦ πρὸς ἐπίδειξιν μετὰ καμάτου καὶ πόνου ταύτην ζητοῦντος καὶ μὴ εὑρίσκοντος· καὶ γεννᾷ τῷ ἄφρονι φθόνον εἰκῇ πρὸς τὸν ἀδελφόν—καὶ φόνου μελέτην—καὶ ἑαυτῷ λύπην διὰ τὸ μὴ ἔχειν τὴν ἐκ τῶν ἐπαίνων φυσίωσιν.

19 Οἱ ζητοῦντες μετὰ πόνου γνῶσιν καὶ ἀποτυγχάνοντες, ἢ διὰ ἀπιστίαν ἀποτυγχάνουσι, ἢ τυχὸν διὰ τὸ ἀφυῶς μέλλειν αὐτοὺς ἀντιφιλονεικοῦντας ἐπαίρεσθαι κατὰ τῶν γινωσκόντων, ὡς ὁ λαὸς πάλαι κατὰ Μωϋσέως· πρὸς οὓς ὁ νόμος ἐρεῖ δεόντως,

been purified, is illuminated; and he who has been illuminated is made worthy to lie with the bridegroom Word in the chamber of the mysteries.[22]

1.17 Just as a farmer who, looking for some suitable space for the transplantation of wild trees, happens across an unexpected treasure, so also every humble and forthright ascetic, in whom the hairiness of materiality has been smoothed away from the soul after the manner of the most blessed Jacob,[23] being asked by his Father about his manner of knowing: "What is this you have found so suddenly, child?" replies, saying: "What the Lord God has bestowed upon me."[24] For whenever God gives us the wise contemplations of his wisdom without labor, when we have not expected it, we ought to believe we will have found a spiritual treasure immediately. For the genuine ascetic is the spiritual farmer who, transplanting his contemplation toward sensory perception of visible realities—like a wild tree—into the space of intelligible realities, finds a treasure, namely, the manifestation by grace of the wisdom in beings.

1.18 Knowledge of divine contemplations, suddenly having come upon the ascetic not expecting it because of his humility, aggrieves the thought process of one who, seeking it with labor and toil for showing off, does not find it; moreover, in the senseless man it randomly produces envy toward his brother—even the entertainment of the idea of murder—and in himself it produces grief in virtue of not having a natural tendency derived from praiseworthy traits.

1.19 Those who are aiming at knowledge with toil and miss, either miss because of disbelief, or perhaps because they, who are striving jealously, are stupidly about to vaunt themselves over those with knowledge, as of old the people against Moses; to them the

[22]Cf. Sg of Sgs 1:4.
[23]Cf. Gen 27:11.
[24]Gen 27:20. Cf. Philo, *Quod Deus sit immut.* 91–92.

ὅτι παραβιασάμενοί τινες ἀνέβησαν εἰς τὸ ὄρος, καί ἐξῆλθεν ὁ Ἀμορραῖος ὁ οἰκῶν ἐν τῷ ὄρει ἐκείνῳ καί ἐτίτρωσκεν αὐτούς. Ἀνάγκη γὰρ τοὺς ἐπιδείξεως ἕνεκεν ἐπιμορφιζομένους τὴν ἀρετήν μὴ μόνον σφάλλεσθαι δολοῦντας τὴν εὐσέβειαν, ἀλλὰ καὶ ὑπὸ τοῦ συνειδότος τιτρώσκεσθαι.

20   [1092] Ὁ πρὸς ἐπίδειξιν ἐφιέμενος γνώσεως, καὶ ἀποτυγχάνων, μήτε φθονείτω τῷ πέλας, μήτε λυπείσθω, ἀλλ᾽ ἔν τινι τῶν ὁμόρων ποιείτω τὴν παρασκευήν, ὡς προστέτακται, κατὰ τὴν πρᾶξιν ἐν τῷ σώματι πρότερον φιλοπονῶν τῇ ψυχῇ τὴν ἑτοιμασίαν τῆς γνώσεως.

21   Οἱ ὀρθῶς μετ᾽ εὐσεβείας τοῖς οὖσι προσβάλλοντες, καὶ μηδένα φιλενδειξίας τρόπον ἐπινοοῦντες, εὑρήσουσι προϋπαντώσας αὐτοῖς τὰς τῶν ὄντων παμφαεῖς θεωρίας, ἀκριβεστάτην αὐτοῖς ἐμποιούσας ἑαυτῶν τὴν κατάληψιν· πρὸς οὓς ὁ νόμος φησίν· Εἰσελθόντες κληρονομήσατε πόλεις μεγάλας καὶ καλάς, καὶ οἰκίας πλήρεις πάντων ἀγαθῶν, ἃς οὐκ οἰκοδομήσατε, καὶ λάκκους λελατομημένους, οὓς οὐκ ἐλατομήσατε, καὶ ἀμπελῶνας καὶ ἐλαιῶνας, οὓς οὐκ ἐφυτεύσατε. Ὁ γὰρ μὴ ἑαυτῷ ζῶν, ἀλλὰ τῷ Θεῷ, πάντων γίνεται πλήρης τῶν θείων χαρισμάτων· τῶν τέως διὰ τὴν ἐπικειμένην τῶν παθῶν ὄχλησιν μὴ φαινομένων.

22   Ὥσπερ διχῶς ἡ αἴσθησις λέγεται (ἡ μέν, καθ᾽ ἕξιν, ἥτις καὶ κοιμωμένων ἡμῶν ἐστι μηδενὸς ἀντιλαμβανομένη τῶν ὑποκειμένων, ἧς οὐδὲν ὄφελος, μὴ πρὸς ἐνέργειαν τεινομένης· ἡ δέ, κατ᾽ ἐνέργειαν, δι᾽ ἧς ἀντιλαμβανόμεθα τῶν αἰσθητῶν), οὕτω καὶ ἡ γνῶσις διττή· ἡ μὲν, ἐπιστημονική, καθ᾽ ἕξιν μόνην τοὺς λόγους ἀναλεγομένη τῶν ὄντων, ἧς οὐδὲν ὄφελος, μὴ πρὸς τὴν τῶν ἐντολῶν ἐνέργειαν

law says, as it should, that certain impetuous types went up to the mountain, and the Amorite who dwelled in that mountain came out and trounced them.[25] For it is necessary that those who dissimulate virtue for the sake of showing off not only be cast down while making a false show of piety, but even that they be trounced by their conscience.

1.20   Let him who is desirous of knowledge for the sake of showing off, and who fails to find it, neither envy one who is near it, nor grieve, but rather, let him make the Preparation with one of his neighbors, as was enjoined,[26] working zealously first with the body in accordance with the practical life to bring about readiness for knowledge in the soul.

1.21   Those who rightly attend to beings with piety, and in no way are intending ostentation, will find the resplendent contemplations of beings going out to encounter them, enabling for them the most precise direct apprehension of themselves; the Law says to them: "Having gone in, inherit great and good cities, and houses full of all good things, which you did not build, and reservoirs, which you did not dig, and vineyards and olive yards, which you did not plant."[27] For he who does not live for himself, but for God,[28] becomes full of all the divine gifts; until then, they are not manifest on account of the insistent disturbance of the passions.

1.22   Just as sensory perception is meant in a twofold manner (the one accords with a capacity, which is with us even when asleep yet has no perception of subsisting realities and is of no use, since it is not aiming to actualization; the other is meant in terms of actual reality, through which we have perceptions of sensory objects), so also is knowledge twofold: the one, scientific, refers only to the

---

[25]Cf. Deut 1:43–44.
[26]Cf. Ex 12:4ff.
[27]Deut 6:10–11; Jos 24:13.
[28]Cf. 2 Cor 5:15.

ἐκτεινομένης· ἡ δέ, κατ᾽ ἐνέργειαν πρακτική, αὐτὴν ἀληθῆ διὰ τῆς πείρας τῶν ὄντων κομίζουσα τὴν κατάληψιν.

23   Ὁ ὑποκριτής, ἕως μὲν δοκεῖ λανθάνειν, ἠρεμεῖ, τὴν ἐκ τοῦ δοκεῖν δίκαιος εἶναι δόξαν θηρώμενος. Ἐπειδὰν δὲ φωραθῇ, θανατηφόρους προΐσχεται λόγους, ταῖς κατ᾽ ἄλλων λοιδορίαις δοκῶν τὴν οἰκείαν συγκαλύπτειν ἀσχημοσύνην· ὄν, ἐχίδνης γεννήματι παρεικάσας ὁ λόγος, ὡς παλίμβολον, ἀξίους τῆς μετανοίας προσέταξεν αὐτῷ ποιεῖσθαι καρπούς, τουτέστι, πρὸς τοὺς φαινομένους τρόπους μεταποιῆσαι τὴν κρυπτομένην τῆς καρδίας διάθεσιν.

24   Φασί τινες θηρίον εἶναι πᾶν ὃ μὴ τῷ νόμῳ τῶν ἐν ἀέρι τε καὶ γῇ καὶ θαλάττῃ ζώων κέκριται καθαρόν, κἂν ἥμερον εἶναι τῷ ἤθει δοκῇ· οἷς ἕκαστον τῶν ἀνθρώπων ἐκ τοῦ οἰκείου πάθους ὁ λόγος προσαγορεύει.

25   Ὁ ἐπὶ βλάβῃ τῶν πέλας μορφιζόμενος φιλίαν, λύκος ἐστὶ κωδίῳ ἐπικρύπτων τὴν ἑαυτοῦ κακουργίαν. Ὃς ἐπειδὰν εὕρῃ ψιλὸν ἦθος ἢ ῥῆμα κατὰ [1093] Χριστὸν ἁπλοϊκῶς, ἢ γινόμενον ἢ λεγόμενον, ἥρπασε καὶ διέφθειρε· μυρίους καταχέων μώμους ὢν τοῖς λόγοις ἢ τοῖς ἤθεσιν ἐπιτίθεται, ὥσπερ κατάσκοπος τῆς ἐν Χριστῷ ἀδελφῶν ἐλευθερίας.

26   Ὁ ὑποκρινόμενος σιωπὴν κακουργίας χάριν, τῷ πλησίον τεκταίνεται δόλον, οὐ ἀποτυγχάνων ἄπεισι, τῷ ἰδίῳ πάθει

capacity of reckoning the *logoi* of beings and is of no use, since it does not extend to the actualization of the commandments; the other, practical in operation, conveys true comprehension of beings itself, through experience.[29]

1.23 The hypocrite, so long as he figures that he escapes notice, keeps quiet, hunting glory by seeming to be just. But when he is found out, he fires off lethal words, by his own railings against others thinking to hide his own deformity. Scripture, having compared him to a "brood of vipers," since <they are> duplicitous, enjoins him to make fruits worthy of repentance,[30] that is, to align the hidden disposition of his heart with the behaviors that are shown.[31]

1.24 Some say a beast is any animal in the air, on the ground, or in the sea not pronounced pure by the Law,[32] even if it seems to be tame in character; with such words Scripture assigns a name to each human depending on his own particular passion.

1.25 He who feigns friendship to the harm of his neighbors is a wolf in sheepskin hiding his own malice.[33] Whenever he finds an unadorned custom or phrase that is done or said simply, after the manner of Christ,[34] he seizes and corrupts it,[35] pouring out myriad reproaches with which he attacks the words and customs as an inquisitor of the freedom of his brothers in Christ.[36]

1.26 He who is feigning silence for the sake of malice contrives deceit against his neighbor, falling short of which he withdraws,

---

[29]Cf. Philo, *Leg. alleg. lib.* 2.36.
[30]Matt 3:7–8.
[31]Cf. *Ambig.* 10.117.
[32]Cf. Lev 11:1ff.
[33]Cf. Matt 7:15.
[34]Literally, "according with Christ."
[35]Cf. Jn 10:12.
[36]Cf. Gal 2:4.

προσθέμενος ὀδύνην. Ὁ δὲ σιωπῶν ὠφελείας χάριν, ηὔξησε φιλίαν καὶ ἀπελεύσεται χαίρων, ὡς λαβὼν φωτισμὸν σκότους λυτήριον.

27   Ὁ ἐν συνεδρίῳ λόγων ἀκρόασιν προπετῶς ἀνακόπτων οὐκ ἔλαθε φιλοδοξίαν νοσῶν· ὑφ᾽ ἧς ἁλισκόμενος, μυρίους προβάλλεται δρόμους καὶ περιδρόμους προτάσεων, τὴν εἱρμόν τῶν λεγομένων διαστῆσαι βουλόμενος.

28   Ὁ σοφός, καὶ διδάσκων καὶ διδασκόμενος, μόνα βούλεται τὰ ὠφελοῦντα διδάσκεσθαι καὶ διδάσκειν· ὁ δὲ δοκήσει σοφός, καὶ ἐρωτῶν καὶ ἐρωτώμενος, τὰ περιεργότερα μόνον προβάλλεται.

29   Ὧν μετέσχε τις κατὰ Θεοῦ χάριν ἀγαθῶν, καὶ ἄλλοις ἀφθόνως μεταδοῦναι χρεώστης ἐστί. Δωρεὰν γάρ, φησίν, ἐλάβετε, δωρεὰν δότε. Ὁ γὰρ ὑπὸ γῆν κρύπτων τὴν δωρεάν ὡς σκληρὸν διαβάλλει τὸν Κύριον, φειδοῖ τῆς σαρκός τὴν ἀρετὴν ἐξομνύμενος. Ὁ δὲ πιπράσκων ἐχθροῖς τὴν Ἀλήθειαν, ὕστερον ἁλοὺς ὡς φιλόδοξος, μὴ φέρων τὴν αἰσχύνην, ἀπάγχεται.

30   Τοὺς ἔτι δειλιῶντας τὸν πρὸς τὰ πάθη πόλεμον καὶ φοβουμένους τὴν τῶν ἀοράτων ἐχθρῶν ἐπιδρομήν σιωπᾶν δεῖ, τουτέστι, τὸν ὑπὲρ ἀρετῆς ἀντιρρητικὸν μὴ μεταχειρίζεσθαι τρόπον, ἀλλὰ παραχωρεῖν τῷ Θεῷ δι᾽ εὐχῆς τὴν ὑπὲρ ἑαυτῶν μέριμναν· πρὸς οὕς ἐν Ἐξόδῳ λέγεται· Κύριος πολεμήσει περὶ ὑμῶν καὶ ὑμεῖς σιγήσεσθε. Τοὺς δέ, ἤδη μετὰ τὴν ἀναίρεσιν τῶν διωκόντων, τοὺς τῶν ἀρετῶν ἐπιζητοῦντας τρόπους πρὸς εὐγνώμονα μάθησιν, δέον ἔχειν μόνον ἠνεῳγμένον τῆς διανοίας τὸ οὖς· πρὸς οὕς φησιν· Ἄκουε Ἰσραήλ.

adding distress to his own passion. He who is being silent for the sake of profiting enhances friendliness and will walk away rejoicing, since he receives the light delivering him from darkness.

1.27   He who during a gathering rashly cuts off the recitation of words does not conceal that he is sick with vanity; when he has been overcome by it, he goes round and round propounding a myriad of propositions, wanting to interrupt the sequence of what was being said.

1.28   The wise man, when teaching and being taught, wills only to be taught and to teach profitable things; but he who would appear wise, when asking and being asked, propounds only rather pretentious statements.

1.29   The goods in which a man participates according to the grace of God also indebt him to share ungrudgingly with others. For "Freely," it says, "you received, freely give."[37] Thus, one who conceals the gift underground charges the Lord with harshness, thereby renouncing virtue out of parsimony for the flesh. But he who sells the Truth to enemies, when he is later found out as being vainglorious, hangs himself, being unable to bear the shame.[38]

1.30   It is necessary for those who are still being cowardly in the war against the passions and who are fearing the assault of invisible enemies to remain silent, that is, not to take an adversarial posture for the sake of virtue, but rather to yield their anxiety to God through prayer. To them it is said in Exodus: "The Lord will fight on your behalf and you will be silent."[39] Moreover, for those who, immediately following the annihilation of the persecutors, are seeking the ways of the virtues for reasonable instruction, it is necessary to keep

[37]Matt 10:8.
[38]Matt 26:15, 27:5.
[39]Ex 14:14.

Τῷ δὲ σφόδρα διὰ τὴν κάθαρσιν τῆς θείας ἐφιεμένῳ γνώσεως, ἁρμόδιος ἡ εὐλαβὴς παρρησία· πρὸς ὅν εἰρήσεται· Τί βοᾷς πρός με; Οὐκοῦν ὅτῳ μὲν σιωπῇ διὰ φόβον προστέτακται, πρόσφορος μόνον ἡ πρὸς Θεὸν καταφυγή· ὅτῳ δὲ ἀκούειν παρακελεύεται, ἁρμόδιος ἡ πρὸς ὑπακοὴν τῶν θείων ἐντολῶν ἑτοιμότης· τῷ δὲ γνωστικῷ, τί δι᾽ ἱκεσίαν ἀπαύστως βοᾶν ἐπιτήδειον, ὑπέρ τε τῆς τῶν κακῶν ἀποτροπῆς καὶ εὐχαριστίας τῆς τῶν ἀγαθῶν μετουσίας.

31 Οὐδέποτε ψυχὴ δύναται πρὸς γνῶσιν ἐκταθῆναι Θεοῦ εἰ μὴ αὐτὸς ὁ Θεὸς συγκαταβάσει χρησάμενος ἅψηται αὐτῆς καὶ ἀναγάγῃ πρὸς ἑαυτόν. [1096] Οὐ γὰρ ἄν τοσοῦτον ἴσχυσεν ἀναδραμεῖν ἀνθρώπινος νοῦς—ὡς ἀντιλαβέσθαι τινὸς θείας ἐλλάμψεως, εἰ μὴ αὐτὸς ὁ Θεὸς ἀνέσπασεν αὐτόν, ὡς δυνατὸν ἦν ἀνθρώπινον νοῦν ἀνασπασθῆναι καὶ ταῖς θείαις αὐγαῖς κατεφώτισεν.

32 Ὁ τοὺς μαθητὰς τοῦ Κυρίου μιμούμενος, οὐ παραιτεῖται διὰ τοὺς Φαρισαίους ὁδὸν ποιεῖν ἐν Σαββάτῳ διὰ τῶν σπορίμων καὶ στάχυας τίλλειν, ἀλλὰ μετὰ τὴν πρακτικὴν ἐν τῇ ἀπαθείᾳ γενόμενος, τοὺς λόγους ἀναλέγεται τῶν γεγονότων, εὐσεβῶς τὴν θείαν τῶν ὄντων ἐπιστήμην τρεφόμενος.

33 Ὁ κατὰ τὸ Εὐαγγέλιον μόνον πιστὸς τὸ ὅρος τῆς κακίας αὐτοῦ διὰ πράξεως μετατίθησιν, ἀπωθούμενος ἑαυτοῦ τῇ ἀστάτῳ περιφορᾷ τῶν ὑπὸ αἴσθησιν τὴν ἐπ᾽ αὐτοῖς προτέραν διάθεσιν. Ὁ δὲ μαθητὴς εἶναι δυνάμενος, ἐκ τοῦ Λόγου δεχόμενος χερσὶ τῶν γνωστικῶν ἄρτων τὰ κλάσματα, διατρέφει χιλιάδας, πράξει δεικνὺς πληθυνομένην τοῦ Λόγου τὴν δύναμιν. Ὁ δὲ καὶ ἀπόστολος ἰσχύσας

only the ear of their understanding open. To them it is said: "Listen, O Israel."[40] For him who has great desire of divine knowledge on account of his purification, reverent freedom of speech is suitable. To him it will be said, "Why are you crying out to me?"[41] Consequently then, to him who on account of his fear silence has been enjoined, flight toward God alone is useful; and to him who is ordered to listen, readiness for the hearing of the divine commandments is suitable; but for the one with knowledge, it is of course appropriate ceaselessly to be crying out in supplication, both for the prevention of evils and as a thanksgiving for participation in good things.

1.31   Never can a soul reach out toward the knowledge of God if God himself does not, having condescended, lay hold of it and lead it up to himself. For a human mind is not strong enough to ascend such a distance—as if to seize for its part some divine illumination, if God himself did not draw it upward, as far as is possible for a human mind to be drawn upward, and enlighten it with divine radiances.

1.32   He who imitates the disciples of the Lord, does not on account of the Pharisees decline to make his way through ripe fields and pluck ears of corn on the Sabbath,[42] but having come to be in dispassion after the practical life, he picks the *logoi* of beings that have come into existence, piously nourishing his God-like science of beings.

1.33   He who according to the Gospel only has faith displaces the mountain of his own vice through a practical life,[43] thrusting away from himself his former disposition for the unstable fluctuation of things in the sphere of sensory perception on which it was based. And he who has been empowered to be a disciple, receiving in his hands the pieces of gnostic loaves from the Word, feeds thousands,[44]

[40]Deut 4:6.
[41]Ex 14:15.
[42]Cf. Matt 12:1–2.
[43]Cf. Matt 17:20.
[44]Cf. Matt 14:19–20.

εἶναι, πᾶσαν ἰατρεύει νόσον καὶ μαλακίαν, ἐκβάλλων δαιμόνια, τουτέστι, τὴν τῶν παθῶν φυγαδεύων ἐνέργειαν. Νοσοῦντας ἰώμενος, πρὸς ἕξιν εὐσεβείας τοὺς στερηθέντας αὐτῆς δι᾽ ἐλπίδος ἐπανάγων καὶ τοὺς δι᾽ ὄκνον μαλακισθέντας ἐπιστύφων τῷ λόγῳ τῆς κρίσεως. Πατεῖν γὰρ ἐπάνω ὄφεων καὶ σκορπίων κελευσθείς, ἀρχὴν καὶ τέλος τῆς ἁμαρτίας ἐξαφανίζει.

34 Ὁ ἀπόστολος καὶ μαθητὴς πάντως ἐστὶ καὶ πιστός. Ὁ δὲ μαθητής, οὐ πάντως μὲν καὶ ἀπόστολος, πάντως δὲ πιστός. Ὁ δὲ μόνον πιστός, οὔτε μαθητὴς οὔτε ἀπόστολός ἐστι· πλὴν δύναται διὰ βίου καὶ θεωρίας καὶ ὁ τρίτος εἰς τὴν τοῦ δευτέρου καὶ ὁ δεύτερος εἰς τὴν τοῦ πρώτου μετενεχθῆναι τάξιν καὶ ἀξίαν.

35 Ὅσα μὲν ἐν χρόνῳ κατὰ χρόνον δημιουργεῖται, τελειωθέντα ἵσταται, λήγοντα τῆς κατὰ φύσιν αὐξήσεως. Ὅσα δὲ κατ᾽ ἀρετὴν ἐπιστήμη Θεοῦ κατεργάζεται, τελειωθέντα, πάλιν κινεῖται πρὸς αὔξησιν. Τὰ γὰρ τέλη αὐτῶν ἑτέρων ἀρχαὶ καθεστήκασιν. Ὁ γὰρ καταπαύσας ἐν ἑαυτῷ διὰ τῶν ἀρετῶν κατὰ τὴν πρᾶξιν τὴν τῶν φθειρομένων ὑπόστασιν, ἑτέρων ἀπήρξατο θειοτέρων διατυπώσεων· παύεται γὰρ οὐδέποτε τῶν καλῶν ὁ Θεός, ὧν οὐδὲ ἀρχήν ἔσχεν. Ὡς γὰρ φωτὸς ἴδιον τὸ φωτίζειν, οὕτως ἴδιον Θεοῦ τὸ εὖ ποιεῖν. Διὸ τῷ μὲν νόμῳ τὴν κατὰ χρόνον τῶν ἐν γενέσει καὶ φθορᾷ σύστασιν ἀφηγουμένῳ τιμᾶται δι᾽ ἀργίας τὸ Σάββατον· τῷ Εὐαγγελίῳ δὲ τὴν τῶν νοητῶν εἰσηγουμένῳ κατάστασιν, δι᾽ εὐποιίας καλῶν ἔργων τοῦτο φαιδρύνεται· κἄν ἀγανακτῶσιν οἱ μήπω γνόντες ὅτι διὰ τὸν ἄνθρωπον τὸ Σάββατον γέγονεν, ἀλλ᾽ οὐ διὰ τὸ Σάββατον

showing by the practical life the multiplying power of the Word. And he who has been strengthened to be even an apostle, heals every illness and debility, casting out demons,[45] that is, putting the activity of the passions to flight. He heals ailing people, through hope restoring to a capacity for piety those who have been deprived of it and with a discerning word bandaging up those who have been debilitated by losing heart. For having been ordered to trample serpents and scorpions underfoot,[46] he obliterates the beginning and end of sin.

1.34 The apostle is necessarily both a disciple and faithful. The disciple, while not necessarily also an apostle, is nevertheless faithful necessarily. Yet, he who is faithful only is neither a disciple nor an apostle; nevertheless, the third is able through a holy life and contemplation to be transferred to the order and dignity of the second, and the second into that of the first.[47]

1.35 Whatever things exist in time are being fashioned in accordance with time and, having been perfected, they are brought to a standstill, thereby having ceased from growth according to nature. Whatever things God's science effects in the realm of virtue, when they have been perfected, they move again for increase, for their ends have established the starting points of further ends. For, he who through the virtues puts an end to the ground of corruptible things in himself, in accordance with the practical life has made a beginning of other more divine configurations, for God never rests from good things, of which there is also no beginning. For just as it is the property of light to shine, just so it is the property of God to do good. Thus, while in the Law, which recounts in accordance with time the structure of things liable to generation and corruption, the Sabbath is honored by rest,[48] in the Gospel, which illumines the constitution of intelligible realities, the Sabbath is celebrated through the

[45]Cf. Matt 10:8; Lk 10:17.
[46]Cf. Lk 10:19.
[47]Cf. Origen, *Hom. in Gen.* 1.7.
[48]Cf. Ex 31:14.

ὁ ἄνθρωπος· καὶ ὅτι κύριός ἐστι καὶ τοῦ Σαββάτου ὁ Υἱὸς τοῦ
ἀνθρώπου.

36   Ἔστι τῷ νόμῳ καὶ τοῖς προφήταις καὶ Σάββατον καὶ Σάββατα καὶ
Σάββατα Σαββάτων· ὥσπερ καὶ περιτομὴ καὶ περιτομῆς περιτομή·
καὶ θέρος καὶ θέρους θέρος, κατὰ τὸ εἰρημένον· Ὅταν θερίσητε τὸν
θερισμὸν ὑμῶν. Ἔστιν οὖν τὸ μὲν πρῶτον, πρακτικῆς καὶ φυσικῆς καὶ
θεολογικῆς φιλοσοφίας ἀποπεράτωσις. Τὸ δεύτερον δέ, γενέσεως καὶ
τῶν κατὰ γένεσιν λόγων ἀπόλυσις. Τὸ δὲ τρίτον, τῶν κατ᾽ αἴσθησιν
καὶ νοῦν πνευτικωτέρων λόγων εἰσφορὰ καὶ ἀπόλαυσις. Καὶ τοῦτο
τρισσῶς ἐφ᾽ ἑκάστῳ δηλονότι τῶν εἰρημένων γινόμενον, ἵνα γνῷ
τοὺς λόγους ὁ γνωστικὸς καθ᾽ οὕς ὁ μὲν Μωϋσῆς ἔξω τῆς ἁγίας γῆς
σαββατίζει τελευτῶν· ὁ δὲ τοῦ Ναυῆ Ἰησοῦς, περιτέμνει περάσας τὸν
Ἰορδάνην· οἱ δὲ τὴν ἀγαθὴν γῆν κληρονομοῦντες, τὴν εἰσφορὰν τοῦ
καθ᾽ ὑπέρθεσιν διπλοῦ θέρους τῷ Θεῷ προσκομίζουσιν.

37   Σάββατόν ἐστιν ἀπάθεια ψυχῆς λογικῆς, κατὰ τὴν πρακτικὴν
παντελῶς ἀποβαλομένης τῆς ἁμαρτίας τὰ στίγματα.

beneficence of good deeds,[49] even should those be infuriated who have not yet realized that "the Sabbath has come to be for the sake of humanity and not humanity for the sake of the Sabbath," and that "the Son of Man is Lord even of the Sabbath."[50]

1.36 In the Law and the Prophets there is a Sabbath,[51] Sabbaths,[52] and Sabbaths of Sabbaths,[53] just as there are a circumcision and a circumcision of circumcision,[54] or a harvest[55] and a harvest of harvest, according to what was said, "When you harvest your harvest."[56] The first, therefore, is the accomplishment of practical, natural, and theological philosophy. The second is the deliverance from generation and the principles in accordance with generation. And the third is the gathering and enjoyment of the more spiritual principles regarding sensory perception and mind. And clearly this occurs triply in each of the cases mentioned, so that the gnostic might comprehend the rationales according to which Moses, while outside the Holy Land, in dying keeps the Sabbath,[57] while Joshua, son of Nun, after crossing the Jordan, circumcised;[58] and those who inherited the good land brought to God a gathering from the harvest's overabundant double yield.[59]

1.37 "Sabbath" means the dispassion of a rational soul, by the practical life entirely removing sin's scars.

---

[49]Cf. Lk 6:9; Jn 5:16–17.
[50]Mk 2:27–28. See Evagrius, *Cent.* 4.44.
[51]Cf. Is 66:23
[52]Cf. Ex 31:13
[53]Cf. Lev 16:31
[54]Cf. Gen 17:10–13.
[55]Cf. Gen 8:22.
[56]Cf. Lev 23:10. Philo brings up numerous of these themes, *De somn.* 2 and *De spec. leg.* 2. Origen also brings up these themes in *De princ.* 2.3.5.
[57]Cf. Deut 34:5.
[58]Cf. Jos 5:3.
[59]Cf. Lev 23:11.

38   Σάββατά ἐστιν ἐλευθερία ψυχῆς λογικῆς, καὶ αὐτὴν τὴν κατὰ φύσιν πρὸς αἴσθησιν, διὰ τῆς ἐν πνεύματι φυσικῆς θεωρίας, ἀποθεμένης ἐνέργειαν.

39   Σάββατα Σαββάτων ἐστὶν ἠρεμία πνευματικὴ ψυχῆς λογικῆς καὶ ἀπ᾽ αὐτῶν πάντων τῶν ἐν τοῖς οὖσι θειοτέρων λόγων τὸν νοῦν συστειλάσης, καὶ μόνῳ τῷ Θεῷ κατ᾽ ἐρωτικὴν ἔκστασιν ὁλικῶς ἐνδησάσης καὶ παντελῶς ἀκίνητον αὐτὸν τοῦ Θεοῦ διὰ τῆς μυστικῆς θεολογίας ποιησάσης.

40   Περιτομή ἐστιν ἡ περὶ γένεσιν τῆς κατὰ ψυχὴν ἐμπαθοῦς ἀπόθεσις διαθέσεως.

41   Περιτομὴ περιτομῆς ἐστιν ἡ καὶ αὐτῶν τῶν κατὰ ψυχὴν περὶ τὴν γένεσιν φυσικῶν κινημάτων, παντελὴς ἀποβολὴ καὶ περιαίρεσις.

42   Θέρος ἐστὶ ψυχῆς λογικῆς ἡ τῶν κατ᾽ ἀρετὴν [1100] καὶ φύσιν τῶν ὄντων πνευματικωτέρων λόγων μετ᾽ ἐπιστήμης συλλογὴ καὶ ἐπίγνωσις.

43   Θέρους θέρος ἐστὶν ἡ πᾶσιν ἄβατος μετὰ τὴν τῶν νοητῶν μυστικὴν θεωρίαν περὶ νοῦν ἀγνώστως συνισταμένη τοῦ Θεοῦ κατανόησις, ἥν προσφέρει δεόντως ὁ ἐκ τῶν ὁρατῶν καὶ ἀοράτων κτισμάτων ἀξίως γεραίρων τὸν Κτίσαντα.

44   Ἔστι καί ἄλλο πνευματικώτερον θέρος, αὐτοῦ λεγόμενον εἶναι τοῦ Θεοῦ, καὶ ἄλλη μυστικωτέρα περιτομή, καὶ ἄλλο κρυφιώτερον Σάββατον, ἐν ᾧ, ἀπὸ τῶν ἰδίων ἔργων σαββατίζων, ὁ Θεὸς ἀναπαύει

1.38 "Sabbaths" means the freedom of a rational soul, through natural contemplation by the Spirit having put off the very activity according to nature directed at sensory perception.

1.39 "Sabbath of Sabbaths" means the spiritual quietude of the rational soul, having contracted the mind away even from all the truly divine *logoi* themselves which are in beings, and wholly having put on God alone in an erotic ecstasy, and altogether making it unmovable from God through mystical theology.

1.40 "A circumcision" means the putting off of the impassioned disposition in the soul connected with generation.[60]

1.41 "A circumcision of circumcision" means the absolute removal and stripping off of even the natural movements themselves in the soul connected with generation.

1.42 "A harvest" of a rational soul means the collection and recognition with science of the more spiritual *logoi* of beings according to virtue and nature.

1.43 "A harvest of harvest" means the universally inaccessible thought of God that in the mind takes place by unknowing beyond the mystical contemplation of intelligible realities,[61] which he who is worthily honoring the Creator from visible and invisible creations duly presents.

1.44 There is yet another more spiritual harvest, said to be of God himself, and another more mystical circumcision, and another more hidden Sabbath, in which, keeping the Sabbath from his own works,

---

[60]Cf. Evagrius, *KG* 4.12, and Maximus, *Ambig.* 30.2.

[61]This is a distinctly Dionysian theme, where the absolute cessation of intellectual activities serves as precondition for rendering oneself passible to the divine. Cf. *Myst.* 1.3 and *Cap. theol.* 1.54 below.

κατὰ τό· Ὁ μὲν θερισμὸς πολύς, οἱ δὲ ἐργάται ὀλίγοι. Καί· Περιτομὴ καρδίας ἐν πνεύματι. Καί· Εὐλόγησεν ὁ Θεὸς τὴν ἡμέραν τὴν ἑβδόμην καὶ ἡγίασεν αὐτήν, ὅτι ἐν αὐτῇ κατέπαυσεν ἀπὸ πάντων τῶν ἔργων αὐτοῦ ὧν ἤρξατο ὁ Θεὸς ποιῆσαι.

45   Θεοῦ θέρος ἐστὶν ἡ εἰς αὐτὸν κατὰ τὴν τῶν αἰώνων ἀποπεράτωσιν γινομένη τῶν ἀξίων καθόλου μονή τε καὶ ἵδρυσις.

46   Ἐν πνεύματι περιτομὴ καρδίας ἐστὶν ἡ γινομένη τῶν κατ᾽ αἴσθησιν καὶ νοῦν περὶ τὰ αἰσθητὰ καὶ τὰ νοητὰ φυσικῶν ἐνεργειῶν παντελὴς περιαίρεσις, διὰ τῆς ἀμέσως τό τε σῶμα καὶ τὴν ψυχὴν ὁλικῶς μεταμορφούσης πρὸς τὸ θειότερον παρουσίας τοῦ Πνεύματος.

47   Θεοῦ σαββατισμός ἐστιν ἡ εἰς αὐτὸν διόλου τῶν πεποιημένων κατάντησις, καθ᾽ ἥν καταπαύει τῆς ἐπ᾽ αὐτοῖς φυσικῆς ἐνεργείας, τὴν αὐτοῦ θειοτάτην ἀρρήτως ἐνεργουμένοις ἐνέργειαν. Παύεται γὰρ ὁ Θεὸς τῆς ἐν ἑκάστῳ τῶν ὄντων τυχὸν φυσικῆς ἐνεργείας, καθ᾽ ἥν ἕκαστον τῶν ὄντων φυσικῶς κινεῖσθαι πέφυκεν, ὁπόταν ἕκαστον, τῆς θείας ἀναλόγως ἐπιλαβόμενον ἐνεργείας, τὴν κατὰ φύσιν οἰκείαν περὶ αὐτὸν ὁρίσῃ τὸν Θεόν ἐνέργειαν.

48   Ζητητέον τοῖς σπουδαίοις τίνα καθήκει νοεῖν εἶναι τὰ ἔργα ὧν ἤρξατο τῆς γενέσεως ὁ Θεὸς καὶ τίνα, πάλιν, ὧν οὐκ ἤρξατο. Εἰ γὰρ πάντων κατέπαυσε τῶν ἔργων ὧν ἤρξατο ποιῆσαι, δῆλον ἐκείνων οὐ κατέπαυσεν ὧν οὐκ ἤρξατο ποιῆσαι. Μήποτε, οὖν, ἔργα μὲν Θεοῦ

God rested,[62] as in the passages: "While the harvest is abundant, the workers are nevertheless few,"[63] and "A circumcision of the heart in the Spirit,"[64] and "God blessed the seventh day and hallowed it, since on it he rested from all of his works which he himself had begun to make."[65]

1.45 A "harvest of God" means both the complete abiding and foundation of the worthy ones taking place in him at the culmination of the ages.

1.46 A "circumcision of the heart in the Spirit" means the absolute stripping off of the natural activities in sensory perception and mind in connection with sensory and intelligible realities, which immediately and holistically transfigures both the body and the soul into what is more divine through the presence of the Spirit.

1.47 "God's keeping of the Sabbath day" means the creations' complete conversion unto him, wherein he rests from his natural activity toward those who inexpressibly are enacting his most divine activity. For God perchance rests from the natural activity in each being, by which each being by nature acquires its natural motion, whenever each one, having taken on the divine activity in a way appropriate to itself, defines its own natural activity in connection with God himself.[66]

1.48 It is for the virtuous to investigate what particular works it is proper to consider to be those whose origin God began and, again, what particular ones he did not begin. For if he rested from all the works which he began to make, it is clear he did not rest from those

[62]Cf. Gen 2:2.
[63]Mt 9:37.
[64]Rom 2:29.
[65]Gen 2:3.
[66]Cf. Proclus, *In. Th.* 35; Dionysius the Areopagite *C.h.* 1.1, Maximus *Carit.* 2.62, *Ambig.* 7.22, 20.2, and *Opusc.* 1, PG 91.33B.

χρονικῶς ἠργμένα τοῦ εἶναί ἐστι πάντα τὰ ὄντα μετέχοντα, οἷον αἱ διάφοροι τῶν ὄντων οὐσίαι. Τὸ γὰρ μή ὄν, ἔχουσι αὐτῶν τοῦ εἶναι πρεσβύτερον. Ἦν γὰρ ποτε ὅτε τὰ ὄντα μετέχοντα οὐκ ἦν. Θεοῦ δὲ ἔργα τυχὸν οὐκ ἠργμένα τοῦ εἶναι χρονικῶς τὰ ὄντα μεθεκτά, ὧν κατὰ χάριν μετέχουσι τὰ ὄντα μετέχοντα· οἷον ἡ ἀγαθότης καὶ πᾶν εἴ τι ἀγαθότητος ἐμπεριέχεται λόγῳ. Καί ἁπλῶς, πᾶσα ζωὴ καὶ ἀθανασία καὶ ἁπλότης καὶ ἀτρεψία καὶ ἀπειρία καὶ ὅσα περὶ αὐτὸν οὐσιωδῶς θεωρεῖται, ἅτινα καὶ ἔργα Θεοῦ εἰσι καὶ οὐκ ἠργμένα χρονικῶς. Οὐ γὰρ ποτε πρεσβύτερον ἀρετῆς τὸ οὐκ ἦν· οὐδὲ τινος ἄλλου τῶν εἰρημένων, κἄν τὰ μετέχοντα αὐτῶν καθ᾽ αὐτὰ ἦρκται τοῦ εἶναι χρονικῶς. [1101] Ἄναρχος γὰρ πᾶσα ἀρετή, μὴ ἔχουσα τὸν χρόνον ἑαυτῆς πρεσβύτερον, οἷα τὸν Θεὸν ἔχουσα τοῦ εἶναι μονώτατον ἀϊδίως γεννήτορα.

49 Πάντων τῶν ὄντων καὶ μετεχόντων καὶ μεθεκτῶν ἀπειράκις ἀπείρως, ὁ Θεὸς ὑπεξήρηται. Πᾶν γὰρ εἴ τι τὸν τοῦ εἶναι λόγον ἔχει κατηγορούμενον, ἔργον Θεοῦ τυγχάνει. Κἄν τὸ μὲν κατὰ γένεσιν ἦρκται τοῦ εἶναι χρονικῶς, τὸ δὲ κατὰ χάριν τοῖς γεγονόσιν ἐμπέφυκεν, οἷα τις δύναμις ἔμφυτος, τὸν ἐν πᾶσι ὄντα Θεὸν διαπρυσίως κηρύττουσα.

50 Τὰ ἀθάνατα πάντα καὶ αὐτὴ ἡ ἀθανασία· καὶ τὰ ζῶντα πάντα καὶ αὐτὴ ἡ ζωή· καὶ τὰ ἅγια πάντα καὶ αὐτὴ ἡ ἁγιότης· καὶ τὰ ἐνάρετα

which he did not begin to make. Perhaps, therefore, the works of God beginning their existence temporally are all participating beings, such as the different substances of beings, since they have non-being prior to their existence. For there once was a "when" when participating beings were not. On the other hand, the works of God not beginning their existence temporally are perhaps participated realities, of which participating beings participate by grace, such as goodness and anything particular that is encompassed by the principle of goodness. Put simply, all life, immortality, simplicity, immutability, infinity, and as many things as substantively are contemplated with reference to him, which very things are also works of God, yet not beginning temporally. For non-being never was prior to virtue, nor to any of the other things listed, although participating beings in themselves have begun to exist temporally from them. For all virtue is unoriginated, not having time prior to itself, since it is the kind of reality eternally having God as the most exclusive author of its existence.

1.49 God incomprehensibly eludes infinitely[67] all beings, both participating and participated.[68] For anything particular that has the term "existence" for a predicate is a work of God. Although the former has begun to exist temporally, the latter has by grace been implanted in originated beings, as if a kind of implanted potentiality, loudly proclaiming that God is in all beings.[69]

1.50 All things immortal and immortality itself, all things living and life itself, all things holy and holiness itself, all things virtuous

[67] A linchpin Dionysian phrase, *D.n.* 8.2.

[68] Cf. Proclus, *In. Th.* 116.

[69] This phrase must be read carefully in light of *Ambig.* 20.2 and *Op*usc. 1, PG 91.33B, since the Confessor does not mean to say that divinity is a natural potentiality of the human substance, since its realization would make the human divine by nature, which is impossible. This is why he carefully qualifies it with "as if a kind of," by which I take him to mean that humans have the potential to become divine inasmuch as can, in fact, be deified, but cannot naturally achieve it by any effort of their own or by virtue of any underlying potentiality of their human substance to be realized. Deification represents a supernatural condition.

πάντα καὶ αὐτὴ ἡ ἀρετή· καὶ τὰ ἀγαθὰ πάντα καὶ αὐτὴ ἡ ἀγαθότης· καὶ τὰ ὄντα πάντα καὶ αὐτὴ ἡ ὀντότης, Θεοῦ προδήλως ἔργα τυγχάνουσιν· ἀλλὰ τὰ μὲν τοῦ εἶναι χρονικῶς ἠργμένα· ἦν γὰρ ποτε ὅτε οὐκ ἦν· τὰ δὲ τοῦ εἶναι χρονικῶς οὐκ ἠργμένα. Οὐκ ἦν γὰρ ποτε ὅτε οὐκ ἦν ἀρετὰ καὶ ἀγαθότης καὶ ἁγιότης καὶ ἀθανασία. Καὶ τὰ μὲν ἠργμένα χρονικῶς τῇ μετοχῇ τῶν οὐκ ἠργμένων χρονικῶς εἰσι καὶ λέγονται τοῦθ᾽ ὅπερ καί εἰσι καὶ λέγονται. Πάσης γὰρ ζωῆς καὶ ἀθανασίας, ἁγιότητός τε καὶ ἀρετῆς δημιουργός ἐστιν ὁ Θεός· ὑπὲρ οὐσίαν γὰρ πάντων τῶν τε νοουμένων καὶ λεγομένων ἐξῄρηται.

51 Ἡ ἕκτη κατὰ τὴν Γραφὴν ἡμέρα τὴν τῶν ὑπὸ φύσιν ὄντων εἰσηγεῖται συμπλήρωσιν· ἡ δὲ ἑβδόμη τῆς χρονικῆς ἰδιότητος περιγράφει τὴν κίνησιν· ἡ δὲ ὀγδόη τῆς ὑπὲρ φύσιν καὶ χρόνον ὑποδηλοῖ καταστάσεως τὸν τρόπον.

52 Ὁ τὴν ἕκτην μόνον κατὰ τὸν νόμον ἄγων ἡμέραν, τὴν κατ᾽ ἐνέργειαν ἐκθλίβουσαν τὴν ψυχὴν τῶν παθῶν φεύγων δυναστείαν, διὰ τῆς θαλάσσης ἀφόβως ἐπὶ τὴν ἔρημον διαβαίνει, τὴν τῶν παθῶν ἀργίαν μόνην σαββατίζων. Ὁ δὲ τὸν Ἰορδάνην διαβὰς καὶ αὐτήν ἀπολιπὼν τὴν τῶν παθῶν μόνον ἀργοῦσαν κατάστασιν, ἦλθεν εἰς τὴν τῶν ἀρετῶν κληρονομίαν.

53 Ὁ τὴν ἕκτην εὐαγγελικῶς ἄγων ἡμέραν, ἀποκτείνας πρότερον τὰ τῆς ἁμαρτίας πρῶτα κινήματα, τὴν πάσης κακίας ἔρημον διὰ τῶν ἀρετῶν καταλαμβάνει τῆς ἀπαθείας κατάστασιν· σαββατίζων κατὰ νοῦν καὶ αὐτῆς ψιλῆς τῆς τῶν παθῶν φαντασίας. [1104] Ὁ δὲ Ἰορδάνην διαπεράσας, εἰς τὴν τῆς γνώσεως μετατίθεται χώραν, καθ᾽ ἥν ὁ νοῦς, ναὸς μυστικῶς ὑπὸ τῆς εἰρήνης οἰκοδομούμενος, Θεοῦ κατοικητήριον γίνεται ἐν Πνεύματι.

and virtue itself, all things good and goodness itself, and all things existing and existence itself clearly occur as works of God; but the first began to be temporally, since there was once when they were not; the second did not begin to be temporally, thus, there never was when there were neither virtue, nor goodness, nor holiness, nor immortality. And the first, beginning temporally, are and are called whatever they are and are called by participation in the ones not beginning temporally. So, God is the fashioner of all life, immortality, holiness, and virtue, and being beyond substance he transcends the substance of all intelligible and utterable realities.[70]

1.51 The sixth day, according to Scripture, presents the completion of beings subject to nature; the seventh circumscribes the motion of what is of a temporal character; and the eighth hints at the manner of the condition beyond nature and time.[71]

1.52 He who carries out the sixth day only in accord with the Law, fleeing the tyranny of the passions actively oppressing the soul, crosses fearlessly through the sea into the desert,[72] keeping the Sabbath by rest from the passions only. But he who crosses the Jordan,[73] also leaving behind this very state that rests only from the passions, comes into the inheritance of the virtues.

1.53 He who carries out the sixth day in accord with the Gospel, having already mortified the first motions of sin, through virtue reaches the state of dispassion, deserted by every vice; he keeps the Sabbath in the mind, even from the very simple impression of the passions. But he who has crossed the Jordan is transferred into the land of knowledge, wherein the mind, a temple mystically built by peace, becomes the abode of God in the Spirit.[74]

[70]Cf. Dionysius the Areopagite, *D.n.* 11.6.

[71]Cf. Evagrius, *KG* 5.8, 83, and 6.7.

[72]Cf. Ex 16:1.

[73]Cf. Jos 3:17.

[74]Cf. 2 Sam/2 Kgs 7:11–13; 1 Chron 28:3. It is Solomon (shalom/peace) not David (the warrior) who builds the temple. With especial thanks to Joshua Lollar for pointing out this reference.

54   Ὁ τὴν ἕκτην θεϊκῶς μετὰ τῶν προσφόρων ἔργων καὶ ἐννοιῶν
ἑαυτῷ συμπληρώσας ἡμέραν, καὶ αὐτὸς μετὰ τοῦ Θεοῦ καλῶς τὰ
ἑαυτοῦ συντελέσας ἔργα, διέβη τῇ κατανοήσει πᾶσαν τὴν τῶν
ὑπὸ φύσιν καὶ χρόνον ὑπόστασιν καὶ εἰς τὴν τῶν αἰώνων καὶ τῶν
αἰωνίων μετετάξατο μυστικὶν θεωρίαν. Σαββατίζων ἀγνώστως κατὰ
νοῦν, τὴν ὁλικὴν τῶν ὄντων ἀπόλειψίν τε καὶ ὑπέρβασιν. Ὁ δὲ καὶ
τῆς ὀγδόης ἀξιωθείς, ἐκ τῶν νεκρῶν ἀνέστη, τῶν μετὰ Θεὸν λέγω
πάντων, αἰσθητῶν τε καὶ νοητῶν, καὶ λόγων καὶ νοημάτων, καὶ ἔζησε
τὴν τοῦ Θεοῦ μακαρίαν ζωήν—τοῦ μόνον κατ᾽ ἀλήθειαν κυρίως
ζωῆς καὶ λεγομένου καὶ ὄντος—οἷα καὶ αὐτὸς γενόμενος τῇ θεώσει
θεός.

55   Ἕκτη ἡμέρα ἐστὶν ἡ τῶν πρακτικῶν περὶ ἀρετὴν τῶν κατὰ
φύσιν ἐνεργειῶν, παντελὴς ἀποπλήρωσις· ἑβδόμη δέ ἐστιν ἡ τῶν
θεωρητικῶν περὶ τὴν ἄρρητον γνῶσιν πασῶν τῶν φυσικῶν ἐννοιῶν
ἀποπεράτωσις καὶ ἀπόπαυσις· ὀγδόη δέ, ἡ πρὸς θέωσιν τῶν ἀξίων
μετάταξίς τε καὶ μετάβασις. Καὶ μήποτε ταύτην τὴν ἑβδόμην καὶ τὴν
ὀγδόην τυχὸν μυστικώτερον ὑποφαίνων ὁ Κύριος, προσηγόρευσεν
ἡμέραν συντελείας καὶ ὥραν, ὡς πάντων περιγραφούσαν τὰ
μυστήρια καὶ τοὺς λόγους. Ἃς οὐδὲν οὐδαμῶς τὸ παράπαν τῶν
ἐπουρανίων καὶ ἐπιγείων δυνάμεων γνῶναι πρὸ πείρας τοῦ παθεῖν
δυνήσεται, πλὴν αὐτῆς τῆς ταῦτα ποιούσης μακαρίας θεότητος.

56   Ἡ ἕκτη ἡμέρα τὸν τοῦ εἶναι τῶν ὄντων λόγον ὑποδηλοῖ· ἡ δὲ
ἑβδόμη τὸν τοῦ εὖ εἶναι τῶν ὄντων τρόπον ὑποσημαίνει· ἡ δὲ ὀγδόη
τὸ τοῦ ἀεὶ εὖ εἶναι τῶν ὄντων ἄρρητον μυστήριον ὑπαγορεύει.

1.54 He who divinely has completed the sixth day in himself with presentable deeds and thoughts, and who with God rightly has concluded his deeds, has transcended in his understanding every subsisting thing subject to nature and time and has transposed himself into the mystical contemplation of the ages and eternal things. He is keeping the Sabbath not knowing with his mind,[75] in the total abandonment and transcendence of beings. And he who has also been deemed worthy of the eighth resurrects from the dead, I mean, from all things after God, sense-perceptible and intelligible, words and thoughts, and lives the blessed life of God—since he is both called and is life in the true and proper sense—so much so that he even becomes God by deification.

1.55 The sixth day is the absolute fulfillment of practical natural activities concerning virtue; the seventh is the completion and cessation of all natural contemplative concepts concerning ineffable knowledge; and the eighth is the transposition and transcendence to deification of the worthy. And perhaps the Lord, hinting at this deification, possibly more mystically, called the seventh and eighth day "day and hour of completion,"[76] since it circumscribes the mysteries and *logoi* of all things. Not one of the heavenly or earthly powers will be able to know such things in any way at all[77] before experiencing passivity,[78] except for the blessed divinity itself, maker of these things.

1.56 The sixth day hints at the *logos* of being of beings; the seventh suggests the mode of well-being of beings; and the eighth implies the ineffable mystery of the eternal well-being of beings.[79]

[75]See 1.43 above.
[76]Cf. Dan 12:13, Mt 24:3, and 24:36.
[77]Cf. Mt 24:36.
[78]Deification requires a full cessation of the natural human activities, at which time the human makes him-or herself liable to deification by having the divine activities operating within him or her.
[79]Cf. *Ambig.* 65.2 and *Qu. Thal.* 25, CCSG 7, p. 163.72ff.

57 Πρακτικῆς ἐνεργείας σύμβολον ὑπάρχουσαν τὴν ἕκτην ἡμέραν γινώσκοντες, πᾶσαν ἐν αὐτῇ τῶν ἔργων τῆς ἀρετῆς τὴν ὀφειλὴν ἀποπληρώσωμεν, ὅπως καὶ ἐφ᾽ ἡμῶν ῥηθείη τό· Καὶ εἶδεν ὁ Θεὸς πάντα ὅσα ἐποίησε καὶ ἰδοὺ καλὰ λίαν.

58 Ἀποπληροῖ τὴν ὀφειλὴν τῆς ἐπαινουμένης τῷ Θεῷ καλῆς ἐργασίας, ὁ διὰ σώματος τῇ ψυχῇ φιλοπονῶν τὴν εὔκοσμον ποικιλίαν τῶν ἀρετῶν.

59 Ὁ τὴν παρασκευὴν τῶν ἔργων τῆς δικαιοσύνης πληρώσας, διέβη πρὸς τὴν ἀνάπαυσιν τῆς [1105] γνωστικῆς θεωρίας, καθ᾽ ἣν τοὺς λόγους τῶν ὄντων περιλαβὼν θεοπρεπῶς, τῆς κατὰ νοῦν περὶ αὐτὴν κινήσεως ἀναπαύεται.

60 Ὁ τῆς δι᾽ ἡμᾶς ἑβδοματικῇ τοῦ Θεοῦ μετεσχηκὼς ἀναπαύσεως καὶ τῆς αὐτοῦ δι᾽ ἡμᾶς μεθέξει κατὰ τὴν θέωσιν ὀγδοατικῆς ἐνεργείας, εἴτουν μυστικῆς ἀναστάσεως· ἀφεὶς καὶ αὐτὸς ἐν τῷ τάφῳ κείμενα τὰ ὀθόνια καὶ τὸ ἐπὶ τῆς κεφαλῆς σουδάριον, ἅπερ θεωροῦντες, εἴ τις Πέτρος καὶ Ἰωάννης, πιστεύουσιν ἐγηγέρθαι τὸν Κύριον.

61 Μνημεῖόν ἐστιν ἴσως δεσποτικὸν ἢ ὁ κόσμος οὗτος ἢ ἡ ἑκάστου τῶν πιστῶν καρδία· τὰ δὲ ὀθόνια οἱ τῶν αἰσθητῶν μετὰ τῶν κατ᾽ ἀρετὴν τρόπων ὑπάρχουσι λόγοι· τὸ δὲ σουδάριον ἡ τῶν νοητῶν ἐστι μετὰ τῆς ἐνδεχομένης θεολογίας ἁπλῆ καὶ ἀποίκιλος γνῶσις, δι᾽ ὧν ἐγνωρίζετο πρότερον ὁ Λόγος, ἀχώρητον ἡμῖν ἔχων παντάπασιν δίχα τούτων, τὴν ὑπὲρ ταῦτα κατάληψιν.

1.57   Knowing the sixth day to be the symbol of the accomplishment of the practical life, let us fulfill every requirement of the deeds of virtue in it in such a way that the passage "... and God saw as many things as he did, and look, they were very good"[80] might also be said of us.

1.58   A man would fulfill the requirement of a beautiful craft, commendable to God who through the body industriously elaborates the elegant tapestry of the virtues in the soul.

1.59   He who completes the Day of Preparation of the works of justice passes over to the repose of gnostic contemplation, in which, embracing the *logoi* of beings in a manner worthy of God, he reposes in his mind from the motion surrounding it.[81]

1.60   He who has partaken of God's seventh-day rest, for our sake, also will partake of his eighth-day activity of deification for our sake, that is, of the mystical resurrection; he too has left the shroud and the linen cloths for the head lying in the tomb;[82] those perceiving such objects, as if some kind of Peter and John, believe that the Lord has been raised.[83]

1.61   Maybe the Lord's sepulcher is either this world or the heart of each believer; and the shroud is the *logoi* of sensory realities with their way of being lining up with virtue; and the linen cloths for the head are the simple and uncompounded knowledge of intelligible realities together with theology that is accepted, through which the Word, who is absolutely incomprehensible to us without them, first made known the apprehension that is beyond them.

---

[80]Gen 1:31.
[81]Cf. Evagrius, *KG* 1.90, 4.26, 6.40, 42.
[82]Cf. Jn 20:6–7.
[83]Cf. *Ambig.* 54.2.

62 Οἱ θάπτοντες ἐντίμως τὸν Κύριον, καὶ ἐνδόξως ἀναστάντα θεάσονται· πᾶσιν ὄντα τοῖς μὴ τοιούτοις ἀθέατον. Οὐκ ἔτι γὰρ τοῖς ἐπιβουλεύουσίν ἐστιν ἁλωτός, οὐκ ἔχων τῶν ἐκτὸς τὰ προκαλύμματα, δι᾽ ὧν ἐδόκει θέλων ἁλίσκεσθαι παρὰ τῶν βουλομένων καὶ πάσχειν ὑπὲρ τῆς πάντων σωτηρίας ἠνείχετο.

63 Ὁ θάπτων ἐντίμως τὸν Κύριον πᾶσίν ἐστι τοῖς φιλοθέοις αἰδέσιμος· θριάμβου γάρ αὐτὸν καὶ ὀνείδους καθηκόντως ἐρρύσατο, βλασφημίας ὑπόθεσιν οὐκ ἀφεὶς τοῖς ἀπίστοις τὴν ἐν τῷ ξύλῳ αὐτοῦ προσήλωσιν. Οἱ δὲ σφραγῖδας ἐπιτιθέντες τῷ τάφῳ καὶ στρατιώτας προκαθιστῶντες μισητοὶ τῆς ἐγχειρήσεως· οἵ καὶ ἀναστάντα τὸν Λόγον ὡς κλαπέντα διαβάλλουσιν, ἀργυρίῳ ὥσπερ τὸν νόθον μαθητὴν εἰς προδοσίαν (λέγω δὲ τὸν ἐπιδεικτικὸν τρόπον τῆς ἀρετῆς), οὕτω καὶ τοὺς στρατιώτας πρὸς συκοφαντίαν τοῦ ἀναστάντος Σωτῆρος ὠνούμενοι. Γινώσκει τῶν λεγομένων τὴν ἔμφασιν ὁ γνωστικός, οὐκ ἀγνοῶν πῶς τε καὶ ποσαχῶς σταυροῦται ὁ Κύριος καὶ θάπτεται καὶ ἀνίσταται· ὡσεὶ νεκροὺς μὲν ποιῶν τοὺς ὑπὸ δαιμόνων τῇ καρδίᾳ παρακαθημένους ἐμπαθεῖς λογισμούς, τοὺς διαμεριζομένους ἐν τοῖς πειρασμοῖς, ὥσπερ ἱμάτια, τοὺς τρόπους τῆς ἠθικῆς εὐπρεπείας, καὶ ὑπερβαίνων, ὥσπερ σφραγίδας, τοὺς ἐπικειμένους τῇ ψυχῇ τύπους, τῶν κατὰ πρόληψιν ἁμαρτημάτων.

64 Πᾶς φιλάργυρος, δι᾽ εὐλαβείας τὴν ἀρετὴν ὑποκρινόμενος, ἐπειδὰν εὕρῃ τὴν ποθουμένην ὕλην πορίσασθαι τὸν τρόπον ἐξώμνυται, καθ᾽ ὅν μαθητὴς εἶναι τοῦ Λόγου τὸ πρὶν ἐνομίζετο.

65 Ὅταν ἴδῃς τινὰς ὑπερηφάνους μὴ φέροντας ἐπαινεῖσθαι τοὺς κρείττονας, ἀκήρυκτόν τε μηχανωμένους ποιεῖν τὴν

1.62 Those who are burying the Lord honorably will also see him resurrected gloriously; for all those not acting likewise he remains unseen. For he can no longer be captured by those plotting against him, not having the external coverings through which he seemed willing to be captured by the conspirators and endured to suffer for the salvation of all.

1.63 He who buries the Lord honorably is venerable to all God-loving people; for appropriately he delivers him from the triumphalist song and reproach, not leaving to the unbelievers that subject for blasphemy: his being nailed onto the tree. And those who have placed the seals on the tomb and have stationed soldiers are hateful for the deed.[84] Such types slander the resurrected Word as having been stolen,[85] just as they do with the fake disciple[86] (I mean, the showy kind of virtue) for betrayal, so too do they buy off the soldiers for their false testimony against the resurrected Savior. The gnostic knows the meaning of the things said, not being ignorant of how and in how many ways the Lord is crucified, buried, and resurrected; it is as though he puts to death the impassioned thoughts placed in the heart by demons who during temptations divide, like his garments,[87] the ways of dignified morality, and, like the seals, he goes beyond the underlying impressions of habitual sins that lie upon the soul.[88]

1.64 Every greedy man dissimulating virtue through piety, when he finds he has procured his desired object, swears off the previous manner of life according to which he was reckoned a disciple of the Word.

1.65 Whenever you see some arrogant types unable to bear that those who are more virtuous are being praised, and who contrive

[84]Mt 27:66.
[85]Cf. Mt 28:13.
[86]Cf. Mt 26:15.
[87]Cf. Ps 21/22:18; Mt 27:35; Mk 15:24.
[88]Cf. *Ambig.* 10.49, 32. 4–5, and 47.2.

λαλουμένην ἀλήθειαν, μυρίοις αὐτὴν ἀπείργοντας πειρασμοῖς καὶ ἀθεμίτοις διαβολαῖς, νόει μοι πάλιν ὑπὸ τούτων σταυροῦσθαι τὸν Κύριον [1108] καὶ θάπτεσθαι καὶ στρατώταις καὶ σφραγῖσι φυλάττεσθαι. Οὕς ἑαυτοῖς περιτρέπων ὁ Λόγος ἀνίσταται, πλέον τῷ πολεμεῖσθαι διαφαινόμενος, ὡς πρὸς ἀπάθειαν διὰ τῶν παθημάτων στομούμενος. Πάντων γάρ ἐστιν ἰσχυρότερος, ὡς ἀλήθεια καὶ ὢν καὶ καλούμενος.

66   Τό τῆς ἐνσωματώσεως τοῦ Λόγου μυστήριον πάντων ἔχει τῶν τε κατὰ τὴν Γραφὴν αἰνιγμάτων καὶ τύπων τὴν δύναμιν, καὶ τῶν φαινομένων καὶ νοουμένων κτισμάτων τὴν ἐπιστήμην. Καὶ ὁ μὲν γνοὺς σταυροῦ καὶ ταφῆς τὸ μυστήριον, ἔγνω τῶν προειρημένων τοὺς λόγους· ὁ δὲ τῆς ἀναστάσεως μυηθεὶς τὴν ἀπόρρητον δύναμιν, ἔγνω τὸν ἐφ᾽ ᾧ τὰ πάντα προηγουμένως ὁ Θεὸς ὑπεστήσατο σκοπόν.

67   Τὰ φαινόμενα πάντα δεῖται σταυροῦ, τῆς τῶν ἐπ᾽ αὐτοῖς κατ᾽ αἴσθησιν ἐνεργουμένων ἐπεχούσης τὴν σχέσιν ἕξεως· τὰ δὲ νοούμενα πάντα χρῄζει ταφῆς, τῆς τῶν ἐπ᾽ αὐτοῖς κατὰ νοῦν ἐνεργουμένων ὁλικῆς ἀκινησίας. Τῇ γὰρ σχέσει συναναιρουμένης τῆς περὶ πάντα φυσικῆς ἐνεργείας τε καὶ κινήσεως, ὁ Λόγος μόνος ἐφ᾽ ἑαυτὸν ὑπάρχων, ὥσπερ ἐκ νεκρῶν ἐγηγερμένος ἀναφαίνεται, πάντα κατὰ περιγραφὴν ἔχων τὰ ἐξ αὐτοῦ, μηδενὸς φυσικῇ σχέσει τὴν πρὸς αὐτὸν οἰκειότητα τὸ σύνολον ἔχοντος. Κατὰ χάριν γάρ, ἀλλ᾽ οὐ κατὰ φύσιν, ἐστὶν ἡ τῶν σωζομένων σωτηρία.

to render the spoken truth unproclaimed, preventing it by myriad temptations and slanders without evidence, it means to me that the Lord is yet again crucified and buried by such types and is guarded by soldiers and seals.[89] Yet the Word is resurrected, refuting them by their very own rationales, being all the more proven by being attacked, since he is being tempered to dispassion through his passions. He is stronger than all, since he both is and is called the truth.[90]

1.66 The mystery of the embodiment of the Word contains the power of the entirety of both the figures and types in Scripture, also the science of creatures that appear and of those that are thought. And the one who has come to know the mystery of the cross and tomb, comes to know the *logoi* of the aforementioned creatures; and one who has been initiated into the ineffable power of the resurrection comes to know the purpose toward which God initially established all things.[91]

1.67 All things that appear are in need of the cross, which is the capacity for holding back the relation of things that are actualized upon them in accordance with sensory perception; but all intelligible realities require the tomb, which is the complete immobility of things that are actualized upon them in accordance with mind. For when both natural activity and motion are taken away together with the relation in connection with all things, only the Word in himself remains, just as he appeared when he had been raised from the dead, containing all things that are from him by way of circumscription, since nothing at all has by natural relation kinship with him. For the salvation of the saved is by grace, certainly not by nature.[92]

---

[89]Cf. Mt 27:66.
[90]Cf. Jn 14:6; Origen, *Jo.* 20.6.
[91]Cf. *Ep.* 25, PG 91.613CD.
[92]Cf. Eph 2:5.

68   Τῶν πρός τι καὶ οἱ αἰῶνές εἰσι, καὶ οἱ χρόνοι, καὶ οἱ τόποι, ὧν
ἄνευ οὐδὲν τῶν συνεπινοουμένων τούτοις ἐστίν. Ὁ δὲ Θεός, οὐ τῶν
πρός τι ἐστίν, οὐ γὰρ ἔχει τι καθόλου συνεπινοούμενον. Εἴπερ οὖν
ἄρα κληρονομία τῶν ἀξίων αὐτός ἐστιν ὁ Θεός, ὑπὲρ πάντας αἰῶνας
καὶ χρόνους καὶ τόπους ὁ ταύτης ἀξιούμενος τῆς χάριτος ἔσται,
τόπον ἔχων αὐτὸν τὸν Θεὸν κατὰ τὸ γεγραμμένον· Γενοῦ μοι εἰς
Θεὸν ὑπερασπιστὴν καὶ εἰς τόπον ὀχυρὸν τοῦ σῶσαί με.

69   Τὸ τέλος οὐδὲν τὸ παράπαν ἐμφερὲς ἔχει μεσότητα, ἐπεὶ οὐδὲ
τέλος. Μεσότης δέ ἐστι πάντα τὰ μετὰ τὴν ἀρχὴν κατόπιν ὄντα
τοῦ τέλους. Εἰ τοίνυν πάντες οἱ αἰῶνες καὶ οἱ χρόνοι καὶ οἱ τόποι
μετὰ τῶν συνεπινοουμένων αὐτοῖς ἁπάντων, μετὰ τὸν Θεὸν εἰσιν,
ἀρχὴν ἄναρχον ὄντα· καὶ ὡς ἀπείρου τέλους αὐτοῦ πολὺ κατόπιν
ὑπάρχουσι, μεσότητος οὐδὲν διαφέρουσι· τέλος δὲ τῶν σῳζομένων
ἐστὶν ὁ Θεός, οὐδὲν ἔσται μεσότητος κατὰ τὸ ἀκρότατον τέλος
γενομένοις τοῖς σῳζομένοις συνθεωρούμενον.

70   [1109] Ὁ πᾶς κόσμος, ἰδίοις περιοριζόμενος λόγοις, καὶ τόπος
λέγεται καὶ αἰὼν τῶν ἐν αὐτῷ διαιτωμένων· τρόπους θεωρημάτων
ἔχων κατὰ φύσιν τοὺς ἐν αὐτῷ προσφυεῖς, μερικὴν κατανόησιν
αὐτοῖς ἐμποιῆσαι τῆς ἐπὶ πάντα σοφίας τοῦ Θεοῦ δυναμένους· οἷς
ἕως χρῶνται πρὸς κατανόησιν, οὐ δύνανται δίχα μεσότητος εἶναι καὶ
μερικῆς καταλήψεως. Ἐπειδὴ δὲ τὸ ἐκ μέρους τοῦ τελείου φανέντος
καταργεῖται, καὶ τὰ ἔσοπτρα πάντα καὶ τὰ αἰνίγματα παρέρχονται,
τῆς πρόσωπον πρὸς πρόσωπον παραγινομένης ἀληθείας, ὑπὲρ

1.68   Ages, times, and places belong in the category of "relation;"[93] nothing that is conceptualized together with these exists without them. But God is not in the category of "relation," since he is not something with which anything else at all can be conceptualized. In consequence, therefore, if indeed God himself is the inheritance of the worthy, he who is made worthy of this grace will be beyond all ages, times, and places, having God himself for a place, according to what is written: "Be for me a champion God, and a stronghold to save me."[94]

1.69   The end bears no resemblance at all to the intermediate state, since it would be no end. And the intermediate state is all things after the first principle that fall short of the end. If then all the ages, and all the times, and all the places are with all things co-conceptualized with them, they are after God, their first principle without first principle; moreover, since they fall far short of him, the infinite end, they differ in no way from the intermediate state; finally, since the end of the saved is God, in the highest end nothing from the intermediate state will be co-envisioned with those who have come to be saved.

1.70   The entire world, being defined by the boundaries of its own *logoi*, is called both place and age of the things dwelling within it; it has ways of contemplating by way of nature, ways that naturally grow within it, enabling them to produce a partial apprehension of God's wisdom toward all things; by these ways, so long as they are used for apprehension, acts of contemplation cannot be anything other than an intermediate state and partial understanding. But when what is perfect appears, what is partial is annulled, and all mirrors and all figures will pass away when the truth presents itself face to face;[95] he who is saved, having been perfected in accordance with God, will be

[93]See footnote to 1.7.
[94]Ps 70:3 (71:3 MT).
[95]Cf. 1 Cor 13:12.

πάντας ἔσται κόσμους καὶ αἰῶνας καὶ τόπους, οἷς τέως ὡς νήπιος ἐπαιδαγωγεῖτο, τελειωθεὶς κατὰ Θεὸν ὁ σωζόμενος.

71 Ὁ Πιλάτος τοῦ κατὰ φύσιν τύπος ἐστί, τοῦ δὲ γραπτοῦ νόμου, τὸ πλῆθος τῶν Ἰουδαίων. Ὁ τοίνυν κατὰ πίστιν ὑπὲρ τοὺς δύο μὴ γενόμενος νόμους, οὐ δύναται δέξασθαι τὴν ὑπὲρ φύσιν καὶ λόγον ἀλήθειαν· ἀλλὰ σταυροῖ πάντως τὸν Λόγον ἢ ὡς Ἰουδαῖος σκάνδαλον ἢ ὡς Ἕλλην μωρίαν ἡγούμενος τὸ Εὐαγγέλιον.

72 Ὅταν ἴδῃς Ἡρώδην καὶ Πιλάτον ἀλλήλοις φιλιάζοντας ἐπὶ τῇ ἀναιρέσει τοῦ Ἰησοῦ, τότε νόει τὴν εἰς αὐτὸ συνδρομήν, τοῦ τε τῆς πορνείας καὶ τῆς κενοδοξίας δαίμονος, ἐπὶ τῷ θανατῶσαι τὸν λόγον τῆς ἀρετῆς καὶ τῆς γνώσεως, ἀλλήλοις συμφωνούντων. Ὁ μὲν γὰρ κενόδοξος δαίμων, πνευματικὴν γνῶσιν ὑποκρινόμενος, παραπέμπει τῷ δαίμονι τῆς πορνείας. Διό· Λαμπρὰν περιθεὶς ἐσθῆτα, φησίν, ὁ Ἡρώδης, ἀνέπεμψε Πιλάτῳ τὸν Ἰησοῦν.

73 Καλὸν μὴ συγχωρεῖν σαρκὶ καὶ πάθεσι προσανέχειν τὸν νοῦν. Οὐ γὰρ συλλέγουσι, φησίν, ἐξ ἀκανθῶν σῦκα, τουτέστιν, ἐκ παθῶν, ἀρετήν· οὔτε ἐκ βάτου σταφυλήν, τουτέστιν, ἐκ τῆς σαρκός, τὴν εὐφραίνουσαν γνῶσιν.

74 Διὰ τῆς ὑπομονῆς τῶν πειρασμῶν δοκιμαζόμενος ὁ ἀσκητής, καὶ διὰ τῆς σωματικῆς παιδαγωγίας καθαιρόμενος, καὶ διὰ τῆς ἐπιμελείας τῶν ὑψηλῶν θεωρημάτων τελειούμενος, ἀξιοῦται τῆς θείας παρακλήσεως. Κύριος γάρ, φησὶν ὁ Μωϋσῆς, ἐκ Σινᾶ ἥκει, τουτέστιν, ἐκ τῶν πειρασμῶν· καὶ ἐπεφάνη [1112] ἡμῖν ἐκ Σηείρ, τουτέστιν, ἐκ τῶν σωματικῶν πόνων· καὶ κατέπαυσεν ἐξ ὄρους

beyond all worlds, and ages, and places, wherein—till then—he was reared like an infant.[96]

1.71 Pilate is a type of the law that accords with nature, and the crowd of the Jews, of the written Law. So, he who does not come to be, in accordance with faith, higher than the two laws, cannot receive the truth that is beyond nature and language; rather, he, no doubt, crucifies the Word, deeming the Gospel either a scandal, like a Jew, or nonsense, like a Greek.[97]

1.72 Whenever you see Herod and Pilate befriending each other for Jesus' destruction,[98] notice, then, the converging of the demon of fornication and vainglory[99] for the same purpose, to kill the *logos* of virtue and of knowledge, conspiring with each other. For the vain-glorious demon dissimulating spiritual knowledge sends it along to the demon of fornication. Thus, "Having clothed him with bright raiments," it says, "Herod sent Jesus back to Pilate."[100]

1.73 It is good for the mind not to make room for the flesh or to devote itself to the passions. "For they do not gather," it says, "figs from thistles," that is, virtue from passions, "nor grapes from a bramble bush,"[101] that is, joyous knowledge from the flesh.

1.74 The ascetic who is being tested through the endurance of temptations, cleansed through the disciplining of the body, and per-fected through attentiveness to the contemplations of higher things, is deemed worthy of divine comforting. "For the Lord," says Moses, "comes from Sinai," that is, from temptations, "and appeared to us from Seir," that is, from the bodily toils, "and rested at Mount Paran

---

[96]Cf. 1 Cor 13:11.
[97]Cf. 1 Cor 1:23.
[98]Cf. Lk 23:12.
[99]Cf. Evagrius, *Pra.* 13 and 58.
[100]Lk 23:11.
[101]Cf. Mt 7:16.

Φαρὰν σὺν μυριάσι Κάδης, τουτέστιν, ἐξ ὅρους τῆς πίστεως σὺν μυριάσιν ἁγίων γνώσεων.

75   Ὁ Ἡρώδης φρονήματος λόγον ἐπέχει σαρκός· ὁ δὲ Πιλάτος αἰσθήσεως· ὁ δὲ Καῖσαρ τῶν αἰσθητῶν· οἱ δὲ Ἰουδαῖοι τῶν ψυχικῶν λογισμῶν. Ἐπειδὰν οὖν ἐξ ἀγνοίας ἡ ψυχὴ τοῖς αἰσθητοῖς προστεθῇ, προδίδωσι τῇ αἰσθήσει τὸν Λόγον εἰς θάνατον, καθ᾽ ἑαυτῆς κυροῦσα δι᾽ ὁμολογίας, τὴν τῶν φθαρτῶν βασιλείαν. Φασὶ γὰρ οἱ Ἰουδαῖοι· Οὐκ ἔχομεν βασιλέα εἰ μὴ Καίσαρα.

76   Ὁ Ἡρώδης, ἐνεργείας τόπον ἐπέχει παθῶν· ὁ δὲ Πιλάτος, τῆς ἐπ᾽ αὐτοῖς ἠπατημένης ἕξεως· ὁ δὲ Καῖσαρ, τοῦ σκοτεινοῦ κοσμοκράτορος· οἱ δὲ Ἰουδαῖοι, ψυχῆς. Ὁπηνίκα γοῦν ὑποκλιθεῖσα ψυχὴ τοῖς πάθεσι, τὴν ἀρετὴν παραδῷ τῇ ἕξει τῆς κακίας ὑποχείριον, τὴν μὲν τοῦ Θεοῦ προδήλως ἀρνεῖται βασιλείαν· πρὸς δὲ τὴν τοῦ διαβόλου μετέρχεται φθοροποιὸν τυραννίδα.

77   Οὐκ ἀρκεῖ τῇ ψυχῇ πρὸς εὐφροσύνην πνευματικὴν ἡ ὑποταγὴ τῶν παθῶν, εἰ μὴ τὰς ἀρετὰς κτήσηται τῇ πληρώσει τῶν ἐντολῶν. Μὴ χαίρετε γάρ, φησίν, ὅτι τὰ δαιμόνια ὑμῖν ὑποτάσσεται, τουτέστι, τὰ ἐνεργήματα τῶν παθῶν· ἀλλ᾽ ὅτι τὰ ὀνόματα ὑμῶν ἐγράφη ἐν οὐρανῷ· τῇ δι᾽ ἀρετῶν τῆς υἱοθεσίας χάριτι, πρὸς τὸν τόπον τῆς ἀπαθείας μεταγραφέντα.

78   Ἀναγκαῖος τῷ γνωστικῷ πάντως ἐστὶν ὁ διὰ πράξεως πλοῦτος τῶν ἀρετῶν. Ὁ ἔχων γάρ, φησί, βαλάντιον, τουτέστι, γνῶσιν πνευματικήν· ἀράτω ὁμοίως καὶ πήραν, τουτέστι, τὴν δαψιλῶς τὴν ψυχὴν διατρέφουσαν τῶν ἀρετῶν ἀφθονίαν. Ὁ δὲ μὴ ἔχων, βαλάντιον

with a numberless host of Kadesh,"[102] that is, at the mountain of faith with a numberless host of holy knowledge.

1.75   Herod stands for the fleshly way of thinking, Pilate for that of sensory perception, Caesar for that of sensory realities, and the Jews for that of the soul's thoughts. Thus, whenever the soul out of ignorance is added to sensory reality, they hand the Word over to sensory perception for death, the soul invoking against itself through a declaration the dominion of corruptible realities. For, "The Jews say: 'we have no king but Caesar.'"[103]

1.76   Herod stands for the place of the activity of the passions; and Pilate of the character state that has been tricked by them; and Caesar of the world-ruler of darkness;[104] and the Jews of the soul. In consequence, at such a time as the soul inclines to the passions, it renders virtue captive to the character state of vice; it clearly denies the kingdom of God and crosses over to the corrupting tyranny of the devil.

1.77   The subjection of the passions does not suffice the soul for spiritual gladness if it has not acquired the virtues by the fulfillment of the commandments. "So do not rejoice," it says, "because the demons are subject to you;" that is, the activities of the passions; "but rather, because your names have been written in heaven;"[105] since they have been transcribed into the place of dispassion through the virtues by the grace of adoption.

1.78   Wealth in virtue through the practical life is absolutely necessary for the gnostic. "For he who has," it says, "a purse," that is, spiritual knowledge, "let him likewise also grab a wallet," that is, the liberality of the virtues continuously sustaining the soul. "And he

[102]Deut 33:2.
[103]Jn 19:15.
[104]Eph 6:12.
[105]Lk 10:20.

δηλονότι καὶ πήραν, τουτέστι, γνῶσιν καὶ ἀρετήν· πωλησάτω τὸ ἱμάτιον αὐτοῦ, καὶ ἀγορασάτω μάχαιραν. Ἐκδότω, φησί, προθύμως τὴν ἑαυτοῦ σάρκα τοῖς πόνοις τῶν ἀρετῶν καὶ μεταχειρισάσθω σοφῶς ὑπὲρ τῆς εἰρήνης τοῦ Θεοῦ, τὸν πρὸς τὰ πάθη καὶ τοὺς δαίμονας πόλεμον· ἤγουν, τὴν ἐν ῥήματι Θεοῦ διακρίνουσαν ἕξιν τὸ χεῖρον τοῦ κρείττονος.

79 Τριακοντούτης ὤν, ὁ Κύριος ἀναφαίνεται, τοὺς διορατικοὺς τῷ ἀριθμῷ τούτῳ τὰ περὶ ἑαυτοῦ κρυφίως μυστήρια διδάσκων. Ὁ γὰρ τριάκοντα ἀριθμὸς μυστικῶς κατανοούμενος, χρόνου τε καὶ φύσεως καὶ τῶν ὑπὲρ τὴν ὁρατὴν φύσιν νοητῶν, δημιουργὸν καὶ προνοητὴν εἰσάγει τὸν Κύριον. Χρόνου μὲν διὰ τοῦ ἑπτά, ἑβδοματικὸς γὰρ ὁ χρόνος· φύσεως δὲ διὰ τοῦ πέντε, πενταδικὴ γὰρ ἡ φύσις, διὰ τὴν αἴσθησιν πενταχῶς διαιρουμένην· νοητῶν δὲ διὰ τοῦ ὀκτώ, [1113] ὑπὲρ γὰρ τὴν μετρουμένην τοῦ χρόνου περίοδον, ἡ τῶν νοητῶν ἐστι γένεσις· προνοητὴν δὲ διὰ τοῦ δέκα, διά τε τὴν τῶν ἐντολῶν ἁγίαν δεκάδα, τὴν πρὸς τὸ εὖ τοὺς ἀνθρώπους ἐνάγουσαν καὶ διὰ τὸ τούτου τοῦ γράμματος μυστικῶς ἀπῆρχθαι τῆς προσηγορίας τὸν Κύριον, ἡνίκα γέγονεν ἄνθρωπος. Συνάψας οὖν τὸν πέντε, καὶ τὸν ἑπτά, καὶ τὸν ὀκτώ, καὶ τὸν δέκα, τὸν τριάκοντα πληροῖς ἀριθμόν. Ὁ τοίνυν ὡς ἀρχηγῷ τῷ Κυρίῳ καλῶς ἔπεσθαι γινώσκων, οὐκ ἀγνοήσει τὸν λόγον καθ᾽ ὅν καὶ αὐτὸς τριακοντούτης ἀναφανήσεται κηρύττειν δυνάμενος τὸ Εὐαγγέλιον τῆς βασιλείας. Ὅτε γὰρ ἀμέμπτως, ὥσπερ τινὰ φύσιν ὁρατήν, τὸν κατὰ πρᾶξιν τῶν ἀρετῶν δημιουργήσει κόσμον, τὴν ἐπ᾽ αὐτῆς τῆς ψυχῆς, ὥσπερ τινὰ χρόνον, διὰ τῶν ἐναντίων συμβαίνουσαν μὴ ἀλλοιώσας περίοδον καὶ διὰ θεωρίας τὴν τῶν νοητῶν ἀπταίστως δρέψεται γνῶσιν καὶ τὴν αὐτὴν καὶ ἄλλοις ἕξιν προνοητικῶς ἐνθεῖναι δεδύνηται· τότε καὶ αὐτός, ὡς δ᾽ ἂν ἔχῃ σωματικῆς ἡλικίας,

who does not have" (meaning a purse and a wallet, that is, knowledge and virtue) "let him sell his outer garment and buy a sword."[106] That is to say that one should eagerly hand one's flesh over to the toils of the virtues and contend wisely for the sake of the peace of God in the battle against the passions and the demons—that is, the character state discerning worse from better by the word of God.

1.79 Being thirty years old, the Lord appears,[107] by this number hiddenly teaching those with discernment the mysteries concerning himself. For the number thirty being contemplated mystically introduces the Lord, creator and provider of both time and nature, also of intelligible realities beyond visible nature: of time, through the number seven, for time is sevenfold; of nature, through the number five, for nature is fivefold since sensory perception is divided in a fivefold manner; of intelligible realities, through the number eight; for beyond the measured period of time is the generation of intelligible realities; and provider through the number ten, on account of the holy Decalogue of the commandments that lead humans toward what is right, also on account of the fact that the Lord mystically began his name, when he had become a human, with this letter.[108] So now, having added five, seven, eight, and ten, you have in total the number thirty.[109] He who knows, therefore, properly to follow the Lord like a leader, will not be ignorant about the principle in accordance with which he too will appear to be thirty, able to preach the Gospel of the Kingdom. For when he blamelessly creates a world of the virtues in accordance with the practical life—something like visible nature, and depending on the practical life has not altered the cycle taking place in the soul through contraries—something like time, and through contemplation will securely gain the knowledge of intelligible realities, and will have been able providentially to

[106]Lk 22:36. Cf. Evagrius, *KG* 5.28.

[107]Cf Lk 3:23.

[108]The letter I (Iota) stands for the numeral 10 in Greek numbering; it is also the first letter of Jesus' name in Greek.

[109]Maximus provides another numerology in *Myst.* 5.

τριακοντούτης ἐστὶ τῷ πνεύματι, συνεμφαίνων τῶν οἰκείων ἀγαθῶν τὴν ἐν ἄλλοις ἐνέργειαν.

80   Ὁ ταῖς ἡδοναῖς παρειμένος τοῦ σώματος οὔτε πρὸς ἀρετὴν ἐστιν ἐνεργὸς οὔτε πρὸς γνῶσιν εὐκίνητος. Ὅθεν οὐδὲ ἄνθρωπον ἔχει, τουτέστιν, ἔμφρονα λογισμόν· ἵνα ὅταν ταραχθῇ τὸ ὕδωρ, βάλῃ αὐτὸν εἰς τὴν κολυμβήθραν, τουτέστιν, εἰς τὴν δεκτικὴν τῆς γνώσεως ἀρετὴν τὴν ἰατρεύουσαν πᾶσαν νόσον, εἰ μὴ που διὰ ῥᾳθυμίαν ὁ νοσῶν ἀναβαλλόμενος, ὑπ᾽ ἄλλου προληφθῇ τοῦ κωλύοντος αὐτῷ παραβενέσθαι τὴν ἴασιν. Διὸ καὶ τριάκοντα καὶ ὀκτὼ ἔτη τῇ νόσῳ συγκατακλίνεται. Ὁ γὰρ μὴ πρὸς δόξαν Θεοῦ τὴν ὁρατὴν θεώμενος κτίσιν καὶ πρὸς τὴν νοητὴν φύσιν εὐσεβῶς ἀναβιβάζων τὴν ἔννοιαν, εἰκότως νοσῶν διαμένει τὸν εἰρημένον τῶν ἐτῶν ἀριθμόν. Ὁ γὰρ τριάκοντα φυσικῶς λαμβανόμενος ἀριθμὸς τὴν αἰσθητὴν σημαίνει φύσιν· ὥσπερ καὶ πρακτικῶς σκοπούμενος τὴν πρακτικὴν ἀρετήν. Ὁ δὲ ὀκτὼ φυσικῶς κατανοούμενος, τὴν νοητὴν τῶν ἀσωμάτων παραδηλοῖ φύσιν· ὥσπερ καὶ γνωστικῶς θεωρούμενος, τὴν πάνσοφον θεολογίαν· αἷς ὁ μὴ κινούμενος πρὸς Θεόν, πάρετος μένει, μέχρις ἂν ἐλθὼν ὁ Λόγος, διδάξῃ αὐτὸν τὸν σύντομον τῆς ἰάσεως τρόπον, φάσκων· Ἔγειραι, ἆρον τὸν κράββατόν σου, καὶ περιπάτει· διαναστῆναι τὸν νοῦν τῆς κατεχούσης φιληδονίας, καὶ ἆραι τὸ σῶμα τοῖς ὤμοις τῶν ἀρετῶν, καὶ ἀπελθεῖν εἰς τὸν οἶκον, δηλαδὴ τὸν οὐρανὸν ἐγκελευόμενος. Καλὸν γὰρ ὑπὸ [1116] τοῦ κρείττονος τοῖς ὤμοις τῆς πράξεως τὸ χεῖρον αἴρεσθαι πρὸς ἀρετὴν ἢ τὸ κρεῖττον διὰ θρύψεως πρὸς φιληδονίαν ὑπὸ τοῦ χείρονος φέρεσθαι.

81   Ἕως τῆς ἡμῶν τε καὶ πάντων τῶν μετὰ Θεὸν οὐσίας κατὰ διάνοιαν καθαρῶς οὐκ ἐκβεβήκαμεν, οὔπω τὴν τῆς κατ᾽ ἀρετὴν

instill the same capacity in others, then even he, whatever bodily age he might have, will be thirty in spirit, manifesting simultaneously in others the activity of his own goods.

1.80 He who is sidetracked by the pleasures of the body is neither active for virtue, nor well-moved toward knowledge. Therefore, he has no one, that is, a prudent thought, to cast him into the pool when the water is stirred, that is, into the virtue receptive of knowledge, the kind that heals every illness;[110] unless it should happen that the ailing man, dallying due to laziness, should have been beaten by another who would prevent him from receiving healing. Because of that, he lies around for thirty eight years with the illness. For, he who does not contemplate visible creation for the glory of God, and does not piously elevate the concept to its intelligible nature, spends the mentioned number of years like the ailing man. For when the number thirty is taken as referring to nature, it signifies sensory nature, just as when it is seen as referring to praxis, it signifies practical virtue. When the number eight is conceptualized as referring to nature, it hints at the intelligible nature of the bodiless hosts, just as when it is contemplated as pertaining to knowledge, it hints at the all-wise theology; he who is not moved by these things toward God remains paralyzed, until the Word, having arrived, teaches him the immediate manner of healing, saying: "Get up; grab your mat and walk,"[111] urging him to pick up his mind from the binding love of pleasure, to shoulder the body of the virtues, and to depart to his house, obviously meaning heaven. For it is right for what is worse to be elevated to virtue on the shoulders of the practical life by what is better rather than for what is better to be carried toward love of pleasure by what is worse.[112]

1.81 As long as we have not purely transcended both our own substance and that of all things after God in our mind, we cannot

[110]Cf Jn 5:7.
[111]Jn 5:8.
[112]Cf. *Qu. Dub.* 64, CCSG 10, p. 113.

ἀτρεψίας ἕξιν ἐλάβομεν. Ὁπηνίκα δὲ τοῦτο δι᾽ ἀγάπης ἡμῖν κατορθωθῇ τὸ ἀξίωμα, τότε γνωσόμεθα τῆς θείας ἐπαγγελίας τὴν δύναμιν. Ἐκεῖ γὰρ εἶναι χρὴ πιστεύειν καθ᾽ ἵδρυσιν ἀμετάθετον τοὺς ἀξίους, ἔνθα προλαβὼν ὁ νοῦς δι᾽ ἀγάπης τὴν σφετέραν ἐνερρίζωσε δύναμιν. Ὁ γὰρ μὴ ἐκβὰς ἑαυτοῦ καὶ πάντων τῶν ὁπωσοῦν νοεῖσθαι δυναμένων καὶ εἰς τὴν ὑπὲρ νόησιν σιγὴν καταστάς, οὐ δύναται τροπῆς εἶναι πάμπαν ἐλεύθερος.

82   Πᾶσα νόησις, πλήθους, ἢ τουλάχιστον, δυάδος πάντως ἔμφασιν ἔχει. Μέση γάρ ἐστι τινῶν ἀκροτήτων σχέσις, ἀλλήλοις συνάπτουσα, τό τε νοοῦν καὶ τὸ νοούμενον. Οὐδέτερον δὲ διόλου τὴν ἁπλότητα πέφυκε σώζειν. Τό τε γὰρ νοοῦν, ὑποκείμενόν τί ἐστι, πάντως συνεπινοουμένην αὐτῷ τὴν τοῦ νοεῖν ἔχον δύναμιν. Καὶ τὸ νοούμενον ὑποκείμενόν τι πάντως ἐστὶν ἢ ἐν ὑποκειμένῳ, συνεπινοουμένην αὐτῷ τὴν τοῦ νοεῖσθαι δύναμιν ἔχον ἢ προϋποκειμένην τὴν οὗ ἐστι δύναμις οὐσίαν. Οὐ γάρ τι τῶν ὄντων τὸ σύνολον αὐτὸ καθ᾽ αὑτὸ ἁπλῆ τις οὐσία ἢ νόησίς ἐστιν, ἵνα καὶ μονὰς ἀδιαίρετος. Τὸν δὲ Θεὸν εἴτε οὐσίαν εἴπωμεν, οὐκ ἔχει φυσικῶς συνεπινοουμένην αὐτῷ τὴν τοῦ νοεῖσθαι δύναμιν, ἵνα μὴ σύνθετος, εἴτε νόησιν, οὐκ ἔχει φυσικῶς δεκτικὴν τῆς νοήσεως ὑποκειμένην οὐσίαν· ἀλλ᾽ αὐτὸς κατ᾽ οὐσίαν νόησίς ἐστιν ὁ Θεὸς καὶ ὅλος νόησις, καὶ [1117] μόνον· καὶ αὐτὸς κατὰ τὴν νόησιν οὐσία, καὶ ὅλος οὐσία καὶ μόνον· καὶ ὑπὲρ οὐσίαν ὅλος, καὶ ὑπὲρ νόησιν ὅλος, διότι καὶ μονὰς ἀδιαίρετος καὶ ἀμερὴς καὶ ἁπλῆ. Ὁ τοίνυν καθ᾽ ὁτιοῦν νόησιν ἔχων, οὔπω τῆς δυάδος ἐξῆλθεν· ὁ δὲ ταύτην πάμπαν ἀπολιπών, γέγονε ποσῶς ἐν τῇ μονάδι, τὴν τοῦ νοεῖν ὑπεροχικῶς ἀποθέμενος δύναμιν.

yet acquire the capacity for changelessness in virtue. But at the time when this dignity is rectified in us through love, then we will know the power of the divine promise. For one must believe the worthy to be in an unshakable foundation where the mind, going first, has rooted its power through love. For he who does not transcend himself and everything that can be thought in any way, and does not come to stability in the silence beyond thought, is not at all able to be free from change.

1.82 All thought necessarily entails the appearance of plurality or, at the very least, of duality, since there is a mediating relationship between the two specific extremes—that which thinks and that which is thought—connecting them reciprocally. Moreover, it is not in either of them to maintain simplicity consistently. For that which thinks is a specifically subsisting reality, necessarily possessing the potentiality to think as a concept inherent to it. And that which is thought is necessarily a specifically subsisting reality, or is in a subsisting reality, possessing the potentiality to be thought—or a presupposed substance, which is its potentiality—as a concept inherent to it. For absolutely no being itself, in itself, is a concrete simple substance or thought and therefore not an indivisible singularity. As regards God (were we to call him a substance), neither does he have the capacity of being thought by nature implied in himself, lest he should be composite, nor (were we to call him a thought), does he have an underlying substance naturally receptive of thought; but God himself is in substance thought and entirely thought and only thought; and he is by thought a substance and entirely a substance and only a substance; also entirely beyond substance and entirely beyond thought, thus also an indivisible singularity without parts and simple. Therefore, he who has any thought whatsoever has not yet escaped from the duality; but he who has altogether left it behind, has surely come to be in the singularity, transcendently laying aside the capacity of thought.[113]

---

[113]Cf. Dionysius the Areopagite, *D.n.* 7.4.

83 Ἐν μὲν τοῖς πολλοῖς ἑτερότης, καὶ ἀνομοιότης ἐστί, καὶ διαφορά· ἐν δὲ τῷ Θεῷ, κυρίως ἑνὶ καὶ μόνῳ τυγχάνοντι, ταυτότης, καὶ ἁπλότης μόνον ἐστί, καὶ ὁμοιότης. Οὐκ ἀσφαλὲς οὖν πρὶν ἔξω γενέσθαι τῶν πολλῶν, ἐπιβάλλειν ταῖς περὶ Θεοῦ θεωρίαις· καὶ δηλοῖ τοῦτο Μωϋσῆς, ἔξω τῆς παρεμβολῆς πηγνύμενος τὴν σκηνὴν τῆς διανοίας καὶ τότε προσομιλῶν τῷ Θεῷ. Τὸ γὰρ μετὰ λόγου τοῦ κατὰ προφορὰν πειρᾶσθαι φάναι τὸν ἄρρητον ἐπικίνδυνον· ὅτι δυὰς καὶ πλέον ἐστὶν ὁ κατὰ προφορὰν λόγος. Τὸ δὲ ἄνευ φωνῆς μόνῃ τῇ ψυχῇ τὸ ὂν θεωρεῖν, ἰσχυρότατον, ὅτι κατὰ τὴν ἀδιαίρετον ἵσταται μονάδα καὶ οὐκ ἐν τοῖς πολλοῖς. Ὁ γὰρ ἀρχιερεὺς ἅπαξ τοῦ ἐνιαυτοῦ εἰς τὰ Ἅγια τῶν ἁγίων εἴσω τοῦ καταπετάσματος εἰσιέναι μόλις προστεταγμένος, διδάσκει μόνον δεῖν ἐκεῖνον τὸν τὴν αὐλὴν καὶ τὰ ἅγια διαβάντα καὶ εἰς τὰ Ἅγια τῶν ἁγίων εἴσω γενόμενον, τουτέστι, τὴν ἅπασαν τῶν αἰσθητῶν τε καὶ νοητῶν παρελθόντα φύσιν καὶ πάσης τῆς κατὰ γένεσιν ἰδιότητος γενόμενον καθαρόν, ἀνείμονι καὶ γυμνῇ τῇ διανοίᾳ προσβάλλειν ταῖς περὶ Θεοῦ φαντασίαις.

84 Μωϋσῆς ὁ μέγας ἔξω τῆς παρεμβολῆς πηξάμενος ἑαυτοῦ τὴν σκηνήν, τουτέστι, τὴν γνώμην καὶ τὴν διάνοιαν ἱδρυσάμενος ἔξω τῶν ὁρωμένων, προσκυνεῖν τὸν Θεὸν ἄρχεται· καὶ εἰς τὸν γνόφον εἰσελθών, τὸν ἀειδῆ καὶ ἄϋλον τῆς γνώσεως τόπον, ἐκεῖ μένει τὰς ἱερωτάτας τελούμενος τελετάς.

85 [1120] Ὁ γνόφος ἐστὶν ἡ ἀειδὴς καὶ ἄϋλος καὶ ἀσώματος κατάστασις, ἡ τὴν παραδειγματικὴν τῶν ὄντων ἔχουσα γνῶσιν· ἐν ᾗ ὁ γενόμενος ἐντός, καθάπερ τις ἄλλος Μωϋσῆς, φύσει θνητῇ κατανοεῖ τὰ ἀθέατα, δι' ἧς τῶν θείων ἀρετῶν ἐν ἑαυτῷ ζωγραφήσας τὸ κάλλος, ὥσπερ γραφὴν εὐμιμήτως ἔχουσαν τοῦ ἀρχετύπου

1.83 While in the many there is otherness, dissimilarity, and difference, in God, by being properly one and unique, there is only identity, simplicity, and similarity. Consequently, it is not safe, before coming to be outside of the many, to apply oneself to the contemplations about God; and Moses indicates this, pitching the tent of the intellect outside the camp, and then conversing with God.[114] For it is precarious to attempt to disclose the ineffable with public discourse, since public discourse is twofold, even manifold. Rather, it is most sound to contemplate being in the soul alone, without verbal expression, because it subsists in relation to the undivided singularity and not in the many. For the high priest, having been appointed to enter into the Holy of holies inside the veil only once a year,[115] teaches that it is necessary that only the one who has crossed the courtyard and the sanctuary and has come to be within the Holy of holies—that is, one who has passed by the entirety of the nature of both visible and intelligible realities and has become pure from every property in accordance with generation—attends with unveiled and naked intellect to things that appear about God.

1.84 The great Moses, having pitched his tent outside the camp,[116] that is, having established his will and intellect outside visible realities, begins to worship God; and having entered the dark cloud,[117] the formless and immaterial place of knowledge, he remains there, performing the holiest rites.

1.85 The dark cloud[118] is the formless, immaterial, and incorporeal condition containing the paradigmatic knowledge of beings; he who has come to be inside it, just like another Moses, understands invisible realities in a mortal nature; having depicted the beauty of the divine virtues in himself through this state, like a painting

[114]Cf. Ex 33:7.
[115]Cf. Lev 16:34.
[116]Cf. Ex 33:7.
[117]Cf. Ex 20:21.
[118]Cf. Ex 20:21.

κάλλους τὸ ἀπεικόνισμα, κάτεισιν, ἑαυτὸν προβαλλόμενος τοῖς βουλομένοις μιμεῖσθαι τὴν ἀρετήν, καὶ ἐν τούτῳ δεικνύς, ἧς μετείληφει χάριτος, τὸ φιλάνθρωπόν τε καὶ ἄφθονον.

86   Οἱ ἀσπίλως τὴν κατὰ Θεὸν μετερχόμενοι φιλοσοφίαν, μέγιστον ἐκ τῆς κατ᾽ αὐτὴν ἐπιστήμης κέρδος εὑρίσκουσι, τὸ μηκέτι τὴν γνώμην τοῖς πράγμασι συμμεταβάλλεσθαι, ἀλλὰ μετ᾽ εὐσταθοῦς βεβαιότητος πᾶσιν ἐγχειρεῖν προθύμως τοῖς ἁρμόζουσι τῷ λόγῳ τῆς ἀρετῆς.

87   Τὴν κατὰ σάρκα πρώτην ἐν Χριστῷ διὰ Πνεύματος βαπτισθέντες ἀφθαρσίαν, τὴν ἐσχάτην κατ᾽ αὐτὸν ἐν Πνεύματι· δι᾽ ἐπιδόσεως ἔργων ἀγαθῶν δηλονότι, καὶ τοῦ κατὰ πρόθεσιν θανάτου τὴν προτέραν φυλάξαντες ἀκηλίδωτον ἐκδεχόμεθα· καθ᾽ ἥν τῶν ἐχόντων οὐδεὶς ἀποβολὴν δέδοικε τῶν κτηθέντων ἀγαθῶν.

88   Τοῖς ἐπὶ γῆς τῆς θείας ἀρετῆς ἀπ᾽ οὐρανοῦ δι᾽ ἔλεον τὸν πρὸς ἡμᾶς τὴν χάριν καταπέμψαι βουληθεὶς ὁ Θεός, συμβολικῶς τὴν ἱερὰν σκηνὴν καὶ τὰ ἐν αὐτῇ πάντα κατεσκεύασε, σοφίας οὖσαν ἀπεικόνισμα καὶ τύπον καὶ μίμημα.

89   Ἡ χάρις τῆς Νέας Διαθήκης μυστικῶς τῷ τῆς Παλαιᾶς κέκρυπται γράμματι· διὸ φησιν ὁ Ἀπόστολος ὅτι ὁ νόμος πνευματικὸς ἐστιν. Ὁ οὖν νόμος τῷ μὲν γράμματι παλαιοῦται καὶ γηράσκει καταργούμενος, τῷ δὲ πνεύματι νεάζει διαπαντὸς ἐνεργούμενος. Ἡ γὰρ χάρις παντελῶς ἀπαλαίωτος.

accurately rendering the representation of the archetypal beauty,[119] he descends, offering himself to those willing to imitate virtue, and in this shows both love of humanity and freedom from envy of the grace of which he had partaken.[120]

1.86　Those faultlessly following Godlike philosophy will derive the greatest profit from the structure of science it confers, namely, no longer to change the mentality along with things, but rather, eagerly to undertake with steadfast firmness all things conforming to the principle of virtue.

1.87　Having been baptized in Christ, through the Spirit we receive the first incorruption which pertains to the flesh; when we have been baptized in the Spirit, we receive the last incorruption, which pertains to Christ, through an increase of good deeds, most assuredly, and through rendering our death as an offering, thus keeping the first incorruption undefiled; no one who keeps it in this way fears the loss of the good things he has acquired.

1.88　God having willed, in his mercy, to send the grace of divine virtue from heaven to us who are on earth, prepared symbolically the holy tent and all things in it as a copy, type, and imitation of wisdom.[121]

1.89　The grace of the New Testament is mystically hidden in the letter of the Old; thus, the Apostle says that "the Law is spiritual."[122] The Law, consequently, although in the letter it ages and grows old when not being practiced,[123] nevertheless in the spirit it constantly grows young, being energized. For grace is absolutely unaging.[124]

[119]Cf. Ex 25:40.
[120]Cf. Gregory of Nyssa, *V. Mos.* 1.46, 56, 58, 2.162–65, 169, and 315.
[121]Cf. Philo, *Quis rer. div. her.* 112 and Gregory of Nyssa, *V. Mos.* 2.174.
[122]Rom 7:14.
[123]Cf. Heb 8:13.
[124]Cf. Origen, *Hom. in Num.* 9.4.

90. Ὁ μὲν νόμος σκιὰν ἔχει τοῦ Εὐαγγελίου, τὸ δὲ Εὐαγγέλιον εἰκών ἐστι τῶν μελλόντων ἀγαθῶν. Ὁ μὲν γὰρ κωλύει τὰς τῶν κακῶν ἐνεργείας, τὸ δὲ τὰς πράξεις τῶν ἀγαθῶν παρατίθεται.

91 Τὴν ἁγίαν ὅλην Γραφὴν σαρκὶ διαιρεῖσθαι λέγομεν καὶ πνεύματι, καθάπερ τινὰ πνευματικὸν ἄνθρωπον οὖσαν. Ὁ γὰρ τὸ ῥητὸν τῆς Γραφῆς εἰπὼν [1121] εἶναι σάρκα, τὸν δὲ νοῦν πνεῦμα, ἤγουν ψυχήν, τῆς ἀληθείας οὖν ἁμαρτήσεται. Σοφὸς δὲ προδήλως, ὁ τὸ μὲν φθειρόμενον ἀφείς, ὅλος δὲ τοῦ ἀφθάρτου γενόμενος.

92 Ὁ μὲν νόμος σάρξ ἐστι τοῦ κατὰ τὴν ἁγίαν Γραφὴν πνευματικοῦ ἀνθρώπου, αἴσθησις δὲ οἱ προφῆται, τὸ δὲ Εὐαγγέλιον ψυχὴ νοερά, διὰ σαρκὸς τοῦ νόμου καὶ δι' αἰσθήσεως τῶν προφητῶν ἐνεργοῦσα καὶ τὴν ἑαυτῆς δύναμιν ταῖς ἐνεργείαις ἐμφαίνουσα.

93 Σκιὰν μὲν εἶχεν ὁ νόμος εἰκόνα δὲ οἱ προφῆται τῶν ἐν τῷ Εὐαγγελίῳ θείων καὶ πνευματικῶν ἀγαθῶν. Αὐτὸ δὲ τὸ Εὐαγγέλιον αὐτὴν παροῦσαν ἡμῖν διὰ τῶν γραμμάτων ἔδειξε τὴν ἀλήθειαν, τὴν τῷ νόμῳ προσκιασθεῖσαν καὶ τοῖς προφήταις προεικονισθεῖσαν.

94 Ὁ τὸν νόμον διὰ βίου καὶ πολιτείας ἐπιτελῶν, μόνων τῶν τῆς κακίας ἀργεῖ συμπερασμάτων, καταθύων τῷ Θεῷ τῶν ἀλόγων παθῶν τὴν ἐνέργειαν· καὶ τούτῳ πρὸς σωτηρίαν ἀρκεῖται τῷ τρόπῳ, διὰ τὴν ἐν αὐτῷ πνευματικὴν νηπιότητα.

95 Ὁ τῷ προφητικῷ λόγῳ παιδαγωγούμενος πρὸς τῇ ἀποβολῇ τῆς τῶν παθῶν ἐνεργείας καὶ τὰς κατὰ ψυχὴν συνισταμένας αὐτῶν

1.90 The Law contains a shadow of the Gospel, whereas the Gospel is the figure of good things to come.[125] For the former inhibits the commission of evil deeds, whereas the latter prescribes the performance of good deeds.

1.91 We say that the whole holy Scripture is divided into flesh and spirit, as if it were some spiritual human. For he who says that the literal content of the Scripture is flesh, yet that its sense is spirit or soul, will not fall short of the truth. And clearly he is wise who, having left behind what is corruptible, comes to belong wholly to the incorruptible.

1.92 The Law is the flesh of the spiritual human who stands for the holy Scripture, the Prophets are his sensory perception, and the Gospel is his intellectual soul, operating through the flesh of the Law, through the sensory perception of the Prophets, and manifesting its own power by its activities.[126]

1.93 The Law contains a shadow and the Prophets a figure of the divine and spiritual goods in the Gospel. And the Gospel shows the truth itself as being present to us through the letters, having been foreshadowed by the Law and prefigured by the Prophets.

1.94 He who is fulfilling the Law through his way of life and civic conduct merely staves off the final steps of vice, sacrificing the actualization of irrational possessions for the sake of God; and he is content with this way toward salvation, because of the spiritual infancy in him.[127]

1.95 He who is being instructed by the Prophetic voice for the rejection of the actual commission of the passions also removes

[125]Cf. Heb 10:1.
[126]Cf. Origen, *Hom. in Lev.* 6.2.
[127]Cf. 1 Cor 3:2. See also *Myst.* 24.

ἐκτίθεται συγκαταθέσεις· ἵνα μὴ τῷ χείρονι, φημὴ δὴ τῇ σαρκί, δοκῶν κακίας ἀπέχεσθαι, τῷ κρείττονι, λέγω δὲ τῇ ψυχῇ, λάθῃ ταύτην δαψιλῶς ἐνεργούμενος.

96 Ὁ τὴν εὐαγγελικὴν ζωὴν γνησίως ἀσπαζόμενος, καὶ ἀρχὴν καὶ τέλος ἑαυτοῦ τῆς κακίας ἐξέτεμε· καὶ πᾶσαν ἀρετὴν ἔργῳ τε καὶ λόγῳ μετέρχεται. Θύων θυσίαν αἰνέσεως καὶ ἐξομολογήσεως, πάσης τῆς κατ᾽ ἐνέργειαν τῶν παθῶν ἀπηλλαγμένος ὀχλήσεως, καὶ τῆς κατὰ νοῦν πρὸς αὐτὰ μάχης ὑπάρχων ἐλεύθερος, καὶ μόνην ἔχων τὴν ἐπ᾽ ἐλπίδι τῶν μελλόντων ἀγαθῶν τὴν ψυχὴν διατρέφουσαν ἀκόρεστον ἡδονήν.

97 Τοῖς σπουδαιοτέροις τῶν θείων Γραφῶν ἐπιμεληταῖς, δύο ἔχων ἀναφαίνεται μορφὰς ὁ κατὰ Κύριον Λόγος· τὴν μὲν κοινὴν καὶ δημωδεστέραν καὶ οὐκ ὀλίγοις θεατήν, καθ᾽ ἥν λέγεται τό· Εἴδομεν αὐτόν, καὶ οὐκ εἶχεν εἶδος οὐδὲ κάλλος· τὴν δὲ κρυφιωτέραν καὶ ὀλίγοις ἐφικτήν, τοῖς ἤδη κατὰ Πέτρον καὶ Ἰάκωβον καὶ Ἰωάννην, τοὺς ἁγίους ἀποστόλους γεγονόσιν, ἐφ᾽ ὧν ὁ Κύριος μετεμορφώθη πρὸς δόξαν νικῶσαν τὴν αἴσθησιν· καθ᾽ ἥν ἔστιν ὡραῖος κάλλει παρὰ τοὺς υἱοὺς τῶν [1124] ἀνθρώπων. Τούτων δὲ τῶν δύο μορφῶν, ἡ μὲν προτέρα, τοῖς εἰσαγομένοις ἁρμόδιος· ἡ δευτέρα δέ, τοῖς κατὰ τὴν γνῶσιν ὡς ἐφικτὸν τελειωθεῖσιν ἀνάλογος. Καὶ ἡ μὲν τῆς πρώτης τοῦ Κυρίου παρουσίας ἐστὶν εἰκών, ἐφ᾽ ἧς τὸ ῥητὸν τοῦ Εὐαγγελίου θετέον τῆς διὰ παθημάτων καθαιρούσης τοὺς πρακτικούς· ἡ δὲ τῆς δευτέρας καὶ ἐνδόξου παρουσίας ἐστὶ προδιατύπωσις, ἐφ᾽ ἧς τὸ πνεῦμα νοεῖται, τῆς διὰ σοφίας τούς γνωστικοὺς μεταμορφούσης πρὸς θέωσιν, ἐκ τῆς ἐν αὐτοῖς τοῦ

his implicit approval of them that is in his soul,[128] lest, seeming to abstain from vice in what is lesser (I mean, of course, the flesh) he produces this vice in what is greater (I mean the soul) without realizing it.

1.96 He who genuinely embraces the Gospel life has cut off from himself both the beginning and end of vice; moreover, he pursues all virtue in both deed and word. Sacrificing the sacrifice of praise and thanksgiving,[129] because he has been delivered from the entire multitude of the passions at work, and is becoming free even from the battle in his mind against them; and feels the unceasing pleasure that nourishes the soul with the hope of good things to come.

1.97 To the more diligent superintendents of the divine Scriptures the Word as the Lord appears having two forms. The first is a common and very public appearance and not for the few, according to which it is said that, "We saw him and he had neither shapeliness nor beauty;"[130] yet the other is more hidden and attainable to the few, to those who much like Peter, James, and John have become apostles, before whom the Lord was transfigured into a glory prevailing over sensory perception;[131] it is by this glory that he is "sightly in beauty beyond the sons of humanity."[132] Of these two forms, the first is suitable for the initiates, whereas the second is commensurate with those who have been perfected in knowledge as far as is attainable. Also, the former is the figure of the first coming of the Lord (to which the literal sense of the Gospel must be taken to refer), purifying through sufferings those engaged in the practical life; the latter is the bare outline of the second and glorious coming (in which the spiritual sense is understood), which, through wisdom, transfigures

[128]Cf. Mt 5:27, 15:19–20; Jam 1:14–15.
[129]Cf. Ps 115:8/116:17 and Ps 106/107:22.
[130]Is 53:2.
[131]Cf. Mt 17:2.
[132]Ps 44/45:2.

λόγου μεταμορφώσεως, ἀνακεκαλυμμένῳ προσώπῳ τὴν δόξαν Κυρίου κατοπτριζομένους.

98   Ὁ μὲν ἀκατασείστως ὑπὲρ ἀρετῆς ἐγκαρτερῶν τοῖς δεινοῖς ἐνεργουμένην ἐφ᾽ ἑαυτὸν ἔχει τὴν πρώτην τοῦ Λόγου παρουσίαν, πάσης αὐτὸν κηλίδος καθαίρουσαν· ὁ δὲ τὸν νοῦν πρὸς τὴν τῶν ἀγγέλων διὰ θεωρίας μεταβιβάσας κατάστασιν τῆς δευτέρας ἔχει παρουσίας τὴν δύναμιν, ἐνεργοῦσαν αὐτῷ τὸ ἀπαθὲς καὶ ἀνάλωτον.

99   Αἴσθησις μὲν ἕπεται τῷ πρακτικῷ διὰ πόνον κατορθοῦντι τὰς ἀρετάς· ἀναισθησία δὲ τῷ γνωστικῷ, τὸν νοῦν ἀπὸ τῆς σαρκὸς καὶ τοῦ κόσμου συστείλαντι πρὸς Θεόν. Ὁ μὲν γὰρ λῦσαι τὴν ψυχὴν τῶν κατὰ φύσιν τῆς σχέσεως πρὸς τὴν σάρκα δεσμῶν διὰ τῆς πρακτικῆς ἀγωνιζόμενος, ἔχει τὴν γνώμην τοῖς πόνοις συνεχῶς ἐποκλάζουσαν· ὁ δὲ ταύτης τῆς σχέσεως ἀνασπάσας διὰ τῆς θεωρίας τοὺς ἥλους, οὐδενὶ τὸ σύνολόν ἐστι καθεκτός· καθαρὸς ἤδη τοῦ πάσχειν τε καὶ κρατεῖσθαι πεφυκότος παρὰ τῶν ἑλεῖν βουλομένων γενόμενος.

100   Τὸ μάννα δοθὲν τῷ Ἰσραὴλ κατὰ τὴν ἔρημον ὁ τοῦ Θεοῦ Λόγος ἐστί, πρὸς πᾶσαν ἡδονὴν πνευματικὴν ἁρμῶν τοῖς ἐσθίουσιν αὐτὸν καὶ πρὸς πᾶσαν γεῦσιν κατὰ τὴν διαφορὰν τῆς τῶν ἐσθιόντων ἐπιθυμίας μετακιρνώμενος. Πάσης γὰρ ἔχει πνευματικῆς βρώσεως ποιότητα. Διὸ τοῖς μέν ἄνωθεν ἐκ σπόρου ἀφθάρτου διὰ πνεύματος γεννηθεῖσι λογικὸν ἄδολον γίνεται γάλα· τοῖς δὲ ἀσθενοῦσι

the gnostics to deification, who, from the transfiguration of reason within them, "mirror with unveiled face the glory of the Lord."[133]

1.98 He who unshakably endures terrors for the sake of virtue has the first coming of the Lord operating within him, cleansing him from every impurity; he, however, who through contemplation brings his mind over to the condition of the angels has the power of the second coming accomplishing what is dispassionate and incorruptible in him.

1.99 Sensory perception follows the man engaged in the practical life who brings about the virtues with toil, but asensory perception follows the gnostic who retracts the mind away from the flesh and the world toward God. For the former, struggling through the practical life to release the soul from the strictures of a naturalistic relationship to the flesh, constantly succumbs in his mentality to toils, whereas the latter, having yanked out the nails of this relationship through contemplation,[134] is held back by nothing at all, becoming already pure from what brings forth suffering and domination by those things that want to drag him away.

1.100 The manna that was given Israel in the desert is the Word of God,[135] adjusting for those who eat him for every spiritual pleasure and transmuting to every taste based on the difference of desires of those eating. For it has the quality of every spiritual food.[136] For this reason it becomes pure rational milk[137] to those begotten from above from incorruptible seed;[138] and to those ailing vegetables,[139]

[133]2 Cor 3:18.
[134]Gregory of Nyssa has a similar analogy in *Anim. et res.*, GNO 3.3, p. 72 and *Virg.*, GNO 8.1, p. 277.
[135]Cf. Ex 16:14–15.
[136]Cf. Wis 16:20–21. See also Gregory of Nyssa, *V. Mos.* 2.140 and *Hom. in Cant.* 9, GNO 6, pp. 270–271.
[137]Cf. 1 Pet 2:2.
[138]Cf. Jn 3:3–5.
[139]Cf. Rom 14:2.

λάχανον, τὴν παθοῦσαν τῆς ψυχῆς παραμυθούμενος δύναμιν· τοῖς δὲ διὰ τὴν ἕξιν τὰ αἰσθητήρια τῆς ψυχῆς γεγυμνασμένα ἔχουσι πρὸς διάκρισιν καλοῦ τε καὶ κακοῦ, στερεάν ἑαυτὸν δίδωσι τροφήν. Ἔχει δὲ καὶ ἄλλας ἀπείρους δυνάμεις ὁ τοῦ Θεοῦ λόγος, ἐνταῦθα μὴ χωρουμένας· ἀναλύσας δὲ τις καὶ ἄξιος γενόμενος ἐπὶ πολλῶν ἢ ἐπὶ πάντων κατασταθῆναι, λήψεται κἀκείνας ὅλας ἢ τινας τοῦ Λόγου τὰς δυνάμεις διὰ τὸ ἐν ἐλαχίστῳ αὐτὸν ἐνταῦθα πιστὸν γεγονέναι. Πᾶσα γὰρ τῶν ἐνταῦθα διδομένων θείων χαρισμάτων ἀκρότης, συγκρίσει τῶν μελλόντων, ἐλάχιστόν τι καὶ μέτριόν ἐστιν.

ΕΚΑΤΟΝΤΑΣ β'
ΓΝΩΣΤΙΚΑ ΚΕΦΑΛΑΙΑ

1 Εἷς Θεός, ὅτι μία θεότης· μονὰς ἄναρχος [1125] καὶ ἁπλῆ καὶ ὑπερούσιος· καὶ ἀμερὴς καὶ ἀδιαίρετος· ἡ αὐτὴ μονὰς καὶ Τριάς· ὅλη μονὰς ἡ αὐτή, καὶ ὅλη Τριὰς ἡ αὐτή· μονὰς ὅλη κατὰ τὴν οὐσίαν ἡ αὐτή, καὶ Τριὰς ὅλη κατὰ τὰς ὑποστάσεις ἡ αὐτή. Πατὴρ γάρ, καὶ Υἱός, καὶ Πνεῦμα ἅγιον ἡ θεότης, καὶ ἐν Πατρί, καὶ Υἱῷ, καὶ ἁγίῳ Πνεύματι ἡ θεότης. Ὅλη ἐν ὅλῳ τῷ Πατρί ἡ αὐτή· καὶ ὅλος ἐν ὅλῃ τῇ αὐτῇ ὁ Πατήρ· καὶ ὅλη ἐν ὅλῳ τῷ Υἱῷ ἡ αὐτή· καὶ ὅλος ἐν ὅλῃ τῇ αὐτῇ ὁ Υἱός· καὶ ὅλη ἐν ὅλῳ τῷ Πνεύματι τῷ ἁγίῳ ἡ αὐτή· καὶ ὅλον ἐν ὅλῃ τῇ αὐτῇ τὸ Πνεῦμα τὸ ἅγιον. Ὅλη Πατήρ, καὶ ἐν ὅλῳ τῷ Πατρί· καὶ ὅλος ἐν ὅλῃ ὁ Πατήρ· καὶ ὅλη ὅλος ὁ Πατήρ. Καὶ ὅλη ὅλος ὁ Υἱὸς ἡ αὐτή· καὶ ὅλη ἐν ὅλῳ τῷ Υἱῷ ἡ αὐτή· καὶ ὅλος ὅλη, καὶ ἐν ὅλῃ τῇ αὐτῇ ὁ Υἱός. Καὶ ὅλη Πνεῦμα ἅγιον ἡ αὐτή, καὶ ἐν ὅλῳ τῷ Πνεύματι τῷ ἁγίῳ· καὶ τὸ Πνεῦμα τὸ ἅγιον ὅλον ὅλη, καὶ ὅλον ἐν ὅλῃ τῇ αὐτῇ τὸ Πνεῦμα τὸ ἅγιον. Οὐ γὰρ ἐκ μέρους ἡ θεότης ἐν τῷ Πατρί, ἢ ἐκ μέρους Θεὸς ὁ Πατήρ· οὔτε ἐκ μέρους ἐν τῷ Υἱῷ ἡ θεότης, ἢ ἐκ μέρους Θεὸς ὁ Υἱός· οὔτε ἐκ μέρους ἐν τῷ ἁγίῳ Πνεύματι ἡ θεότης,

assuaging the suffering power of the soul; it gives itself, a solid nourishment,[140] to those who through a character state have trained the sensory faculties of the soul for discernment between good and evil. The word of God has, moreover, even other boundless capacities, not contained herein. Finally, someone who, after having passed away becomes worthy to be set over many things,[141] or over all things, will receive all such or some of the capacities of the Word, on account of the fact that he came to be faithful in a few. For every supreme divine gift granted here, in comparison to the future ones, is something small and modest.

SECOND CENTURY
GNOSTIC CHAPTERS

2.1 God is one, because divinity is one: a unity without first principle, simple, and beyond substance, both inseparable and indivisible. The same is unity and Trinity: the same is a whole unity and the same is a whole Trinity, a whole unity in respect of substance, a whole Trinity in respect of persons.[142] For the divinity is Father, Son, and Holy Spirit, and the divinity is in the Father, and in the Son, and in the Holy Spirit. The same whole is in the whole Father and the whole Father is in the same whole; and the same whole is in the whole Son and the whole Son is in the same whole; and the same whole is in the whole Holy Spirit and the whole Holy Spirit is in the same whole. The same whole is the Father, and is in the whole Father and the whole Father is in the same whole, and the whole Father is the same whole. And the same whole is the whole Son, and the same whole is in the whole Son, and the whole Son is the same whole, and the Son is in same the whole. And the same whole is the Holy Spirit, and in the whole Holy Spirit, and the whole Holy Spirit

[140]Cf. Heb 5:14.
[141]Cf. Mt 25:21.
[142]Cf. Basil of Caesarea, *Ep.* 38; Dionysius the Areopagite, *D.n.* 1.4.

ἤ ἐκ μέρους Θεὸς τὸ Πνεῦμα τὸ ἅγιον. Οὔτε γὰρ μεριστὴ ἡ θεότης·
οὔτε ἀτελὴς ὁ Θεὸς ὁ Πατήρ, ἤ ὁ Υἱός, ἤ τὸ Πνεῦμα τὸ ἅγιον· ἀλλ᾽
ὅλη ἐστὶν ἡ αὐτὴ τελεία τελείως ἐν τελείῳ τῷ Πατρί· καὶ ὅλη τελεία
τελείως ἐν τελείῳ τῷ Υἱῷ ἡ αὐτή· καὶ ὅλη τελεία τελείως ἡ αὐτὴ ἐν
τελείῳ τῷ ἁγίῳ Πνεύματι. Ὅλος γὰρ ἐν ὅλῳ τῷ Υἱῷ καὶ τῷ Πνεύματι
τελείως ἐστὶν ὁ Πατήρ· καὶ ὅλος ἐν ὅλῳ τῷ Πατρὶ καὶ τῷ Πνεύματι
τελείως ἐστὶν ὁ Υἱός· καὶ ὅλον ἐν ὅλῳ τῷ Πατρὶ καὶ τῷ Υἱῷ τελείως
ἐστὶ τὸ Πνεῦμα τὸ ἅγιον. Διὸ καὶ εἷς Θεὸς ὁ Πατὴρ καὶ ὁ Υἱὸς καὶ τὸ
Πνεῦμα τὸ ἅγιον. Μία γὰρ καὶ ἡ αὐτὴ οὐσία καὶ δύναμις καὶ ἐνέργεια
Πατρὸς καὶ Υἱοῦ καὶ ἁγίου Πνεύματος· οὐκ ὄντος οὐδενὸς τοῦ
ἑτέρου χωρὶς ἤ νοουμένου.

2   Πᾶσα νόησις τῶν νοούντων καὶ νοουμένων ἐστίν· ὁ δὲ Θεὸς
οὔτε τῶν νοούντων ἐστὶν οὔτε τῶν νοουμένων, ὑπὲρ ταῦτα γάρ· ἐπεὶ
περιγράφεται τῆς τοῦ νοουμένου σχέσεως, ὡς νοῶν, προσδεόμενος·
ἤ τῷ νοοῦντι φυσικῶς ὑποπίπτων, διὰ τὴν σχέσιν νοούμενος.
Λείπεται γοῦν, μήτε νοεῖν μήτε νοεῖσθαι τὸν Θεὸν ὑπολαμβάνειν,
ἀλλ᾽ ὑπὲρ τὸ νοεῖν εἶναι καὶ νοεῖσθαι. Τῶν γὰρ μετ᾽ αὐτόν, φυσικῶς
ἐστι τὸ νοεῖν καὶ τὸ νοεῖσθαι.

3   Πᾶσα νόησις ὥσπερ ἐν οὐσίᾳ πάντως ἔχει τὴν θέσιν ὡς ποιότης,
οὕτω καὶ περὶ οὐσίαν πεποιωμένην ἔχει τὴν κίνησιν. Οὐ γὰρ ἄφετόν
τι καθόλου καὶ ἁπλοῦν καθ᾽ ἑαυτὸ ὑφεστὼς δυνατόν ἐστιν αὐτὴν
ὑποδέξασθαι, ὅτι μὴ ἄφετός ἐστι καὶ ἁπλῆ. Ὁ δὲ Θεός, κατ᾽ ἄμφω

is the same whole, and the whole Holy Spirit is in the same whole. For the divinity is neither in the Father in part, nor is the Father in part God; neither is the divinity in part in the Son, nor is the Son in part God; neither is the divinity in the Holy Spirit in part, nor is the Holy Spirit in part God. For the divinity is neither separable, nor are the Father, the Son, or the Holy Spirit imperfect God; but the same whole is perfect perfectly in the perfect Father; and the same whole is perfect perfectly in the perfect Son; and the same whole is perfect perfectly in the perfect Holy Spirit. For the whole Father is perfectly in the whole Son and in the Spirit; and the whole Son is perfectly in the whole Father and in the Spirit; and the whole Spirit is perfectly in the whole Father and in the Son. Therefore, the Father, Son, and Holy Spirit are one God. For the substance, potentiality, and actuality of the Father, Son, and Holy Spirit are one and the same, since none of them is or is thought without the other.

2.2   Every thought consists in those thinking and things thought; but God belongs neither to those thinking nor to things thought, for he is beyond these; otherwise he is circumscribed: for instance, if he, as one thinking, is in need of a relationship to that which is thought, or, as one in nature subject to one who thinks, is thought by means of a relation, then he is circumscribed. There remains then, to suppose that God neither thinks nor is thought, but is beyond thinking and being thought, since it is for things after him by nature to think and be thought.[143]

2.3   Just as every thought necessarily takes place in a substance as a quality, so also it entails motion qualified with respect to a substance.[144] For it is not possible that something unrelated, absolutely and simply subsisting in and of itself, admit in itself a thought, since

[143]Cf. 1.82 above. See also Evagrius, *KG* 4.77.

[144]Maximus is very likely deriving much of the content in this and related chapters from Aristotelian psychology, particularly *De an.* 3.4–7, 9–11, 429b23–431a19, 431a15–434a22.

πάμπαν ὑπάρχων ἁπλοῦς—καὶ οὐσία τοῦ ἐν ὑποκειμένῳ χωρὶς καὶ
νόησις μὴ ἔχουσά τι καθάπαξ ὑποκείμενον—οὐκ ἔστι τῶν νοούντων
καὶ νοουμένων, ὡς ὑπὲρ οὐσίαν ὑπάρχων δηλονότι καὶ νόησιν.

4 Ὥσπερ ἐν τῷ κέντρῳ τῶν ἐξ αὐτοῦ κατ᾽ εὐθεῖαν ἐκτεταμένων
γραμμῶν ἀδιαίρετος θεωρεῖται [1128] παντελῶς ἡ θέσις, οὕτως ὁ
ἀξιωθεὶς ἐν τῷ Θεῷ γενέσθαι πάντας εἴσεται τοὺς ἐν αὐτῷ τῶν
γεγονότων προϋφεστῶτας λόγους, καθ᾽ ἁπλῆν τινα ἀδιαίρετον
γνῶσιν.

5 Μορφουμένη τοῖς νοουμένοις νόησις· πολλαί νοήσεις ἡ μία
καθίσταται νόησις, κατ᾽ εἶδος ἕκαστον μορφουμένη τῶν νοουμένων.
Ὁπηνίκα δὲ τῶν μορφούντων αὐτὴν αἰσθητῶν τε καὶ νοητῶν τὸ
πλῆθος περάσασα, γένηται πάμπαν ἀνείδεος, τηνικαῦτα προσφυῶς
αὐτὴν ὁ ὑπὲρ νόησιν οἰκειοῦται Λόγος, καταπαύων τῶν ἀλλοιοῦν
αὐτὴν ταῖς τῶν νοημάτων μορφαῖς πεφυκότων· ὅπερ ὁ παθών, καὶ
αὐτὸς κατέπαυσεν ἀπὸ τῶν ἔργων αὐτοῦ, ὥσπερ ἀπὸ τῶν ἰδίων ὁ
Θεός.

6 Ὁ τὴν ἐφικτὴν ἀνθρώποις ἐνταῦθα τελειότητα φθάσας,
καρποφορεῖ τῷ Θεῷ ἀγάπην, χαράν, εἰρήνην, μακροθυμίαν· πρὸς
δὲ τὸ μέλλον, ἀφθαρσίαν καὶ ἀϊδιότητα, καὶ τὰ τούτοις ὅμοια· καὶ

a thought is not unrelated and simple.[145] But God, subsisting altogether simply in two respects—a substance without underlying subject and a thought entailing absolutely no underlying thing—does not pertain to thinking things and what is thought, since he clearly subsists beyond substance and thought.[146]

2.4   Just as the position of the lines extending outward as radii from the center is theorized to be absolutely undivided,[147] in this way he who has been made worthy of coming to be in God, will know all the preexistent *logoi* of things that have come into being in him, by virtue of a simple, undivided knowledge.

2.5   A thought is shaped by objects that are thought:[148] the single thought is established as many thoughts, itself being shaped relative to the form of each of the things thought. And when it has gone beyond the multitude of both sensory perceptions and thoughts shaping it, it becomes entirely formless, at which time the Word beyond thought deep-rootedly indwells it, by putting an end to the multitude of naturally-occurring realities that alters it with the shape of thought; he who undergoes this very thing, he too has come to rest from his works, just as God from his own.[149]

2.6   He who has arrived at the perfection possible for humans in this world, bears for God the fruits of love, joy, peace, longsuffering;[150] and in the coming world, incorruption, eternity, and fruits

[145]Cf. 1.82 above.

[146]Cf. Dionysius the Areopagite, *Myst.* 1.3.

[147]This was one of Dionysius' favorite images, as in *D.n.* 2.5 and 5.6, which Maximus uses repeatedly, e.g., *Ambig.* 7.20. The center being referred to is strictly a theoretical mathematical proposition, since there is in reality no center of a circle that would fit this particular definition.

[148]Maximus is likely referring to Aristotelian theories of psychological perception and thought, e.g., *De an.* 1.4, 408b15–18, 3.2, 426a3–28, *De sen.* 1, 438b21–26. Cf. Gregory of Nyssa, *Anim. et res.*, GNO 3.3, p. 15.6–9.

[149]Cf. Gen 2:2; Heb 4:10.

[150]Cf. Gal 5:22.

μήποτε τὰ μὲν πρῶτα προσήκει τῷ τὴν πρακτικὴν τελειώσαντι· τὰ δεύτερα δὲ τῷ διὰ γνώσεως ἀληθοῦς ἐκστάντι τῶν πεποιημένων.

7   Ὥσπερ ἴδιον παρακοῆς ἔργον ἐστὶν ἡ ἁμαρτία, οὕτως ἴδιον ὑπακοῆς ἔργον ἐστὶν ἡ ἀρετή· καὶ ὥσπερ τῇ μὲν παρακοῇ παρακολουθεῖ παράβασις ἐντολῶν, καὶ τοῦ ἐντειλαμένου διαίρεσις, οὕτω τῇ ὑπακοῇ ἐφέπεται συντήρησις ἐντολῶν, καὶ ἡ πρὸς τὸν ἐντειλάμενον ἕνωσις. Ὁ γοῦν συντηρήσας δι᾽ ὑπακοῆς ἐντολήν, καὶ δικαιοσύνην εἰργάσατο καὶ πρὸς τὸν ἐντειλάμενον ἕνωσιν διὰ τῆς ἀγάπης ἐτήρησεν ἀδιαίρετον· ὁ δὲ παραβὰς διὰ παρακοῆς ἐντολήν, καὶ τὴν ἁμαρτίαν εἰργάσατο καὶ τῆς κατ᾽ ἀγάπην ἑαυτὸν πρὸς τὸν ἐντειλάμενον διεῖλεν ἑνώσεως.

8   Ὁ ἐκ τῆς κατὰ τὴν παράβασιν διαιρέσεως συναγόμενος πρῶτον χωρίζεται τῶν παθῶν· ἔπειτα, τῶν ἐμπαθῶν λογισμῶν· εἶτα, φύσεως καὶ τῶν περὶ φύσιν λόγων· εἶτα, νοημάτων καὶ τῶν περὶ αὐτὰ γνώσεων· καὶ τελευταῖον, τῶν περὶ προνοίας λόγων διαδρὰς τὸ ποικίλον, εἰς αὐτὸν ἀγνώστως καταντᾷ τὸν περὶ Μονάδος λόγον· καθ᾽ ὃν μόνον θεωρήσας ἑαυτοῦ ἀτρεψίαν ὁ νοῦς, χαίρει τὴν ἀνεκλάλητον χαράν, ὡς τὴν εἰρήνην εἰληφὼς τοῦ Θεοῦ τὴν ὑπερέχουσαν πάντα νοῦν, καὶ φρουροῦσαν διηνεκῶς ἄπτωτον τὸν αὐτῆς ἀξιούμενον.

9   Ὁ τῆς γεέννης φόβος κακίαν φεύγειν παρασκευάζει τοὺς εἰσαγομένους· ὁ δὲ πόθος τῆς τῶν ἀγαθῶν ἀντιδόσεως τοῖς προκόπτουσι τὴν ἐπ᾽ ἐνεργείᾳ τῶν ἀρετῶν χαρίζεται προθυμίαν· τὸ δὲ τῆς ἀγάπης μυστήριον πάντων ὑπεραίρει τῶν γεγονότων [1129] τὸν νοῦν πρὸς πάντα τὰ μετὰ Θεὸν τυφλὸν ἀπεργαζόμενον.

similar to these; and the first are perhaps present in him who has come to be perfect in the practical life, and the second in him who through true knowledge has come to stand outside created things.

2.7   Just as sin is an action characteristic of disobedience, just so virtue is an action pertinent to obedience; and just as a transgression of the commandments and separation from him who enjoined them follows upon disobedience, so also observance of the commandments and union with him who enjoined them follows upon obedience. He then, who through obedience has observed a commandment and has brought about justice, he too has preserved through love the undivided union with him who enjoined it; yet, he who has transgressed a commandment through disobedience and has brought about sin, he too has separated himself from the loving union with him who enjoined it.

2.8   He who has been pulled together from the division stemming from the transgression is first separated from the passions; thereafter, from impassioned thoughts; then, from nature and the principles corresponding to nature; then, from thoughts, and their manners of knowing; finally, fleeing the intricacy of the principles concerning divine Providence, he encounters, by unknowing, the very *logos* concerning divine Oneness, in accordance with which the mind, contemplating solely its very own changelessness, rejoices with inexpressible joy, since he has come to receive the peace of God, which transcends all understanding and continuously keeps him safe who has been made worthy of it.[151]

2.9   The fear of Gehenna prepares beginners to flee from vice; the desire of the reward of good things encourages eagerness for the performance of the virtues in those who are progressing; yet, the mystery of love elevates the mind above all created things, rendering one blind to all things after God. For the Lord makes wise only

[151]Cf. Phil 4:7.

Μόνους γὰρ τοὺς τυφλοὺς πρὸς πάντα τὰ μετὰ Θεὸν γεγενημένους ὁ Κύριος σοφίζει, δεικνὺς τὰ θειότερα.

10   Ὁ τοῦ Θεοῦ Λόγος, κόκκῳ σινάπεως ἐοικώς, πρὸ τῆς γεωργίας πάνυ εἶναι δοκεῖ μικρός· ἐπειδὰν δὲ γεωργηθῇ δεόντως, τοσοῦτον διαδείκνυται μέγας, ὥστε τοὺς τῶν αἰσθητῶν καὶ τῶν νοητῶν κτισμάτων μεγαλοφυεῖς λόγους πτηνῶν δίκην αὐτῷ ἐπαναπαύεσθαι. Πάντων γὰρ οἱ λόγοι καθεστήκασιν αὐτῷ χωρητοί· αὐτὸς δὲ τῶν ὄντων ἐστὶν οὐδενὶ χωρητός. Διό, τὸν ἔχοντα πίστιν ὡς κόκκον σινάπεως δύνασθαι μεταθεῖναι λόγῳ τὸ ὄρος ὁ Κύριος ἔφη· τουτέστι, τὸ καθ᾽ ἡμῶν τοῦ διαβόλου κράτος ἀποδιώκειν καὶ μετατιθέναι τῆς βάσεως.

11   Κόκκος τοῦ σινάπεώς ἐστιν ὁ Κύριος, κατὰ πίστιν ἐν Πνεύματι σπειρόμενος ἐν ταῖς καρδίαις τῶν δεχομένων· ὅν ὁ ἐπιμελῶς διὰ τῶν ἀρετῶν γεωργήσας, τὸ μὲν ὄρος τοῦ χοϊκοῦ φρονήματος μετατίθησι τὴν δυσκίνητον ἕξιν ἑαυτοῦ τῆς κακίας κατ᾽ ἐξουσίαν ἀπωθούμενος, τοὺς δὲ λόγους ἑαυτῷ τῶν ἐντολῶν καὶ τοὺς τρόπους, ἢ καὶ τὰς θείας δυνάμεις, ὥσπερ πετεινὰ οὐρανοῦ ἐπαναπαύει.

12   Τῷ Κυρίῳ, καθάπερ τινὶ θεμελίῳ πίστεως, τὸ ὕψος ἐποικοδομοῦντες τῶν ἀγαθῶν, χρυσίον, ἀργύριον, λίθους τιμίους, ἐπιθώμεθα, τουτέστι, θεολογίαν καθαρὰν καὶ ἀκίβδηλον καὶ βίον διαφανῆ καὶ λαμπρὸν καὶ θείους λογισμοὺς τὰ μαργαρώδη νοήματα· ἀλλὰ μὴ ξύλα μὴ χόρτον μήτε καλάμην, τουτέστι, μήτε εἰδωλολατρείαν· ἤγουν, τὴν περὶ τὰ αἰσθητὰ πτόησιν· μήτε βίον

those who have become blind to all things after God, showing them more divine things.[152]

2.10 The Word of God is similar to a mustard seed,[153] seeming to be altogether small prior to its cultivation; but after it is cultivated appropriately, it is proven to be so great that the magnificent *logoi* of sensory and intelligible creations like birds come to rest in it.[154] For the *logoi* contained in all things are established in it, but he is contained by no being. That is why the Lord said that he who has faith like a mustard seed can move a mountain with a word;[155] that is, drive away the power of the devil against us and remove it from its foundation.

2.11 The Lord is the mustard seed,[156] sown by faith in the Spirit in the hearts of the receptive; he who cultivates it attentively through the virtues, on the one hand, moves the mountain[157] of earthly thought, with authority pushing back from himself the stubborn character state of vice and causes the general principles and particular applications of the commandments, or even the divine powers, to light upon himself like the birds of the sky.[158]

2.12 Building the highest of goods, let us lay on the Lord, as if on a firm foundation, gold, silver, precious stones;[159] that is, a pure and unalloyed theology, and a clear and bright life, and divine strings of rationality, those pearl-like thoughts; but not wood, or hay, or straw;[160] that is to say, not idolatry, or being even more precise, excessive excitement about sensory things; also not an irrational life,

[152]Cf. Evagrius, *Pra.* 62.
[153]Cf. Mt 13:31.
[154]Cf. Mt 13:32; Ps 103/104:12; Dn 4:9, 18.
[155]Cf. Mt 17:20; Mk 11:23.
[156]Cf. Mt 13:31; Mk 11:23.
[157]Cf. Mt 17:20; Mk 11:23.
[158]Cf. Mt 13:32; Ps 103/104:12; Dn 4:9, 18.
[159]Cf. 1 Cor 3:12.
[160]Cf. 1 Cor 3:12.

ἀλόγιστον μήτε λογισμοὺς ἐμπαθεῖς καὶ τῆς κατὰ σοφίαν συνέσεως ὥσπερ ἀσταχύων ἐστερημένους.

13 Ὁ γνώσεως ἐφιέμενος ἀμετακινήτους τὰς βάσεις τῆς ψυχῆς ἐρεισάτω παρὰ τῷ Κυρίῳ, καθά φησιν ὁ Θεὸς τῷ Μωϋσῇ· Σὺ δὲ αὐτοῦ στῆθι μετ᾽ ἐμοῦ. Ἰστέον δὲ ὅτι καὶ ἐν αὐτοῖς τοῖς ἱσταμένοις παρὰ τῷ Κυρίῳ ἐστὶ διαφορά· εἴπερ ἐκεῖνο μὴ παρέργως ἀναγινώσκεται τοῖς φιλομαθέσι, τό· Εἰσί τινες τῶν ὧδε ἑστώτων, οἵτινες οὐ μὴ γεύσωνται θανάτου ἕως ἂν ἴδωσι τὴν βασιλείαν τοῦ Θεοῦ ἐληλυθυῖαν ἐν δυνάμει. Οὐ γὰρ πᾶσιν ἀεὶ μετὰ δόξης ὁ Κύριος ἐπιφαίνεται τοῖς παρ᾽ αὐτῷ ἱσταμένοις, ἀλλὰ τοῖς μὲν εἰσαγομένοις, ἐν δούλου μορφῇ παραγίνεται· τοῖς δὲ δυναμένοις ἀκολουθῆσαι αὐτῷ ἐπὶ τὸ ὑψηλὸν ἀναβαίνοντι τῆς αὐτοῦ μεταμορφώσεως ὄρος, ἐν μορφῇ Θεοῦ ἐπιφαίνεται· ἐν ᾗ ὑπῆρχε [1132] πρὸ τοῦ τὸν κόσμον εἶναι. Δυνατὸν οὖν ἐστι μὴ κατὰ τὸ αὐτὸ τὸν αὐτὸν πᾶσι τοῖς παρ᾽ αὐτῷ τυγχάνουσιν ἐπιφαίνεσθαι Κύριον, ἀλλὰ τοῖς μὲν οὕτως, τοῖς δὲ ἑτέρως, κατὰ τὸ μέτρον τῆς ἐν ἑκάστῳ πίστεως δηλονότι ποικίλλων τὴν θεωρίαν.

14 Ὅταν περιφανὴς καὶ λαμπρὸς ἐν ἡμῖν ὁ τοῦ Θεοῦ γένηται Λόγος καὶ τὸ πρόσωπον αὐτοῦ λάμψοι καθάπερ ἥλιος, τότε καὶ τὰ ἱμάτια αὐτοῦ φαίνεται λευκά, τουτέστι, τὰ ῥήματα τῆς ἁγίας τῶν Εὐαγγελίων Γραφῆς τρανὰ καὶ σαφῆ καὶ μηδὲν ἔχοντα κεκαλυμμένον. Ἀλλὰ καὶ Μωϋσῆς καὶ Ἠλίας μετ᾽ αὐτοῦ παραγίνονται, τουτέστιν, οἱ τοῦ νόμου καὶ τῶν προφητῶν πνευματικώτεροι λόγοι.

nor impassioned rationalizations, which are just as deprived of wise understanding as cornstalks.

2.13   He who is aiming at knowledge, let him establish the foundations of his soul as immovable with the Lord, just as God said to Moses: "But you, stand exactly here, with me."[161] It must be understood, however, that even among those standing with the Lord there is difference, if only that passage ". . . there are some among those standing here who will not taste death until they see the kingdom of God has arrived with power"[162] is not read cursorily by those eager to learn. For the Lord does not always appear with glory to all who are standing with him, but rather, he is near the beginners in the shape of a servant,[163] whereas he appears in the shape of God to those who are able to follow him when he ascends the highest mountain peak of his transfiguration,[164] in which shape he was before the existence of the world. It is possible, therefore, that the same Lord does not appear in the same way to all who happen to be with him; rather, to some he appears in one way, and to others in a different way; in accordance with the measure of the faith in each, clearly he varies the vision.

2.14   When the Word of God becomes altogether radiant and bright in us, his face, too, will radiate just like the sun; then even his garments will appear white;[165] that is, the words of the holy Scripture of the Gospels, clear and distinct, having nothing hidden. But also Moses and Elijah are present with him;[166] that is, the more spiritual principles of the Law and the Prophets.[167]

---

[161]Deut 5:31.
[162]Mt 16:28.
[163]Cf. Phil 2:7.
[164]Cf. Mt 17:1–8.
[165]Cf. Mt 17:2.
[166]Cf. Mt 17:3.
[167]Cf. *Ambig.* 10.28–30.

15 Ὥσπερ ἔρχεται ὁ Υἱὸς τοῦ ἀνθρώπου, ὡς γέγραπται, μετὰ
τῶν ἀγγέλων αὐτοῦ ἐν τῇ δόξῃ τοῦ Πατρός, οὕτως καθ' ἑκάστην
προκοπὴν ἀρετῆς μεταμορφοῦται τοῖς ἀξίοις ὁ τοῦ Θεοῦ Λόγος,
ἐρχόμενος μετὰ τῶν ἀγγέλων αὐτοῦ ἐν τῇ δόξῃ τοῦ Πατρός.
Οἱ γὰρ ἐν νόμῳ καὶ προφήταις πνευματικώτεροι λόγοι, οὓς Μωϋσῆς καὶ
Ἡλίας δι' ἑαυτῶν προτυποῦσι, μετὰ τοῦ Κυρίου φαινόμενοι κατὰ
τὴν μεταμόρφωσιν τοῦ Κυρίου, τὴν ἀναλογίαν σώζουσι τῆς ἐν αὐτοῖς
δόξης, τὴν τέως χωρητὴν τοῖς ἀξίοις ἀποκαλύπτοντες δύναμιν.

16 Ὁ τὸν περὶ μονάδος ποσῶς μυηθεὶς λόγον, πάντως καὶ τοὺς
περὶ προνοίας καὶ κρίσεως ἐπέγνω λόγους συνόντας αὐτῷ. Διὸ
καὶ τρεῖς γενέσθαι σκηνὰς παρ' ἑαυτῷ, κατὰ τὸν ἅγιον Πέτρον,
τοῖς ὁραθεῖσι καλὸν εἶναι ψηφίζεται, τουτέστι, τὰς τρεῖς ἕξεις τῆς
σωτηρίας· τὴν τῆς ἀρετῆς, λέγω, καὶ τὴν τῆς γνώσεως καὶ τὴν
τῆς θεολογίας. Ἡ μὲν γὰρ δεῖται τῆς κατὰ πρᾶξιν ἀνδρείας καὶ
σωφροσύνης, ἧς ὁ μακάριος τύπος ὑπῆρχεν Ἡλίας· ἡ δὲ τῆς κατὰ
τὴν φυσικὴν θεωρίαν δικαιοσύνης, ἥν ὁ μέγας ἐμήνυε δι' ἑαυτοῦ
Μωϋσῆς· ἡ δὲ τῆς κατὰ τὴν φρόνησιν ἀκραιφνοῦς τελειότητος, ἥν
ὁ Κύριος ἐδήλου. Σκηναὶ δὲ προσηγορεύθησαν διὰ τὸ ἄλλας εἶναι
τούτων κρείττους καὶ περιφανεστέρας, τὰς τοὺς ἀξίους κατὰ τὸ
μέλλον διαδεξομένας λήξεις.

17 Ὁ μὲν πρακτικὸς ἐν σαρκὶ λέγεται παροικεῖν, ὡς τῆς ψυχῆς τὴν
πρὸς τὴν σάρκα σχέσιν διὰ τῶν ἀρετῶν ἐκτέμνων καὶ τῶν ὑλικῶν
ἑαυτοῦ περιελόμενος τὴν ἀπάτην. Ὁ δὲ γνωστικὸς καὶ ἐν αὐτῇ τῇ
ἀρετῇ λέγεται παροικεῖν, ὡς ἐν ἐσόπτροις [1133] ἔτι καὶ αἰνίγμασι
θεωρῶν τὴν ἀλήθειαν. Οὔπω γὰρ αὐτῷ τὰ τῶν ἀγαθῶν αὐθυπόστατα

2.15 Just as it is written that the Son of Man comes "with his angels in the glory of the Father,"[168] just so the Word of God is transfigured in the worthy with their every progress in virtue, coming "with his angels in the glory of the Father."[169] For when the more spiritual principles in the Law and the Prophets, which Moses and Elijah through themselves typify, appear with the Lord at the transfiguration of the Lord,[170] they preserve the proportion of glory in themselves, revealing the potentiality till then contained in the worthy.

2.16 He who qualifiedly has been initiated into the rationale behind oneness, has necessarily also come to know the rationales behind providence and judgment, which become conjoined to it. It is by this reason also that one reckons it to be right that three tents be made by himself, like saint Peter, for those who were seen;[171] that is, the three aspects of salvation; I mean: that of virtue, and that of knowledge, and that of theology. For the first requires courage in practice and temperance, of which the blessed Elijah was the type; the second requires justice in accordance with natural contemplation, which the great Moses disclosed by himself; and the third requires inviolate perfection in accordance with prudence, which the Lord exhibited. And tents were spoken about because of the fact that there are other greater and more resplendent things than these, regions through which the worthy will pass in the future.

2.17 The man engaged in the practical life is said to sojourn[172] in the flesh, since he is cutting off from the soul the relation to the flesh through the virtues and peeling off from himself the deception of material realities. Whereas the gnostic is said to sojourn even in virtue itself, since he still sees the truth in mirrors and enigmas.[173]

[168]Mt 16:17.
[169]Mt 16:17.
[170]Cf. Mt 17:1–3.
[171]Cf. Mt 17:4.
[172]Cf. Gen 12:10.
[173]Cf. 1 Cor 13:12.

εἴδη καθὼς εἰσιν ἐθεάσθησαν διὰ τῆς πρόσωπον πρὸς πρόσωπον ἀπολαύσεως. Ἐν εἰκόνι γὰρ τῶν ἀγαθῶν, ὡς πρὸς τὸ μέλλον, πᾶς ἅγιος διαπορεύεται, βοῶν· Πάροικός εἰμι καὶ παρεπίδημος καθὼς πάντες οἱ πατέρες μου.

18 Τὸν εὐχόμενον οὐ δεῖ στῆναί ποτε τῆς ἐπὶ Θεὸν ἀγούσης ὑψηλῆς ἀναβάσεως. Ὡς γὰρ ἀναβάσεις χρὴ νοεῖσθαι κατὰ τήν· ἐκ δυνάμεως εἰς δύναμιν, τὴν ἐν τῇ πρακτικῇ τῶν ἀρετῶν προκοπήν· καὶ τήν· ἀπὸ δόξης εἰς δόξαν, τῶν πνευματικῶν τῆς θεωρίας γνώσεων ἐπανάβασιν· καὶ τὴν ἀπὸ τοῦ ῥητοῦ τῆς ἁγίας καὶ θείας Γραφῆς, ἐπὶ τὸ πνεῦμα μετάβασιν· οὕτω καὶ ἐν τῷ περὶ εὐχῶν τόπῳ γινόμενον χρὴ ποιεῖν, ἐπαίρειν τὸν νοῦν ἀπὸ τῶν ἀνθρωπίνων καὶ τὸ φρόνημα τῆς ψυχῆς ἐπὶ τὰ θειότερα· ἵνα καὶ δυνηθῇ ὁ νοῦς ἀκολουθῆσαι τῷ διεληλυθότι τοὺς οὐρανούς, Ἰησοῦ τῷ Υἱῷ τοῦ Θεοῦ, πανταχοῦ ὄντι καὶ πάντα διερχομένῳ δι᾽ ἡμᾶς οἰκονομικῶς ἵνα καὶ ἡμεῖς, ἀκολουθοῦντες αὐτῷ, πάντα διέλθωμεν τὰ μετ᾽ αὐτόν· καὶ γενώμεθα πρὸς αὐτόν, ἐάν γε νοῶμεν αὐτόν, οὐ κατὰ τὴν σμικρότητα τῆς οἰκονομικῆς συγκαταβάσεως ἀλλὰ κατὰ τὴν μεγαλειότητα τῆς φυσικῆς ἀοριστίας.

19 Καλὸν ἀεὶ σχολάζειν καὶ ζητεῖν τὸν Θεόν, ὡς προσετάγημεν. Κἂν γὰρ κατὰ τὴν παροῦσαν ζωὴν ζητοῦντες ἐπὶ τὸ πέρας ἐλθεῖν τοῦ βάθους τοῦ Θεοῦ οὐ δυνάμεθα, ἀλλ᾽ ἴσως καὶ ἐπ᾽ ὀλίγον τοῦ βάθους αὐτοῦ φθάνοντες θεωροῦμεν ἁγίων ἁγιώτερα καὶ πνευματικῶν πνευματικώτερα. Καὶ δηλοῖ τυπικῶς ὁ ἀρχιερεύς,

For the self-subsisting forms of the goods have not yet been seen by him as they are, through the enjoyment of being face to face.[174] For every holy man travels among the semblance of the goods, as though toward his destination, shouting: "I am a sojourner and a stranger, just like all my forbearers."[175]

2.18 He who is praying must never cease from his upward ascent leading him to God. For just as one must take the various ascents "from capacity to capacity"[176] as the progress in the practical life of the virtues, and "from glory to glory"[177] as the search for the higher principles of the spiritual knowledge of contemplation, and the transposition from the letter of the holy and divine Scripture to the spirit, so also must he who has come to be in the space of prayer elevate his mind and the soul's determination away from human concerns and toward more divine things, so that the soul might be able to follow him who has passed over into the heavens[178]—Jesus the Son of God—who is everywhere and for our sake economically goes through all things, that we also, following him, might go through all things that are after him and might come to be with him—if, of course, we understand him not according to the tininess of his economic condescension, but according to the magnificence of his natural boundlessness.[179]

2.19 It is right always to be devoted to God and to seek him, as we were enjoined.[180] For we cannot, though we try, arrive at the bottom of the depth of God in this present life; but perchance just by reaching into a fraction of his depth, we may see holier things than the holy and more spiritual things than the spiritual. And the high

[174]Cf. 1 Cor 13:12.
[175]Ps 38/39:12.
[176]Ps 83/84:7.
[177]2 Cor 3:18.
[178]Cf. Heb 4:14.
[179]Cf. Origen, *De princ.* 2.11.6.
[180]Cf. Mt 6:33.

ἀπὸ τῶν ἁγίων τῶν τῆς αὐλῆς ἁγιωτέρων, ἐπὶ τὰ ἅγια τῶν Ἁγίων, ἁγιώτερα τῶν ἁγίων εἰσιών.

20   Πᾶς τοῦ Θεοῦ λόγος οὔτε πολύλογος οὔτε πολυλογία ἐστίν· ἀλλ᾽ εἷς, συνεστὼς ἐκ διαφόρων θεωρημάτων, ὧν ἕκαστον μέρος ἐστὶ τοῦ λόγου. Ὥστε ὁ λέγων ὑπὲρ ἀληθείας, κἂν οὕτως εἰπεῖν δυνηθῇ ὡς μηδὲν εἰς τὸ ζητούμενον παραλιπεῖν, ἕνα λόγον εἴρηκε τοῦ Θεοῦ.

21   Ἐν μὲν τῷ Χριστῷ, Θεῷ ὄντι καὶ Λόγῳ τοῦ Πατρός, ὅλον κατ᾽ οὐσίαν οἰκεῖ τὸ πλήρωμα τῆς θεότητος σωματικῶς· ἐν ἡμῖν δὲ κατὰ χάριν οἰκεῖ τὸ πλήρωμα τῆς θεότητος, ἡνίκα πᾶσαν ἐν ἑαυτοῖς ἀθροίσωμεν ἀρετὴν καὶ σοφίαν, μηδενὶ τρόπῳ, κατὰ τὸ δυνατὸν ἀνθρώπῳ, λειπομένην τῆς πρὸς τὸ ἀρχέτυπον ἀληθοῦς ἐκμιμήσεως. Οὐ γὰρ ἀπεικὸς κατὰ τὸν θέσει λόγον καὶ ἐν ἡμῖν οἰκῆσαι τὸ πλήρωμα τῆς θεότητος τὸ ἐκ διαφόρων συνεστηκὸς πνευματικῶν θεωρημάτων.

22   Ὥσπερ ὁ παρ᾽ ἡμῖν λόγος ἐκ τοῦ νοῦ κατὰ [1136] φύσιν προερχόμενος ἄγγελος τῶν κρυπτομένων τοῦ νοῦ κινημάτων ἐστίν, οὕτως ὁ τοῦ Θεοῦ Λόγος, κατ᾽ οὐσίαν ἐγνωκὼς τὸν Πατέρα, καθάπερ Λόγος τὸν γεννήσαντα Νοῦν—οὐδενὸς τῶν γεννητῶν προσβάλλειν αὐτῷ χωρὶς αὐτοῦ δυναμένου—ἀποκαλύπτει ὃν ἔγνω Πατέρα, ὡς κατὰ φύσιν Λόγος, καθὸ καὶ μεγάλης βουλῆς ἄγγελος λέγεται.

23   Μεγάλη βουλὴ τοῦ Θεοῦ καὶ Πατρός ἐστι τὸ σεσιγημένον καὶ ἄγνωστον τῆς οἰκονομίας μυστήριον, ὅπερ πληρώσας διὰ τῆς σαρκώσεως ὁ μονογενὴς Υἱὸς ἀπεκάλυψεν, ἄγγελος γενόμενος

priest shows this typologically, going from the holy place (which is holier than the courtyard) to the holy of Holies (which is holier than the holy place).[181]

2.20   No word of God is wordy or wordiness, but one, rather, having been framed on the basis of differing contemplations, of which each is a part of the word. Logically, therefore, he who is speaking about truth—even granting that he could speak in such a way that the investigated term lacked nothing—has spoken about one *logos* of God.[182]

2.21   In Christ, since he is God and the Word of the Father, "the whole fullness of divinity dwells bodily by substance;"[183] in us, however, the fullness of divinity dwells by grace whenever we gather all virtue and wisdom in ourselves, in such a way that they are lacking nothing in any way—in accordance with what is possible for a human being—of a true imitation in relation to the archetype. For it is not implausible that by reason of our adoption the fullness of divinity dwell in us also, a fullness consisting in diverse spiritual contemplations.

2.22   Just as our word, by nature proceeding from our mind, is a herald of the hidden movements of the mind, so also the Word of God knows the Fathers by substance; inasmuch as the Word reveals the begetting Mind whom He knows as Father—since nothing begotten is able to approach the Mind without the Word—he is therefore also called "herald of great counsel."[184]

2.23   The great counsel[185] of God the Father is the mystery of the economy kept secret and unknown,[186] which the only-begotten Son revealed when he had fulfilled it through his incarnation, having

---

[181]Cf. Lev 16:2ff.
[182]Cf. Origen, *Jo.* 5.5.
[183]Col 2:9.
[184]Isa 9:6. Note the striking parallel to Origen, *Jo.* 1.38.
[185]Isa 9:6.
[186]Cf. Rom 16:25.

τῆς μεγάλης τοῦ Θεοῦ καὶ Πατρὸς καὶ προαιωνίου βουλῆς.
Γίνεται δὲ τῆς μεγάλης τοῦ Θεοῦ βουλῆς ἄγγελος, ὁ γνοὺς τοῦ
μυστηρίου τὸν λόγον καὶ τοσοῦτον ἔργῳ τε καὶ λόγῳ διὰ πάντων
ἀκαταλήκτως ὑψούμενος μέχρις ἄν φθάσῃ τὸν πρὸς αὐτὸν τοσοῦτον
κατελθόντα.

24 Εἰ δι' ἡμᾶς ὁ τοῦ Θεοῦ Λόγος οἰκονομικῶς κατῆλθεν εἰς
τὰ κατώτερα μέρη τῆς γῆς καὶ ἀνῆλθεν ὑπεράνων πάντων τῶν
οὐρανῶν ὁ πάντη κατὰ φύσιν ἀκίνητος· ἐν ἑαυτῷ κατ᾽ οἰκονομίαν
ὡς ἀνθρώπῳ προενεργῶν τὰ ἐσόμενα· σκοπείτω χαίρων μυστικῶς,
ὁ τὴν φιλίαν στέργων τῆς γνώσεως, ὁποῖόν ἐστι τὸ κατ᾽ ἐπαγγελίαν
τέλος τῶν ἀγαπώντων τὸν Κύριον.

25 Εἰ διὰ τοῦτο γέγονεν υἱὸς ἀνθρώπου καὶ ἄνθρωπος ὁ τοῦ Θεοῦ
καὶ Πατρὸς Υἱὸς Θεὸς Λόγος ἵνα ποιήσῃ θεοὺς καὶ υἱοὺς Θεοῦ τοὺς
ἀνθρώπους, ἐκεῖ γενήσεσθαι, πιστεύσωμεν, ἔνθα νῦν αὐτὸς ἐστιν ὁ
Χριστὸς ὡς κεφαλὴ τοῦ ὅλου σώματος, καὶ ὑπὲρ ἡμῶν γενόμενος
πρόδρομος πρὸς τὸν Πατέρα, τὸ καθ᾽ ἡμᾶς. Ἐν γὰρ συναγωγῇ
θεῶν τῶν σωζομένων ἔσται Θεὸς μέσος ἱστάμενος, διανέμων τὰς
ἀξίας τῆς ἐκεῖθεν μακαριότητος, τοπικὴν οὐκ ἔχων ἀπὸ τῶν ἀξίων
διάστασιν.

26 Ὁ τὰς ἐμπαθεῖς τῆς σαρκὸς ὀρέξεις ἔτι πληρῶν, ὡς εἰδωλολά-
τρης καὶ εἰδωλοποιὸς τὴν γῆν οἰκεῖ τῶν Χαλδαίων. Ἐπὰν δὲ μικρὸν
τὰ πράγματα διακρίνας, αἴσθησιν λάβῃ τῶν καθηκόντων τῆς
φύσεως τρόπων· τὴν γῆν τῶν Χαλδαίων ἀφείς, ἔρχεται εἰς Χαρράν τῆς
Μεσοποταμίας, τὴν μεταίχμιον ἀρετῆς καὶ κακίας λέγω κατάστασιν,
τὴν μήπω τῆς κατ᾽ αἴσθησιν πλάνης καθαρὰν γενομένην. Τοῦτο γὰρ

become a herald of the great and pre-eternal counsel of God the Father. One who knows the principle of the mystery becomes a herald of the great counsel of God, even rising unceasingly in word and deed through all things—so much so that he even reaches him who to a commensurate degree descended toward him.

2.24 If the Word of God, who by nature is altogether immobile, for our sake "descended to the lower parts of the earth and ascended higher than all the heavens,"[187] in himself economically as a human he accomplished beforehand what we will be, let him who cares about the love of knowledge consider while rejoicing mystically what the nature of the end—according to the promise—of those who love the Lord is.

2.25 If it is for this reason that God the Son and Word of God the Father has become the Son of Man and a human that he might make humans gods and sons of God, let us believe then—as far as concerns us—that we will come to be there where now the Christ himself is as the head of the whole body;[188] and that, as one of us, he became the forerunner to the Father on our behalf.[189] For God will be standing "in the middle of the assembly of the gods"[190]—who are the saved—conferring honors of the blessedness there, not having any spatial separation from the worthy.

2.26 He who is still satiating the impassioned appetencies of the flesh inhabits the land of the Chaldeans as an idolater and idol maker. When he has considered things a little, he receives the sensation of the proper ways of nature; leaving the land of the Chaldeans, he comes to Haran of Mesopotamia,[191] I mean the condition in between virtue and vice, which has not yet come to be purified

[187]Eph 4:9–10.
[188]Cf. Col 1:18.
[189]Cf. Heb 6:20.
[190]Ps 81/82:1.
[191]Cf. Gen 11:31. Mesopotamia in Greek means "between the rivers."

ἡ Χαρράν. Εἰ δὲ καὶ τὴν δι᾽ αἰσθήσεως γενομένην σύμμετρον τοῦ καλοῦ σύνεσιν ὑπερκύψῃ, πρὸς τὴν γῆν ἐπείξεται τὴν ἀγαθήν· τοῦτ᾽ ἔστιν, εἰς τὴν πάσης κακίας καὶ ἀγνωσίας ἐλευθέραν κατάστασιν, [1137] ἥν ὁ ἀψευδὴς Θεὸς δείκνυσι καὶ ἐπαγγέλλεται δώσειν ὥσπερ ἔπαθλον ἀρετῆς, τοῖς ἀγαπῶσιν αὐτόν.

27 Εἰ ἐσταυρώθη δι᾽ ἡμᾶς ἐξ ἀσθενείας ὁ τοῦ Θεοῦ Λόγος, καὶ ἠγέρθη ἐκ δυνάμεως Θεοῦ, δῆλον ὅτι πνευματικῶς δι᾽ ἡμᾶς ἀεὶ τοῦτο καὶ ποιεῖ καὶ πάσχει· ὡς πᾶσι πάντα γινόμενος ἵνα σώσῃ τοὺς πάντας. Οὐκοῦν καλῶς ὁ θεῖος Ἀπόστολος ἐν τοῖς Κορινθίοις ἀσθενοῦσιν οὐδὲν ἔκρινεν εἰδέναι εἰ μὴ Ἰησοῦν Χριστόν, καὶ τοῦτον ἐσταυρωμένον. Ἐφεσίοις δὲ γράφει, τελείοις οὖσι, τό· Συνήγειρε καὶ συνεκάθισεν ἡμᾶς ὁ Θεὸς ἐν τοῖς ἐπουρανίοις ἐν Χριστῷ Ἰησοῦ· κατὰ τὴν ἀναλογοῦσαν ἑκάστῳ δύναμιν τὸν τοῦ Θεοῦ Λόγον γίνεσθαι φάσκων. Σταυροῦται τοίνυν τοῖς ἔτι πρὸς εὐσέβειαν πρακτικῶς εἰσαγομένοις, τὰς ἐμπαθεῖς αὐτῶν τῷ θείῳ φόβῳ προσηλῶν ἐνεργείας. Ἀνίσταται δὲ καὶ ἄνεισιν εἰς οὐρανούς, τοῖς ὅλον τὸν παλαιὸν ἀπεκδυσαμένοις ἄνθρωπον, τὸν φθειρόμενον κατὰ τὰς ἐπιθυμίας τῆς ἀπάτης· καὶ ὅλον τὸν νέον ἐνδυσαμένοις, τὸν διὰ τοῦ Πνεύματος κατ᾽ εἰκόνα Θεοῦ κτιζόμενον καὶ πρὸς τὸν Πατέρα τῆς ἐν αὐτοῖς χάριτος γενομένοις· Ὑπεράνω πάσης ἀρχῆς καὶ ἐξουσίας καὶ δυνάμεως καὶ κυριότητος, καὶ παντὸς ὀνόματος ὀνομαζομένου εἴτε ἐν τῷ αἰῶνι τούτῳ εἴτε ἐν τῷ μέλλοντι. Πάντα γὰρ τὰ μετὰ Θεόν, καὶ πράγματα καὶ ὀνόματα καὶ ἀξιώματα, ὑπὸ τὸν ἐν τῷ Θεῷ διὰ τῆς χάριτος γενησόμενον ἔσται.

from sensory deception. For Haran means this. But if he also looks beyond his concept of the good formed in a way commensurate with sensory perception, he drives on into the good land, that is, into the condition free from every vice and ignorance, which the guileless God shows and promises to give, as the laurels of virtue, to those who love him.

2.27 If the Word of God was crucified on account of us because of weakness, and was raised "by the power of God,"[192] it is manifest that he ever both does and undergoes this spiritually on our account, as having become all things for all, that he might save all.[193] In consequence, the divine apostle rightly determined to recognize nothing in the enfeebled Corinthians except "Jesus Christ and him crucified,"[194] whereas he writes to the Ephesians, as being perfect, that, "God raised us up together and sat us down together in the heavenly realms in Christ Jesus,"[195] in this way speaking about what the Word of God became in a way appropriate to the capacity in each. Therefore, he is crucified for those who are yet being introduced to piety through the practical life, by divine fear nailing their impassioned activities. But he is raised and ascends into the heavens for those who have wholly stripped off the old human who is being corrupted by the desires of deceit,[196] and who have wholly put on the new one,[197] who through the Spirit is created according to the image of God, and who come to be, with the Father of the grace within them, "Higher than every rule, and authority, and power, and lordship, and every name that is named, whether in this or the future age."[198] For everything after God, whether things, or names, or dignities, will be beneath him who will have come to be in God through grace.

[192] 2 Cor 13:4.
[193] 1 Cor 9:22.
[194] 1 Cor 2:2.
[195] Eph 2:6.
[196] Eph 4:22.
[197] Cf. Col 3:10.
[198] Eph 1:21.

28 Ὥσπερ πρὸ τῆς ἐμφανοῦς καὶ κατὰ σάρκα παρουσίας, νοητῶς ὁ τοῦ Θεοῦ Λόγος τοῖς πατριάρχαις καὶ προφήταις ἐνεδήμει, προτυπῶν τὰ μυστήρια τῆς αὐτοῦ παρουσίας· οὕτω καὶ μετὰ ταύτην τὴν ἐνδημίαν, οὐ μόνον ἐν τοῖς ἔτι νηπίοις παραγίνεται, διατρέφων πνευματικῶς καὶ ἄγων πρὸς ἡλικίαν τῆς κατὰ Θεὸν τελειότητος, ἀλλὰ καὶ ἐν τοῖς τελείοις, προδιαγράφων αὐτοῖς κρυφίως τῆς μελλούσης αὐτοῦ παρουσίας ὡς ἐν εἰκόνι τοὺς χαρακτῆρας.

29 Ὥσπερ οἱ τοῦ νόμου καὶ τῶν προφητῶν λόγοι, πρόδρομοι τυγχάνοντες τῆς κατὰ σάρκα τοῦ Λόγου παρουσίας, τὰς ψυχὰς εἰς Χριστὸν ἐπαιδαγώγουν, οὕτω καὶ αὐτὸς ὁ δεδοξασμένος τοῦ Θεοῦ Λόγος, σαρκωθείς, πρόδρομος τῆς πνευματικῆς αὐτοῦ παρουσίας γεγένηται· παιδαγωγῶν τὰς ψυχὰς διὰ τῶν οἰκείων λόγων πρὸς ὑποδοχὴν τῆς ἐμφανοῦς αὐτοῦ θεϊκῆς παρουσίας, ἥν ἀεὶ μὲν ποιεῖται, μεταβάλλων ἀπὸ τῆς σαρκὸς πρὸς τὸ πνεῦμα διὰ τῶν ἀρετῶν τοὺς ἀξίους· ποιήσει δὲ καὶ ἐπὶ τέλει τοῦ αἰῶνος, ἐμφανῶς ἀποκαλύπτων τὰ τέως πᾶσιν ἀπόρρητα.

30 Ὅσον ἐγώ εἰμι ἀτελὴς καὶ ἀνυπότακτος, μὴ ὑπακούων τοῦ Θεοῦ διὰ τῆς ἐργασίας τῶν ἐντολῶν μήτε γινόμενος κατὰ τὴν γνῶσιν τέλειος ταῖς φρεσίν, ἀτελὴς καὶ ἀνυπόκτατος τὸ κατ᾽ ἐμὲ καὶ Χριστὸς νομίζεται δι᾽ ἐμέ· μειῶ γὰρ αὐτὸν καὶ [1140] κολοβῶ, μὴ συναυξάνων αὐτῷ κατὰ πνεῦμα ὡς σῶμα Χριστοῦ τυγχάνων καὶ μέλη ἐκ μέρους.

31 Ἀνατέλλει ὁ ἥλιος καὶ δύνει ὁ ἥλιος, φησὶν ἡ Γραφή. Οὐκοῦν καὶ ὁ Λόγος, ποτὲ μὲν νομίζεται ἄνω, ποτὲ δὲ κάτω, κατὰ τὴν ἀξίαν

2.28 Just as the Word of God, before the manifest and incarnate presence, mentally indwelled the patriarchs and prophets, prefiguring the mysteries of his own presence, so also after this indwelling does he come to be not only in those who are still infants, spiritually nourishing and leading them to the full maturity according to godly perfection, but also in the perfect, hiddenly pre-inscribing in them, as if in an image, the distinctive marks of his own impending presence.[199]

2.29 Just as the words of the Law and the Prophets, which are forerunners of the presence of the Word in the flesh, trained souls unto Christ,[200] so also the glorified Word of God himself, having been infleshed, has become the forerunner of his own spiritual presence; he is raising souls through appropriate words for the reception of his manifest divine presence, which he is ever bringing about,[201] turning the worthy away from the flesh toward the spirit through the virtues; and he will be bringing it about also until the end of the age,[202] revealing manifestly those things till now ineffable to all.[203]

2.30 As long as I am imperfect and unruly, neither being obedient to God through the practice of the commandments, nor becoming perfect in knowledge in my mental faculties, Christ must be reckoned—because of me—to be imperfect and unruly insofar as I am in view. For I disparage and restrain him, not growing together with him in my spirit, since I am "the body of Christ and an individual limb."[204]

2.31 "The sun rises and the sun sets,"[205] says the Scripture. Accordingly also the Word is now reckoned above, now below, that is, by

[199]Cf. Origen, Prologue to *Jo.*
[200]Cf. Gal 3:24.
[201]Cf. *Ambig.* 7.22.
[202]Cf. Mt 28:20.
[203]Cf. *Ambig.* 21.16.
[204]1 Cor 12:27.
[205]Eccl 1:5.

δηλονότι, καὶ αὐτὸν τὸν λόγον ἢ τὸν τρόπον τῶν μετερχομένων τὴν ἀρετὴν καὶ περὶ τὴν θείαν κινουμένων γνῶσιν. Μακάριος δὲ ὁ κρατῶν ἄδυτον ἐν ἑαυτῷ, κατὰ τὸν τοῦ Ναυῆ Ἰησοῦν, τὸν τῆς δικαιοσύνης ἥλιον· ὅλον τὸ μέτρον τῆς κατὰ τὴν παροῦσαν ζωὴν ἡμέρας, κακίας ἑσπέρᾳ καὶ ἀγνωσίας μὴ περιγραφόμενον, ἵνα δυνηθῇ νομίμως τροπώσασθαι τοὺς ἐπανισταμένους αὐτοῦ πονηροὺς δαίμονας.

32 Ὑψούμενος ἐν ἡμῖν ὁ τοῦ Θεοῦ Λόγος διὰ πράξεως καὶ θεωρίας, πάντας ἕλκει πρὸς ἑαυτόν, τούς τε περὶ σάρκα καὶ ψυχὴν καὶ φύσιν τῶν ὄντων ἡμετέρους λογισμούς τε καὶ λόγους, καὶ αὐτὰ τὰ μέλη τοῦ σώματος καὶ τὰς αἰσθήσεις κατ᾽ ἀρετὴν καὶ γνῶσιν ἁγιάζων καὶ ὑπὸ τὸν αὐτοῦ ζυγὸν ποιούμενος. Ὁ τοίνυν θεατὴς τῶν θείων ἀναβαινέτω κατὰ σπουδήν, ἀκολουθῶν τῷ Λόγῳ, μέχρις οὗ φθάσῃ τὸν τόπον, οὗ ἐστιν. Ἐκεῖ γὰρ ἕλκει, καθὼς φησιν ὁ Ἐκκλησιαστής· Καὶ εἰς τόπον αὐτοῦ ἕλκει, δηλονότι τοὺς ἀκολουθοῦντας αὐτῷ, ὡς μεγάλῳ Ἀρχιερεῖ καὶ εἰσάγοντι εἰς τὰ Ἅγια τῶν ἁγίων, ἔνθα, τὸ καθ᾽ ἡμᾶς, αὐτὸς ὑπὲρ ἡμῶν πρόδρομος εἰσῆλθεν.

33 Ὁ τὴν κατ᾽ εὐσέβειαν μετιὼν φιλοσοφίαν καὶ πρὸς τὰς ἀοράτους παρατασσόμενος δυνάμεις εὐχέσθω τήν τε φυσικὴν διάκρισιν αὐτῷ παραμεῖναι (φῶς ἔχουσαν σύμμετρον), καὶ τὴν φωτιστικὴν τοῦ Πνεύματος χάριν. Ἡ μὲν γὰρ παιδαγωγεῖ τὴν σάρκα πρὸς ἀρετὴν διὰ πράξεως, ἡ δὲ φωταγωγεῖ τὸν νοῦν, τὴν τῆς σοφίας πάντων προκρῖναι συμβίωσιν, καθ᾽ ἣν τῶν τε τῆς κακίας ὀχυρωμάτων καὶ παντὸς ὑψώματος ἐπαιρομένου κατὰ τῆς γνώσεως τοῦ Θεοῦ ποιεῖται τὴν καθαίρεσιν· καὶ δηλοῖ δι᾽ εὐχῆς αἰτῶν ὁ τοῦ Ναυῆ

the measure of worthiness, and by the measure of the *logos* itself or the way of being of those pursuing virtue and moving around the divine knowledge. And blessed is he who in himself, like Joshua son of Nun, can keep the sun of righteousness from setting and the whole length of the day[206] of this present life from being engulfed by the night of vice and ignorance, that he might be able rightfully to rout the wicked demons rebelling against him.

2.32 When the Word of God is exalted in us through the practical life and contemplation, he draws everyone toward himself,[207] sanctifying both our thoughts and words concerning flesh, soul, and the nature of beings and, in accordance with virtue and knowledge, even the limbs and sensory perceptions of the body, making them come under his yoke.[208] Therefore, let the spectator of divine things ascend hastily, following the Word until he arrives at the place where he is.[209] For he draws there, just as Ecclesiastes says: "and he draws to his place,"[210] that is, those following him as the great High Priest, and he enters into the Holy of holies,[211] wherein he enters, as one of us, as a forerunner on our behalf.[212]

2.33 He who is piously pursuing philosophy and is drawing himself up alongside the invisible powers, let him pray that natural discernment (which has a moderate light) and the illuminating grace of the Spirit remain in him. The former trains the flesh toward virtue by the practical life, the latter enlightens the mind to prefer the companionship of wisdom to everything else, by which it cleanses both from the strongholds of vice and from every "prideful thought that exalts itself against the knowledge of God."[213] And Joshua son

[206]Cf. Jos 10:12–13.
[207]Cf. Jn 12:32.
[208]Cf. Mt 11:30.
[209]Cf. Ex 24:18.
[210]Eccl 1:5.
[211]Cf. Lev 16:2ff; Heb 10:19.
[212]Heb 6:20.
[213]2 Cor 10:5.

Ἰησοῦς στῆναι τὸν ἥλιον κατὰ Γαβαώ, τουτέστιν, ἄδυτον αὐτῷ τὸ φῶς τῆς γνώσεως τοῦ Θεοῦ κατὰ τὸ ὄρος τῆς κατὰ νοῦν θεωρίας φυλαχθῆναι· καὶ τὴν σελήνην κατὰ φάραγγα, τουτέστι, τὴν φυσικὴν διάκρισιν ἐπὶ τῆς σαρκικῆς ἀσθενείας κειμένην ἀπὸ τῆς ἀρετῆς ἀναλλοίωτον διαμεῖναι.

34   [1141] Ἡ Γαβαὼ ἐστιν ὁ ὑψηλὸς νοῦς· ἡ δὲ φάραγξ ἐστὶν ἡ τῷ θανάτῳ ταπεινωθεῖσα σάρξ. Καὶ ὁ μὲν ἥλιός ἐστιν ὁ φωτίζων τὸν νοῦν Λόγος καὶ χορηγῶν αὐτῷ θεωρημάτων δύναμιν, καὶ πάσης ἀγνοίας αὐτὸν ἀπαλλάσσων· ἡ δὲ σελήνη ὁ κατὰ φύσιν νόμος ἐστίν, ὁ πείθων τὴν σάρκα νομίμως ὑποταγῆναι τῷ Πνεύματι πρὸς τὸ δέξασθαι τῶν ἐντολῶν τὴν ζυγόν. Φύσεως δὲ σύμβολον ἡ σελήνη, διὰ τὸ τρεπτόν, ἀλλ᾽ ἐν τοῖς ἁγίοις ἄτρεπτος διαμένει διὰ τὴν ἀναλλοίωτον ἕξιν τῆς ἀρετῆς.

35   Οὐκ ἔξω τῶν ζητούντων χρὴ ζητεῖσθαι τὸν Κύριον, ἀλλ᾽ ἐν ἑαυτοῖς, διὰ τῆς ἐν ἔργοις πίστεως αὐτὸν χρὴ ζητεῖν τοὺς ζητοῦντας. Ἐγγὺς γάρ σου, φησί, τὸ ῥῆμά ἐστιν ἐν τῷ στόματί σου καὶ ἐν τῇ καρδίᾳ σου, τουτέστι τὸ ῥῆμα τῆς πίστεως· ὡς αὐτοῦ ὄντος τοῦ Χριστοῦ καὶ ῥήματος τοῦ ζητουμένου.

36   Μήτε τὸ ὕψος τῆς θεϊκῆς ἀπειρίας ἐννοήσαντες ἀπελπίσωμεν τὴν τοῦ Θεοῦ φιλανθρωπίαν, ὡς οὐ φθάνουσαν διὰ τὸ ὕψος μέχρις ἡμῶν, μήτε ἄπειρον βάθος τῆς ἡμῶν διὰ τὴν ἁμαρτίαν πτώσεως ἐνθυμηθέντες ἀνάστασιν γίνεσθαι τῆς ἐν ἡμῖν νεκρωθείσης ἀρετῆς ἀπιστήσωμεν. Ἀμφότερα γὰρ δυνατὰ τῷ Θεῷ· καὶ τὸ κατελθεῖν καὶ φωτίσαι τὸν νοῦν ἡμῶν διὰ γνώσεως καὶ τὸ ἀναστῆσαι πάλιν τὴν ἀρετὴν ἐν ἡμῖν, καὶ ἑαυτῷ συνυψῶσαι διὰ τῶν ἔργων τῆς δικαιοσύνης. Μὴ γὰρ εἴπῃς, φησίν, ἐν τῇ καρδίᾳ σου· Τίς ἀναβήσεται

of Nun indicates this, asking through prayer that "the sun" stand still "at Gibeon;" that is, that the knowledge of the light of God be kept from setting for him at the mountain of intellectual contemplation; also asking that "the moon" stand still "in the valley;"[214] that is, that the natural discernment that is lying in the flesh's frailty remain unchangeable from virtue.

2.34 Gibeon[215] is the lofty mind, whereas the valley is the flesh humbled by death. The sun is the Word enlightening the mind, both granting it the capacity of contemplations and delivering it from all ignorance; whereas the moon is the law according to nature, which convinces the flesh rightfully to be subject to the Spirit in order to receive the yoke of the commandments.[216] The moon is a symbol of nature because of its changeability, but it remains unchanging in the holy ones on account of the inalterable character state of virtue.

2.35 It is not necessary for the Lord to be sought outside of those seeking him; rather, it is necessary for those seeking him to seek him in themselves through faith in deeds. For "Near you," it says, "is the word: in your mouth and in your heart, that is, the word of faith;"[217] since Christ himself is also the word of him who seeks.

2.36 Let us neither lose hope in God's love of humanity by envisioning the height of the divine boundlessness, as if it does not reach us because of the height, nor reflecting upon the boundless abyss of our fall through sin, disbelieve that a resurrection of our deadened virtue does happen. For both are possible for God: both to descend to enlighten our mind through knowledge and to resurrect again the virtue in us, so to lift us together with himself through the deeds of righteousness. For, "Do not say," it says, "in your heart: 'Who

---

[214]Jos 10:12–13.
[215]Continuing from the previous chapter, cf. Jos 10:12–13.
[216]Cf. Mt 11:30.
[217]Rom 10:8.

εἰς τὸν οὐρανόν; τουτέστι, Χριστὸν καταγαγεῖν· ἤ, Τίς καταβήσεται εἰς τὴν ἄβυσσον; τουτέστι Χριστὸν ἐκ νεκρῶν ἀναγαγεῖν. Τυχὸν δὲ κατ᾽ ἄλλην ἐκδοχήν, ἄβυσσός ἐστι πάντα τὰ μετὰ Θεόν, ἐν οἷς ὅλος ὅλοις κατὰ πρόνοιαν ὁ τοῦ Θεοῦ γίνεται Λόγος, ὡς ζωὴ νεκροῖς ἐπιφοιτῶσα τοῖς οὖσι. Νεκρὰ γὰρ πάντα τὰ ζῶντα μεθέξει ζωῆς. Οὐρανὸν δὲ τὴν φυσικὴν τοῦ Θεοῦ κρυφιότητα, καθ᾽ ἥν πᾶσίν ἐστιν ἀκατάληπτος. Εἰ δὲ τις ἐκλάβοι πάλιν, οὐρανὸν μὲν εἶναι τὸν τῆς θεολογίας λόγον· ἄβυσσον δὲ τὸ τῆς οἰκονομίας μυστήριον οὐκ ἀπεικότως ἐρεῖ κατὰ τὸν ἐμὸν λόγον. Ἀμφότερα γὰρ δυσεπίβατα τοῖς ἀποδεικτικῶς ζητεῖν ἐπιχειροῦσι· μᾶλλον δέ, παντελῶς ἄβατα δίχα πίστεως ἐρευνώμενα.

37 Ἐν μὲν πρακτικῷ τοῖς τῶν ἀρετῶν τρόποις παχυνόμενος ὁ Λόγος γίνεται σάρξ· ἐν δὲ τῷ θεωρητικῷ τοῖς πνευματικοῖς νοήμασι λεπτυνόμενος γίνεται ὥσπερ ἦν ἐν ἀρχῇ· Θεὸς Λόγος.

38 Ποιεῖ σάρκα τὸν Λόγον ὁ παραδείγμασι καὶ ῥήμασι παχυτέροις διὰ τὴν ἀνάλογον τῶν ἀκουόντων δύναμιν, ἠθικὴν τοῦ Λόγου τὴν διδασκαλίαν ποιούμενος· καὶ πάλιν ποιεῖ πνεῦμα τὸν Λόγον ὁ τοῖς ὑψηλοῖς θεωρήμασι τὴν μυστικὴν ἐκτιθέμενος θεολογίαν.

39 Ὁ μὲν ἐκ τῶν θέσεων καταφατικῶς θεολογῶν, σάρκα ποιεῖ τὸν Λόγον, οὐκ ἔχων ἄλλοθεν ἢ ἐκ τῶν ὁρωμένων καὶ ψηλαφωμένων τὸν Θεὸν γινώσκειν [1144] ὡς αἴτιον· ὁ δὲ ἀποφατικῶς ἐκ τῶν ἀφαιρέσεων θεολογῶν, πνεῦμα ποιεῖ τὸν Λόγον, ὡς ἐν ἀρχῇ Θεὸν

will ascend to heaven?' That is, to bring Christ down; or: 'Who will descend into the abyss?' That is, to bring Christ up from the dead."[218] But perhaps, by another interpretation, the abyss means everything after God, in the whole of which the whole Word of God providentially comes to be, as life returning to those who are dead. For all things that are dead will partake of life. And heaven is the natural hiddenness of God, in virtue of which he is incomprehensible to all. And if one were again to take it in a different sense, heaven is the principle of theology, whereas one will not say unreasonably, by my rationale, that the abyss is the mystery of the economy. For both are inaccessible to those undertaking to inquire by way of logical demonstration; better yet, altogether inaccessible when being examined without faith.

2.37 In the man engaged in the practical life, the Word, being thickened by the ways of life of the virtues, becomes flesh;[219] whereas in the man engaged in the contemplative life, growing lean by spiritual thoughts, he becomes what he was in the beginning: God the Word.[220]

2.38 He makes the Word flesh who by somewhat obvious examples and explanations, because of a commensurate capacity of the listeners, makes a moral teaching of the Word. Conversely, he makes the Word spirit who by lofty contemplations is expounding the mystical theology.

2.39 He who theologizes cataphatically on the basis of affirmations makes the Word flesh,[221] being unable to know God as cause from any source other than visible and tangible realities; he, however, who theologizes apophatically on the basis of negations, makes the

[218]Deut 9:4, 30:12; Ps 106/107:26; Bar 3:29; Rom 10:6–7.
[219]Cf. Jn 1:14.
[220]Cf. Jn 1:1–2. See Origen, *De princ.* 1.1.2.
[221]Cf. Jn 1:14.

ὄντα, καὶ πρὸς Θεὸν ὄντα, ἐξ οὐδενὸς τὸ παράπαν τῶν γνωσθῆναι δυναμένων, καλῶς γινώσκων τὸν ὑπεράγνωστον.

40　Ὁ μαθὼν ὀρρύσσειν κατὰ τοὺς πατριάρχας (διὰ πράξεως καὶ θεωρίας) τὰ ἐν αὐτῷ τῆς ἀρετῆς καὶ τῆς γνώσεως φρέατα, τὸν Χριστὸν ἔνδον εὑρήσει, τὴν πηγὴν τῆς ζωῆς, ἀφ᾽ ἧς πίνειν ἡμᾶς ἡ σοφία παρακελεύεται, λέγουσα· Πίνε ὕδατα ἀπὸ σῶν ἀγγείων καὶ ἀπὸ σῶν φρεάτων πηγῆς, ὅπερ ποιοῦντες, εὑρήσομεν ἔνδον ἡμῶν ὄντας τοὺς αὐτῆς θησαυρούς.

41　Οἱ κτηνωδῶς πρὸς μόνην τὴν αἴσθησιν ζῶντες, ἐπισφαλῶς ἑαυτοῖς σάρκα ποιοῦσι τὸν Λόγον· εἰς ὑπηρεσίαν μὲν παθῶν, τοῖς τοῦ Θεοῦ καταχρώμενοι κτίσμασι, τὸν δὲ τῆς σοφίας τῆς πᾶσιν ἐμφαινομένης, οὐ κατανοοῦντες λόγον πρὸς τὸ γνῶναι καὶ δοξάσαι τὸν Θεὸν ἐκ τῶν αὐτοῦ ποιημάτων καὶ συνιέναι πόθεν, καὶ τί, καὶ ἐπὶ τίνι, καὶ ποῦ φέρεσθαι διὰ τῶν ὁρωμένων γεγόναμεν· ἀλλ᾽ ἐν σκότει τὸν αἰῶνα τοῦτον διαπορευόμενοι, μόνην τὴν περὶ Θεὸν ἀμφοῖν ταῖν χεροῖν ψηλαφῶσιν ἀγνωσίαν.

42　Οἱ μόνῳ τῷ ῥητῷ τῆς ἁγίας Γραφῆς παρακαθήμενοι καὶ τῇ σωματικῇ τοῦ νόμου λατρείᾳ δεσμοῦντες τῆς ψυχῆς τὸ ἀξίωμα, ψεκτῶς ποιοῦσιν ἑαυτοῖς σάρκα τὸν Λόγον· ἀλόγων ζώων θυσίαις εὐαρεστεῖσθαι νομίζοντες τὸν Θεόν· οἷς πολὺ τὸ σῶμα πεφρόντισται τοῖς ἐκτὸς καθαρσίοις· τῆς δὲ ψυχῆς παρημέληται τὸ κάλλος, ταῖς

Word spirit, since in the beginning he was God and was with God,[222] rightly knowing the utterly unknowable on the basis of nothing at all that can be known.[223]

2.40 He who like the patriarchs learns to dig (by the practical and contemplative life) the wells of virtue and knowledge in himself, will find Christ inside, the fountain of life,[224] from which wisdom orders us to drink, saying: "Drink water from your containers and from the fountain of your wells,"[225] doing which very thing, we will find its treasures are inside of us.[226]

2.41 Those who like animals are living only for sensory perception, precariously make the Word flesh for themselves; suffering in bondage, they exploit God's creation, but also, do not recognize the principle of wisdom apparent in all things, so that they would know and glorify God from his own works[227] and to be carried through visible realities to understand from where, why, in dependence upon what, and where we came into being; rather, wandering through this present age in darkness,[228] they handle with both hands only their ignorance about God.[229]

2.42 Those who remain on the literal level of the holy Scripture only, and who fetter the dignity of the soul to the bodily worship of the Law, blameworthily make the Word flesh for themselves, reckoning that they please God by sacrifices of irrational animals,[230] they for whom the body has become a great preoccupation for external

[222]Cf. Jn 1:1–2.

[223]Cf. Dionysius the Areopagite, *D.n.* 5.10. See also *Cap. theol.* 1.85.

[224]Cf. Gen 26:15–18.

[225]Prov 5:15.

[226]Cf. Origen, *Hom. in Gen.* 13 (with special thanks to Joshua Lollar for catching the reference).

[227]Cf. Ps 18/19:1.

[228]Cf. Ps 81/82:5.

[229]Cf. *Ambig.* 45.2.

[230]Cf. 1 Sam/1 Kgs 15:22, Isa 1:11.

τῶν παθῶν κηλῖσι στιζόμενον, ὑπὲρ ἧς ἡ πᾶσα τῶν ὁρωμένων προβέβληται δύναμις καὶ πᾶς λόγος θεῖος καὶ νόμος ἐκδέδοται.

43 Εἰς πτῶσιν καὶ ἀνάστασιν πολλῶν κεῖσθαι τὸν Κύριον λέγει τὸ ἅγιον Εὐαγγέλιον. Οὐκοῦν, σκοπήσωμεν μήπως εἰς πτῶσιν μὲν τῶν τε πρὸς μόνην τὴν αἴσθησιν τὴν ὁρωμένην θεωρούντων κτίσιν καὶ τῶν μόνῳ τῷ ῥητῷ στοιχούντων τῆς ἁγίας Γραφῆς, ὡς μὴ δυναμένων πρὸς τὸ καινὸν πνεῦμα διαβῆναι τῆς χάριτος διὰ τὴν ἄνοιαν· ἀνάστασιν δὲ τῶν πνευματικῶς τά τε κτίσματα τοῦ Θεοῦ καὶ τὰ ῥήματα θεωρούντων τε καὶ ἀκουόντων, καὶ τοῖς καθήκουσι τρόποις μόνης τῆς κατὰ ψυχὴν θείας εἰκόνος ἐπιμελουμένων.

44 Τό· κεῖσθαι τὸν Κύριον εἰς πτῶσιν πολλῶν καὶ ἀνάστασιν ἐν τῷ Ἰσραήλ, ἐπαινετῶς μόνον νοούμενον, εἰς πτῶσιν μὲν νοεῖται τῶν ἐν ἑκάστῳ τῶν πιστευόντων τῶν παθῶν τε καὶ πονηρῶν λογισμῶν, ἀνάστασιν δὲ τῶν ἀρετῶν καὶ παντὸς θεοφιλοῦς λογισμοῦ.

45 Ὁ μόνον τῶν ἐν γενέσει καὶ φθορᾷ δημιουργὸν [1145] νομίζων τὸν Κύριον, εἰς κηπουρὸν αὐτὸν παραγνωρίζει, κατὰ τὴν Μαγδαληνὴν Μαρίαν. Διὸ πρὸς ὠφέλειαν φεύγει τοῦ τοιούτου τὴν ἁφὴν ὁ Δεσπότης, μήπω παρ᾽ αὐτῷ δυνηθεὶς ἀναβῆναι πρὸς τὸν Πατέρα, λέγων· Μή μου ἅπτου. Γινώσκει γὰρ βλάπτεσθαι τὸν μετὰ τοιαύτης αὐτῷ προσερχόμενον ταπεινοτέρας προλήψεως.

<rites of> purification; the beauty of the soul, however, for the sake of which the full power of visible realities has been set up and every divine principle and law has been prescribed, stained by the blemishes of the passions, goes neglected.

2.43 The holy Gospel says that the Lord is appointed "for the collapse and resurrection of many."[231] So, let us consider whether he is appointed "for the collapse" of those beholding visible creation with reference only to sensation and who are content only with the literal level of the holy Scripture, as if unable to cross over to the new spirit of grace because of their mindlessness; and "for . . . the resurrection" of those spiritually beholding the creations of God and listening to his words, and who in suitable manners are cultivating only the divine image in the soul.

2.44 The phrase about the Lord being appointed "for the collapse and resurrection of many in Israel,"[232] is only understood rightly when "for the collapse" is taken as that of the passions and wicked thoughts in each one of the believers; and the resurrection as that of the virtues and every God-loving thought.

2.45 He who only reckons the Lord the creator of things subject to generation and corruption, mistakes him for a gardener, like Mary, the Magdalene.[233] Therefore, the Master beneficially flees from the grip of such a one, who is not yet able to ascend with him to the Father, saying: "Do not cling to me."[234] For he knows that he who approaches him with such an inferior preconception will be deceived.[235]

---

[231]Lk 2:34. Cf. Origen, *Hom. in Lc.* 17.
[232]Lk 2:34.
[233]Cf. Jn 20:15.
[234]Jn 20:17.
[235]Cf. *Ambig.* 10.32–34.

46 Οἱ διὰ τὸν φόβον τῶν Ἰουδαίων κατὰ τὴν Γαλιλαίαν ἐν τῷ ὑπερῴῳ κλείσαντες τὰς θύρας καθήμενοι, τουτέστι, οἱ διὰ τὸν φόβον τῶν πνευμάτων τῆς πονηρίας κατὰ τὴν χώραν τῶν ἀποκαλύψεων ἐν τῷ ὕψει τῶν θείων θεωρημάτων ἀσφαλῶς βεβηκότες, θυρῶν δίκην μύσαντες τὰς αἰσθήσεις, παραγινόμενον ἀγνώστως δέχονται τὸν τοῦ Θεοῦ Λόγον, ἄνευ τῆς κατ᾽ αἴσθησιν ἐνεργείας αὐτοῖς ἐπιφαινόμενον· ἀπάθειάν τε διὰ τῆς ἐμπνεύσεως δωρούμενον καὶ τὴν κατὰ πνευμάτων πονηρῶν ἐξουσίαν παρέχοντα καὶ δεικνύοντα τῶν αὐτοῦ μυστηρίων τὰ σύμβολα.

47 Τοῖς μὲν κατὰ σάρκα τὸν περὶ τοῦ Θεοῦ Λόγον ἐρευνῶσιν, ὁ Κύριος οὐκ ἀναβαίνει πρὸς τὸν Πατέρα· τοῖς δὲ κατὰ πνεῦμα διὰ τῶν ὑψηλῶν θεωρημάτων ἐκζητοῦσιν αὐτόν, ἀναβαίνει πρὸς τὸν Πατέρα. Μὴ τοίνυν διὰ παντὸς κρατῶμεν κάτω τὸν ὑπὲρ ἡμῶν κάτω διὰ φιλανθρωπίαν γενόμενον, ἀλλ᾽ ἄνω πρὸς τὸν Πατέρα σὺν αὐτῷ γενώμεθα, τὴν γῆν ἀφέντες καὶ τὰ περὶ τὴν γῆν, ἵνα μὴ καὶ ἡμῖν εἴπῃ τὸ ῥηθὲν τοῖς Ἰουδαίοις ἀδιορθώτοις μείνασιν· ὑπάγω ὅπου ὑμεῖς οὐ δύνασθε ἐλθεῖν. Χωρὶς γὰρ τοῦ Λόγου, πρὸς τὸν Πατέρα τοῦ Λόγου γενέσθαι ἀμήχανον.

48 Ἡ γῆ τῶν Χαλδαίων ἐστὶν ὁ ἐμπαθὴς βίος, ἐν ᾧ τῶν ἁμαρτημάτων δημιουργεῖται καὶ προσκυνεῖται τὰ εἴδωλα. Ἡ δὲ Μέση τῶν ποταμῶν ἐστιν ὁ ἐπαμφοτερίζων τοῖς ἐναντίοις τρόπος. Ἡ δὲ γῆ τῆς ἐπαγγελίας ἐστὶν ἡ παντὸς ἀγαθοῦ πεπληρωμένη κατάστασις. Πᾶς οὖν ὁ ταύτης κατὰ τὸν παλαιὸν Ἰσραὴλ ἀμελῶν τῆς ἕξεως πρὸς δουλείαν πάλιν κατασύρεται παθῶν, τῆς δοθείσης ἐλευθερίας στερούμενος.

2.46 Those who, having secured the doors for fear of the Jews, are seated in the upper chamber in Galilee,[236] that is, those who for fear of the spirits of wickedness in the realm of revelations have stepped securely into the height of divine contemplations, having closed off their sensory perception like doors, receive in their unknowing the Word of God who is present,[237] appearing to those without the activity of sensory perception; and he grants dispassion through insufflation,[238] and confers authority against wicked spirits,[239] and elucidates the significance of his symbols.

2.47 For those who seek the Word of God according to the flesh, the Lord does not ascend to the Father; but to those who seek him out according to the spirit through lofty contemplations, he ascends to the Father. Therefore, let us not constantly hold here below him who for our sake came to be here below out of his love for humanity, but rather let us come to be with him above with the Father, leaving the earth and all things about the earth, lest he say to us also what he said to the Jews who remained incorrigible: "I go where you cannot go."[240] For without the Word it is impossible to come to be with the Father.

2.48 The land of the Chaldeans is the impassioned life, in which the idols of sins are created and worshiped. Mesopotamia[241] is the way of life wavering between opposites. The Promised Land is the condition replete with every good. Everyone who, therefore, neglects this character state like the old Israel, again will be dragged away to the slavery of the passions, being deprived of the freedom granted.

---

[236]Cf. Jn 20:19. Maximus is likely referring to this by memory, since the disciples were in Jerusalem, not Galilee at the time.

[237]Cf. Jn 20:26.

[238]Cf. Jn 20:22.

[239]Cf. Mk 16:17; Lk 10:19.

[240]Jn 8:21.

[241]In Greek Mesopotamia means "between the rivers."

49 Σημειωτέον ὡς οὐδεὶς τῶν ἁγίων ἑκουσίως φαίνεται κατελθὼν εἰς τὴν Βαβυλωνίαν. Οὐ γὰρ θέμις, οὔτε συνέσεώς ἐστι λογικῆς, τῶν ἀγαθῶν ἀνθαιρεῖσθαι τὰ χείρονα τοὺς τὸν Θεὸν ἀγαπῶντας. Εἰ δὲ τινες αὐτῶν κατὰ βίαν ἐκεῖ τῷ λαῷ συναπήχθησαν, νοοῦμεν διὰ τούτων τούς—μὴ προηγουμένως, ἀλλὰ κατὰ περίστασιν—σωτηρίας ἕνεκεν τῶν χρῃζόντων [1148] χειραγωγίας ἀφέντας τὸν ὑψηλότερον τῆς γνώσεως λόγον καὶ τὴν περὶ παθῶν μετερχομένους διδασκαλίαν· καθ᾽ ἥν καὶ ὁ μέγας Ἀπόστολος ἐν σαρκὶ λυσιτελέστερον ἔκρινεν εἶναι, τουτέστι, τῇ ἠθικῇ διδασκαλίᾳ διὰ τοὺς μαθητάς· ὅλον ἔχων τὸν πόθον ἀναλῦσαι τῆς ἠθικῆς διδασκαλίας, καὶ σὺν Χριστῷ γενέσθαι, διὰ τῆς κατὰ νοῦν ὑπερκοσμίου καὶ ἁπλῆς θεωρίας.

50 Ὥσπερ πνιγόμενον τῷ πονηρῷ πνεύματι τὸν Σαούλ, ψάλλων μετὰ τῆς κιννύρας ἀνέπαυεν ὁ μακάριος Δαβίδ, οὕτω καὶ πᾶς λόγος πνευματικός, γνωστικοῖς ἡδυνόμενος θεωρήμασιν, ἀναπαύει τὸν ἐπιληπτευόμενον νοῦν τῆς πνιγούσης αὐτὸν πονηρᾶς ἐλευθερῶν συνειδήσεως.

51 Πυρράκης μετὰ κάλλους ὀφθαλμῶν ἐστι κατὰ τὸν μέγα Δαβὶδ ὁ τῷ φαιδρῷ τοῦ κατὰ Θεὸν βίου τὸν τῆς γνώσεως λόγον ἔχων συνεπιλάμποντα· καθ᾽ οὕς ἡ πρᾶξίς τε καὶ ἡ θεωρία συνεστήκασιν, ἡ μὲν ἀρετῶν λαμπρυνομένη τρόποις, ἡ δὲ θείοις φωτιζομένη νοήμασιν.

52 Ἡ μὲν τοῦ Σαούλ βασιλεία τῆς σωματικῆς τοῦ νόμου λατρείας ἐστὶν εἰκών, ἥν ὁ Κύριος κατήργησεν ὡς μηδὲν τελειώσασαν. Οὐδὲν γάρ, φησίν, ἐτελείωσεν ὁ νόμος. Ἡ δὲ τοῦ μεγάλου Δαβὶδ βασιλεία

2.49 It should be noted that not one of the saints seemed to go down to Babylon willingly. For it is not permitted, nor does it even suit rational intelligence, that those who love God prefer lesser things over good things. And if some of them are by force led there with the people,[242] by these words we understand them to have left the higher principle of knowledge—not for its own sake, but because of circumstance—and to have taken over the teaching about the passions for the sake of the salvation of those needing guidance; for the sake of this teaching also the great Apostle determined it more profitable to remain in the flesh, that is, in ethical teaching, for the sake of his disciples,[243] although having the full intention to abandon ethical teaching and to go to be with Christ through a supra-cosmic and simple contemplation in the mind.

2.50 Just as the blessed David singing with his lyre soothed Saul, who was being tormented by the wicked spirit,[244] so also every spiritual word, sweetened by gnostic contemplations, soothes the frenzied mind, freeing it from the bad conscience tormenting it.

2.51 Red-haired with beautiful eyes is he, like the great David,[245] who has the principle of knowledge, which illuminates him along with the splendor of a godly life; by virtue of these the practical and the contemplative life come to be established, the former being illumined by the ways of the virtues, the latter being enlightened by divine thoughts.

2.52 The kingdom of Saul is an image of the bodily worship of the Law, which the Lord abolished, since it had perfected nothing. For "Nothing" it says "did the Law perfect."[246] Whereas the kingdom of

---

[242]Cf. 2/4 Kgs 25:1ff; 2 Chr 36:1ff.
[243]Cf. Phil 1:23.
[244]1 Sam/1 Kgs 16:14–23.
[245]Cf. 1 Sam/1 Kgs 16:12. See also *Qu. Thal.* 53, CCSG 7, p. 431.
[246]Cf. Heb 7:19.

τῆς εὐαγγελικῆς ἐστι λατρείας προδιατύπωσις, πάντα γὰρ τὰ ἐν καρδίᾳ τοῦ Θεοῦ θελήματα τελείως περιέχει.

53   Ὁ Σαοὺλ ὁ φυσικός ἐστι νόμος, ὁ κατ' ἀρχὰς κυριεύειν τῆς φύσεως παρὰ τοῦ Κυρίου λαχών. Ὃς ἐπειδὴ παρέβη τὴν ἐντολὴν διὰ παρακοῆς, φεισάμενος τοῦ Ἀγὰγ βασιλέως Ἀμαλήκ, τουτέστι τοῦ σώματος, καὶ πρὸς τὰ πάθη κατώλισθεν· ἐξωθεῖται τῆς βασιλείας ἵνα παραλάβῃ τὸν Ἰσραὴλ ὁ Δαβίδ, τουτέστιν ὁ νόμος τοῦ Πνεύματος ὁ γεννῶν τὴν εἰρήνην τὴν οἰκοδομοῦσαν περιφανῶς τῷ Θεῷ τὸν τῆς θεωρίας ναόν.

54   Σαμουὴλ ὑπακοὴ Θεοῦ ἑρμηνεύεται. Οὐκοῦν ἕως ἄν καθ' ὑπακοὴν ὁ Λόγος ἐν ἡμῖν ἱερατεύῃ, κἂν φείσηται τοῦ Ἀγὰγ ὁ Σαούλ, τουτέστι, τοῦ χοϊκοῦ φρονήματος, ἀλλ' οὖν ἀποκτενεῖ τοῦτον ζηλώσας ὁ ἱερεὺς Λόγος καὶ πλήττει καταισχύνων τὸν φιλαμαρτήμονα νοῦν ὡς παραβάτην τῶν θείων δικαιωμάτων.

55   Ἐπὰν ὁ νοῦς, ὑψηλοφρονήσας τὸν κατὰ παθῶν αὐτὸν χρίσαντα τῆς διδασκαλίας λόγον, διὰ τῆς [1149] προσηκούσης ἐρεύνης ἐπερωτῶν περὶ τῶν ποιητέων καὶ οὐ ποιητέων παύσαιτο, τοῖς πάθεσι πάντως ἐξ ἀγνοίας ἁλίσκεται· δι' ὧν κατὰ μέρος τοῦ Θεοῦ χωριζόμενος, ἐν ταῖς ἀκουσίοις περιστάσεσι προσχωρεῖ τοῖς δαίμοσι, τὴν κοιλίαν θεοποιῶν· ἐκεῖθεν εὑρέσθαι θέλων τῶν πιεζόντων παράκλησιν. Καὶ πειθέτω σε Σαούλ, ἐν πᾶσι σύμβουλον μὴ λαμβάνων τὸν Σαμουήλ, ἐξ ἀνάγκης πρὸς εἰδωλολατρίαν μεταστρεφόμενος καὶ τὴν Ἐγγαστρίμυθον ὡς δὴ τινα Θεὸν ἐπερωτᾶν ἀνεχόμενος.

the great David is a prefiguration of the Gospel-based worship, for it encompasses perfectly every will in God's heart.[247]

2.53 Saul is the law of nature, which was allotted by the Lord to have rule of nature at the beginning,[248] who, when he transgressed the commandment through disobedience by sparing Agag, king of Amalek,[249] that is, the body, also slipped down toward the passions; he was exiled from the realm that David could take over Israel, that is, the law of the Spirit, which births that peace that erects for God the temple of contemplation for all to see.[250]

2.54 "Samuel" interpreted is "obedience to God." Therefore, as long as the Word presides as priest in us by virtue of our obedience, though Saul spare Agag, that is, the earthly mind, even yet the priestly Word, being diligent, kills him,[251] and shamingly strikes the sin-loving mind, as a transgressor of the divine ordinances.

2.55 When the mind, having scorned the norm of the teaching that anointed it against the passions, ceases from inquiring through suitable examination about things to be done and not to be done, it is certainly conquered by the passions on the basis of ignorance; being gradually separated from God by them, it goes over to the demons in involuntary circumstances, making the stomach a god,[252] for this reason wanting to find succor from its oppressors. And let Saul convince you: not accepting Samuel for an adviser in everything, necessarily he was perverted into idolatry and was content to ask the soothsayer as if indeed she were some god.[253]

[247]Cf. 1 Sam/1 Kgs 13:14.
[248]Cf. Gen 1:26.
[249]Cf. 1 Sam/1 Kgs 15:8–16:13.
[250]Cf. 1/3 Kgs 6:1ff.
[251]Cf. 1 Sam/1 Kgs 15:33.
[252]Cf. Phil 3:19.
[253]Cf. 1 Sam/1 Kgs 28:7–20.

56 Ὁ τὸν ἄρτον εὐχόμενος λαβεῖν τὸν ἐπιούσιον, οὐ πάντως ὅλον δέχεται καθὼς αὐτός ὁ ἄρτος ἐστίν, ἀλλὰ καθὼς αὐτὸς ὁ δεχόμενος δύναται. Πᾶσι μὲν γὰρ ἑαυτὸν δίδωσι τοῖς αἰτοῦσι ὁ τῆς ζωῆς ἄρτος ὡς φιλάνθρωπος, οὐ κατὰ τὸ αὐτὸ δὲ πᾶσιν, ἀλλὰ τοῖς μὲν μεγάλα δικαιοσύνης ἔργα πεποιηκόσι, πλείονως τοῖς δὲ τούτων ἥττοσιν, ἡττόνως ἑκάστῳ καθώς ἡ κατὰ νοῦν ἀξία δέξασθαι δύναται.

57 Ὁ Κύριος ποτὲ μὲν ἀποδημεῖ, ποτὲ δὲ ἐνδημεῖ. Ἀποδημεῖ κατὰ τὴν πρόσωπον πρὸς πρόσωπον θεωρίαν· ἐνδημεῖ κατὰ τὴν ἐν ἐσόπτρῳ καὶ αἰνίγμασι θεωρίαν.

58 Τῷ μὲν πρακτικῷ, ἐνδημεῖ διὰ τῶν ἀρετῶν ὁ Κύριος· τοῦ δὲ μηδένα λόγον ποιουμένου τῆς ἀρετῆς ἀποδημεῖ. Καὶ πάλιν, τῷ μὲν θεωρητικῷ, διὰ γνώσεως τῶν ὄντων ἀληθοῦς ἐνδημεῖ, τοῦ δὲ ταύτης κατὰ τι παρασφαλέντος ἀποδημεῖ.

59 Ἀποδημεῖ σαρκὸς ὁ πρὸς τὴν γνωστικὴν ἕξιν μεταβὰς ἀπὸ τῆς πρακτικῆς· ἁρπαζόμενος ὡς ἐν νεφέλαις, τοῖς ὑψηλοτέροις νοήμασιν, εἰς τὸν διαφανῆ τῆς μυστικῆς θεωρίας ἀέρα, καθ᾽ ὅν σὺν Κυρίῳ εἶναι δυνήσεται πάντοτε. Ἐκδημεῖ δὲ ἀπὸ τοῦ Κυρίου, ὁ μήπω δίχα τῶν κατ᾽ αἴσθησιν ἐνεργειῶν καθαρῷ νοΐ θεωρῆσαι κατὰ τὸ ἐφικτὸν τὰ νοήματα δυνάμενος καὶ τὸν περὶ τοῦ Κυρίου λόγον ἁπλοῦν χωρὶς αἰνιγμάτων μὴ χωρῶν.

60 Ὁ τοῦ Θεοῦ Λόγος οὐ μόνον καθότι σεσάρκωται λέγεται σάρξ, ἀλλὰ καθότι Θεὸς Λόγος ἁπλῶς νοούμενος ἐν ἀρχῇ πρὸς

2.56 He who prays to receive his daily bread,[254] does not in fact receive the bread as it is in itself; rather, he receives it as he is able. For, although the Bread of Life,[255] since he loves humankind, gives himself to all who ask, he does not give himself in the same way to all; rather, to those who have done great works of justice he gives himself in a fuller way, to those who have done less than these, in a lesser: to each as the dignity in the mind is able to receive.[256]

2.57 The Lord is sometimes absent and sometimes present. He is absent in a face to face contemplation; he is present in a contemplation through a mirror and enigmas.[257]

2.58 The Lord is present in the man exercising the practical life through the virtues, but absent from him who in principle does not produce virtue. And again, to the contemplative man he is present through true knowledge of beings, but absent from him who in some respect errs in such knowledge.

2.59 He is absent from the flesh[258] who passes from the practical character state over to the gnostic; he is snatched up as if in clouds by higher thoughts into the resplendent air of mystical contemplation, where he is able constantly to be with the Lord.[259] But he who is not yet able to contemplate thoughts—inasmuch as is possible—with a pure mind devoid of sensory activities and who cannot admit the simple *logos* about the Lord without enigmas is absent from the Lord.[260]

2.60 The Word of God, is not only called flesh when he is incarnate; rather, when God the Word is thought simply in the beginning,

[254]Cf. Mt 6:11.
[255]Cf. Jn 6:35.
[256]Cf. Origen, *Jo.* 13.33 and Gregory of Nyssa, *Hom. in Cant.* 3, GNO 6, p. 96.
[257]Cf. 1 Cor 13:12.
[258]Cf. 2 Cor 5:8.
[259]Cf. 1 Thes 4:17.
[260]Cf. 2 Cor 5:6.

τὸν Θεὸν καὶ Πατέρα, καὶ σαφεῖς καὶ γυμνοὺς τοὺς τῆς ἀληθείας περὶ τῶν ὅλων ἔχων τύπους, οὐ περιέχει παραβολὰς καὶ αἰνίγματα οὐδὲ ἱστορίας δεομένας ἀλληγορίας· ἐπὰν δὲ ἀνθρώποις ἐπιδημήσῃ μὴ δυναμένοις γυμνῷ τῷ νοῖ γυμνοῖς προσβάλλειν νοητοῖς, ἀπὸ τῶν αὐτοῖς συνήθων διαλεγόμενος—διὰ τῆς τῶν ἱστοριῶν καὶ αἰνιγμάτων καὶ παραβολῶν καὶ σκοτεινῶν λόγων ποικιλίας [1152] συντιθέμενος—γίνεται σάρξ. Κατὰ γὰρ τὴν πρώτην προσβολὴν οὐ γυμνῷ προσβάλλει Λόγῳ ὁ ἡμέτερος νοῦς, ἀλλὰ Λόγῳ σεσαρκωμένῳ, δηλαδὴ τῇ ποικιλίᾳ τῶν λέξεων· Λόγῳ μὲν ὄντι τῇ φύσει, σαρκὶ δὲ τῇ ὄψει, ὥστε τοὺς πολλοὺς σάρκα καὶ οὐ Λόγον ὁρᾶν δοκεῖν κἂν εἰ κατὰ ἀλήθειάν ἐστι Λόγος. Οὐ γὰρ ὅπερ δοκεῖ τοῖς πολλοῖς τοῦτο τῆς Γραφῆς ἐστιν ὁ νοῦς, ἀλλ᾽ ἕτερον παρὰ τὸ δοκοῦν. Ὁ γὰρ Λόγος δι᾽ ἑκάστου τῶν ἀναγεγραμμένων ῥημάτων γίνεται σάρξ.

61   Ἡ ἀπαρχὴ τῆς πρὸς εὐσέβειαν μαθητείας τῶν ἀνθρώπων ὡς πρὸς σάρκα γίνεσθαι πέφυκε. Γράμματι γάρ, ἀλλ᾽ οὐ πνεύματι, κατὰ τὴν πρώτην εἰς θεοσέβειαν προσβολὴν ὁμιλοῦμεν. Κατὰ μέρος δὲ προσβαίνοντες τῷ πνεύματι κατὰ τὸ παχὺ τῶν ῥημάτων τοῖς λεπτοτέροις θεωρήμασιν ἀποξέοντες, ἐν καθαρῷ καθαρῶς τῷ Χριστῷ γινόμεθα κατὰ τὸ δυνατὸν ἀνθρώποις, εἰς τὸ δύνασθαι λέγειν κατὰ τὸν Ἀπόστολον· Εἰ καὶ ἐγνώκαμεν κατὰ σάρκα Χριστόν, ἀλλὰ νῦν οὐκέτι γινώσκομεν· διὰ τὴν ἁπλῆν δηλονότι πρὸς τὸν Λόγον χωρὶς τῶν ἐπ᾽ αὐτῷ καλυμμάτων τοῦ νοὸς προσβολὴν ἀπὸ τοῦ σάρκα τὸν Λόγον γινώσκειν, εἰς τήν ὡς Μονογενοῦς παρὰ Πατρὸς αὐτοῦ δόξαν προκόψαντες.

62   Ὁ τὴν ἐν Χριστῷ ζήσας ζωὴν τήν τε τοῦ νόμου καὶ τῆς φύσεως ὑπερέβη δικαιοσύνην, ὅπερ ὁ θεῖος ἐνδεικνύμενος Ἀπόστολος φησιν· Ἐν γὰρ Χριστῷ Ἰησοῦ οὔτε περιτομὴ ἐστιν οὔτε ἀκροβυστία. Διὰ μὲν τῆς περιτομῆς τὴν νομικὴν δικαιοσύνην δηλώσας, διὰ δὲ τῆς ἀκροβυστίας τὴν φυσικὴν ἰσονομίαν αἰνιξάμενος·

being with God the Father[261] and having the clear and denuded types of truth of everything, he does not include parables and enigmas, nor necessary stories and allegories; but when he is present to humans incapable of approaching denuded thoughts with a denuded mind, discoursing on the basis of means customary for them—framed through a diversity of stories, enigmas, parables, and obscure words—he becomes flesh. For according to the first approach, our mind does not approach the denuded Word, but the incarnate Word—clearly by a diversity of accounts—who is Word by nature, but flesh by sight, so that the many see him seeming to be flesh and not Word, even though he is Word in truth. For that which does not seem to be the case to the many, but is other than what it seems, that is the meaning of Scripture. For the Word becomes flesh through every single written word.

2.61 The first offerings of humanity's education in piety in nature occur as in relation to the flesh. For in our first attempt in divine reverence we relate to the letter, not the spirit. But drawing close to the spirit gradually by scraping off the coarseness of the words with more refined insights, we come to be purely in the pure Christ as much as is possible for humans, so we might be able to say like the Apostle: "Although we have known Christ by the flesh, nevertheless now we do not know him as such any more,"[262] that is to say, by virtue of the mind's simple approach to the Word without the veils pertaining to him we know the Word as flesh and advance to his glory as the only-begotten by the Father.

2.62 He who has lived his life in Christ has transcended the justice of both the Law and nature, indicating which very thing the divine Apostle says: "In Christ Jesus there is neither circumcision, nor uncircumcision."[263] Through "circumcision" he indicated the Law's justice; through "uncircumcision" he hinted at natural equality.

[261]Cf. Jn 1:1–2.
[262]2 Cor 5:16.
[263]Gal 5:6.

63. Οἱ μὲν δι᾽ ὕδατος ἀναγεννῶνται καὶ Πνεύματος, οἱ δὲ ἐν Πνεύματι ἁγίῳ καὶ πυρὶ τὸ βάπτισμα δέχονται. Τὰ τέσσαρα δὲ ταῦτα, τὸ ὕδωρ τέ φημι καὶ τὸ Πνεῦμα καὶ τὸ πῦρ καὶ τὸ Πνεῦμα ἅγιον, τὸ ἕν καὶ τὸ αὐτὸ Πνεῦμα νοῶ τοῦ Θεοῦ. Τοῖς μὲν γὰρ ὕδωρ ἐστὸ τὸ Πνεῦμα τὸ ἅγιον, ὡς ῥυπτικὸν τῶν ἐκτὸς περὶ τὸ σῶμα μολυσμῶν· τοῖς δὲ πνεῦμα μόνον, ὡς ἐνεργητικὸν τῶν κατ᾽ ἀρετὴν ἀγαθῶν· τοῖς δὲ πῦρ, ὡς καθαρτικὸν τῶν ἐντὸς κατὰ τὸ βάθος περὶ ψυχὴν κηλίδων· τοῖς δὲ κατὰ τὸν μέγαν Δανιήλ, Πνεῦμα ἅγιον, ὡς σοφίας καὶ γνώσεως χορηγόν. Ἐκ γὰρ τῆς διαφόρου περὶ τὸ ὑποκείμενον ἐνεργείας, διαφόρους λαμβάνει τὸ ἕν καὶ αὐτὸ Πνεῦμα τὰς προσηγορίας.

64 Ὁ νόμος τὸ Σάββατον δέδωκεν· Ἵνα, φησίν, ἀναπαύσηται τὸ ὑποζύγιόν σου καὶ ὁ παῖς σου. Ἀμφότερα δὲ ταῦτα δι᾽ αἰνιγμάτων τὸ σῶμα δηλοῦσι. Τοῦ γὰρ πρακτικοῦ νοὸς ὑποζύγιόν ἐστι τὸ σῶμα, ἀχθοφορεῖν βίᾳ τοῖς τρόποις τῶν ἀρετῶν κατὰ τὴν πρᾶξιν ἀναγκαζόμενον. Τοῦ δὲ θεωρητικοῦ παῖς, ὡς ἤδη λογισθὲν θεωρήμασι καὶ λογικῶς ταῖς γνωστικαῖς ἐπιταγαῖς τοῦ νοὸς ὑπηρετούμενον. [1153] Ἀμφοτέροις δὲ Σάββατόν ἐστι τῶν αὐτοῖς ἐνεργουμένων κατά τε πρᾶξιν καὶ θεωρίαν καλῶν, τὸ πέρας, τὴν πρόσφορον ἑκάστῳ παρέχον ἀνάπαυσιν.

65 Ὁ τὴν ἀρετὴν μετὰ τῆς πρεπούσης γνώσεως ἐξανύων, ὑποζύγιον ἔχει τὸ σῶμα, λόγῳ ἐλαύνων πρὸς τὴν τῶν καθηκόντων ἐνέργειαν· παῖδα δὲ τὸν ἐπ᾽ ἀρετῇ κατὰ τὴν πρᾶξιν τρόπον, ἤγουν, αὐτὸν τὸν καθ᾽ ὃν ἡ ἀρετὴ πέφυκε γίνεσθαι τρόπον, ὥσπερ ἀργυρίῳ τοῖς διακριτικοῖς ὠνηθέντα λογισμοῖς. Σάββατον δὲ ἡ κατ᾽ ἀρετὴν ἀπαθὴς καὶ εἰρηναία τῆς τε ψυχῆς καὶ τοῦ σώματος κατάστασις, ἤγουν, ἀναλλοίωτος ἕξις.

2.63 Some are born again through water and the Spirit,[264] others receive the baptism in the Holy Spirit and fire.[265] These four, I mean water, Spirit, fire, and the Holy Spirit, I take to be the one and the same Spirit of God. For to some the Holy Spirit is water, as a cleanser of the external filth on the body; to others, he is Spirit only, as productive of the good deeds of virtue; to others he is fire, as a purifier from the internal impurities in the depth of the soul; and to others, as with the great Daniel, he is the Holy Spirit, as the giver of wisdom and knowledge.[266] For on the basis of the subject's different activity, the one and the same Spirit receives different titles.

2.64 The Law has provided the Sabbath: "That" it says, "your yoked beast and hired hand might rest."[267] Both of these, through enigmas, indicate the body. For the body is the yoked beast of the mind engaged in the practical life, being compelled by the ways of virtue, as required by the practical life, to bear burdens with bodily strength. The hired hand is the body of the contemplative, since <it is> considered to be already in contemplations, and being subject rationally to the commandments of the mind. For both the Sabbath is the end of the goods, practical or contemplative, accomplished by them, granting to each their due rest.

2.65 He who makes virtue effective with the knowledge that becomes it, keeps the body as a yoked beast, with reason driving it on to the accomplishment of its duties; and he keeps the body as a hired hand by way of the practical life leading to virtue, that is, the specific way in line with which virtue naturally comes about, as though hired with money for discerning thoughts. And the Sabbath is the dispassionate and peaceful condition of both soul and body, that is, an unchanging character state.

[264]Cf. Jn 3:5.
[265]Cf. Mt 3:11.
[266]Cf. Dn 1:17; 5:11–12.
[267]Cf. Ex 20:10. See Origen, *Jo.* 13.33.

66 Ὁ τοῦ Θεοῦ λόγος τοῖς μὲν ἔτι περὶ τὰ σωματικὰ τῆς ἀρετῆς
εἴδη τὸ πλέον ἔχουσι τῆς φροντίδος ἄχυρον γίνεται καὶ χόρτος,
διατρέφων αὐτῶν τὸ παθητικὸν τῆς ψυχῆς μέρος πρὸς τὴν τῶν
ἀρετῶν ὑπηρεσίαν· τοῖς ἀνηγμένοις δὲ τῇ θεωρίᾳ τῆς ἀληθοῦς τῶν
θείων κατανοήσεως ἔστιν ἄρτος διατρέφων αὐτῶν τῆς ψυχῆς τὸ
νοερὸν πρὸς θεοειδῆ τελειότητα. Διὸ τοὺς πατριάρχας εὑρίσκομεν
ἐπισιτιζομένους ἐν τῇ ὁδῷ καὶ ἑαυτοῖς ἄρτους καὶ τοῖς ὄνοις
αὐτῶν χορτάσματα. Καὶ ὁ ἐν τοῖς Κριταῖς δὲ Λευΐτης τῷ ἐν Γαβαᾷ
ξεναγήσαντι αὐτὸν πρεσβύτῃ φησίν· Εἰσὶ καὶ ἡμῖν ἄρτοι, καὶ τοῖς
ὄνοις ἡμῶν ἄχυρα· καὶ οὐκ ἔστιν ὑστέρημα τοῖς παισί σου, παντὸς
τινος.

67 Ὁ τοῦ Θεοῦ Λόγος καὶ δρόσος λέγεται καὶ ἔστιν· καὶ ὕδωρ καὶ
πηγὴ καὶ ποταμός, ὡς γέγραπται, κατὰ τὴν ὑποκειμενικὴν δηλονότι
τῶν δεχομένων δύναμιν, ταῦτα καὶ ὢν καὶ γινόμενος. Τοῖς μὲν γάρ
ἐστι δρόσος, ὡς τῆς ἔξωθεν ἐπικειμένης αὐτοῖς περὶ τὸ σῶμα τῶν
παθῶν πυρώσεώς τε καὶ ἐνεργείας σβεστικός. Τοῖς δὲ τὸ βάθος τῷ ἰῷ
τῆς κακίας φρυσσομένοις ἐστὶν ὕδωρ, οὐ μόνον ὡς δι᾽ ἀντιπαθείας
τοῦ ἀντικειμένου φθαρτικός, ἀλλὰ καὶ ὡς μεταδοτικὸς ζωτικῆς πρὸς
τὸ εὖ εἶναι δυνάμεως. Πηγὴ δὲ ἀεννάως ἔχουσιν ἀναβλύζουσαν τὴν
ἕξιν τῆς θεωρίας ὡς σοφίας χορηγός. Ποταμὸς δὲ τοῖς τὴν εὐσεβῆ
καὶ ὀρθὴν [1156] καὶ σωτήριον ποταμηδὸν προχέουσι διδασκαλίαν,
ὡς ἀνθρώπους καὶ κτήνη καὶ θηρία καὶ φυτὰ δαψιλῶς ποτίζων, ἵνα
καὶ ἄνθρωποι θεωθῶσι τοῖς τῶν λεγομένων ὑψωθέντες νοήμασι·
καὶ οἱ κτηνωθέντες τοῖς πάθεσι, διὰ τῆς ἀκριβοῦς τῶν κατ᾽ ἀρετὴν
τρόπων ἀποδείξεως ἀνθρωπισθέντες, τὴν φυσικὴν ἐπαναλάβωσι
λογιότητα· καὶ οἱ θηριωθέντες ταῖς πονηραῖς ἕξεσι καὶ κακοπραγίαις,
διὰ τῆς προσηνοῦς τε καὶ εὐαφοῦς παραινέσεως τιθασσευθέντες,
πρὸς τὴν τῆς φύσεως ἐπανέλθωσιν ἡμερότητα· καὶ οἱ φυτῶν

2.66   The Word of God becomes bran and hay to those the greater part of whose attention still revolves around the bodily forms of virtue, nourishing the passible part of their souls for the service of the virtues; but to those who have been led up to the contemplation of the true thought of divine things, he is the bread nourishing the thinking part of their souls for godlike perfection. This is why we find the patriarchs being furnished with food on the way: bread for themselves and fodder for their donkeys.[268] And the Levite in the book of the Judges says to the old man in Gibeah who hosted him, "We also have bread, and our donkeys bran, and your hired hands have need of nothing at all."[269]

2.67   The Word of God both is called and is dew,[270] and water, and fountain,[271] and river,[272] as it is written; to be clear, he both is and comes to be these things in accordance with the underlying capacity of those receiving him. For to some he is dew, as an extinguisher of the burning desire and perpetration of the passions, externally hemming them in all over the body. To those burning in their innermost parts by the poison of wickedness he is water, not only as though destructive of what is harmful through an antidote, but also as a bestower of vivifying force for well-being. And fountain for those who have the character state of contemplation ever gushing forth, as the giver of wisdom. And a river to those who pour forth like a stream with the pious, right, and salvific teaching, as abundantly giving humans, cattle, beasts, and plants to drink, that also humans might be deified, being exalted by the contemplations of the things here said; and that those turned cattle by the passions might be humanized by the precise indication of the ways of the virtues, taking up again their natural rationality; and those who have become wild beasts by wicked character states and vicious actions, being

[268]Cf. Gen 24:25, 42:25, 27.
[269]Jdgs 19:19.
[270]Cf. Deut 32:2, Sir 15:3, 24:28–29.
[271]Cf. Jn 4:14.
[272]Cf. Jn 7:38.

δίκην ἀναισθητοῦντες τῶν ἀγαθῶν, διὰ τῆς εἰς βάθος τοῦ Λόγου διαβάσεως ἀπαλυθέντες, λάβωσιν αἴσθησιν πρὸς καρπογονίαν καὶ δύναμιν τὴν αὐτοὺς διατρέφουσαν, τοῦ Λόγου ποιότητα.

68　Ὁδός ἐστιν ὁ τοῦ Θεοῦ Λόγος τοῖς καλῶς κατὰ τὴν πρακτικὴν καὶ εὐτόνως τὸ τῆς ἀρετῆς τρέχουσι στάδιον (καὶ μήτε δεξιὰ διὰ κενοδοξίας μήτε ἀριστερὰ διὰ τῆς πρὸς τὰ πάθη ῥοπῆς ἐκκλίνουσιν) εὐθύνων κατὰ Θεὸν τὰ διαβήματα· ὅπερ εἰς τέλος μὴ φυλάξας Ἀσὰ ὁ βασιλεὺς Ἰούδα, λέγεται περὶ τὸ γῆρας αὐτοῦ πεπονηκέναι τοὺς πόδας, ὡς περὶ τὸν δρόμον τοῦ κατὰ Θεὸν βίου ἀσθενήσας.

69　Θύρα λέγεται τοῦ Θεοῦ Λόγος, ὡς τοὺς καλῶς πᾶσαν διηνυκότας τὴν ὁδὸν τῶν ἀρετῶν κατὰ τὸν ἄμεμπτον δρόμον τῆς πράξεως πρὸς γνῶσιν εἰσάγων· καὶ ὡς φῶς, δεικνὺς τοὺς πολυφαεῖς τῆς σοφίας θησαυρούς. Ὁ αὐτὸς γὰρ καὶ ὁδός ἐστι καὶ θύρα καὶ κλεὶς καὶ βασιλεία· ὁδὸς μὲν ὡς ὁδηγός· κλεὶς δὲ ὡς ἀνοίγων τοῖς ἀξίοις τῶν θείων καὶ ἀνοιγόμενος· θύρα δὲ ὡς εἰσαγωγεύς· βασιλεία δὲ ὡς κληρονομούμενος καὶ κατὰ μέθεξιν ἐν πᾶσι γινόμενος.

domesticated through kindly and delicate exhortation, might return to the gentleness of their nature; and those who like plants have no sensation of good things, being softened through the Word's passing through to their depths, might receive sensory perception for bearing fruits, and vital force to nourish them, which are a quality of the Word.

2.68 The Word of God is the way[273] to those who in the practical life are running well and vigorously in the stadium of virtue[274] (inclining neither to the right because of vainglory nor to the left by influence of the passions), who aligns their strides straight toward God. Asa the king of Judah, not preserving this very thing until the end, is said to have struggled with his feet when his old age came round,[275] since he became feeble in his pursuit of a Godlike life.[276]

2.69 The Word of God is called a door,[277] since he leads into knowledge those who have completed well the entire course of the virtues in accordance with the blameless race[278] of the practical life; and as a light he shows the resplendent treasures of wisdom. For the same one is way,[279] door,[280] key,[281] and kingdom:[282] way as leader; key as opening and being open to those worthy of divine things; door as one who lets in; and kingdom as being inherited and coming to be in all things by participation.

[273]Cf. Jn 14:6.
[274]Cf. Acts 20:24; 2 Tim 4:7.
[275]Cf. 1/3 Kgs 15:23.
[276]Cf. Evagrius, *Or.* 120.
[277]Cf. Jn 10:9.
[278]Cf. 2 Tim 4:7.
[279]Cf. Jn 14:6.
[280]Cf. Jn 10:6.
[281]Cf. Rev 1:18.
[282]Cf. Jn 18:36.

70   Φῶς ὁ Κύριος λέγεται, καὶ ζωὴ καὶ ἀνάστασις καὶ ἀλήθεια. Φῶς μὲν καὶ ὡς λαμπρότης ψυχῶν, καὶ ὡς ἀγνοίας σκότους διώκτης· καὶ ὡς φωτίζων τὸν νοῦν πρὸς κατανόησιν τῶν ἀπορρήτων καὶ δεικνὺς τὰ μόνοις θεατὰ τοῖς καθαροῖς μυστήρια· ζωὴ δὲ ὡς τὴν πρέπουσαν ψυχαῖς ἀγαπώσαις τὸν Κύριον ἐν τοῖς θείοις παρεχόμενος κίνησιν· ἀνάστασις δὲ ὡς τῆς νεκρᾶς τῶν ὑλικῶν προσπαθείας ἐγείρων τὸν νοῦν, φθορᾶς παντοίας καθαρὸν καὶ νεκρότητος· ἀλήθεια δὲ ὡς ἕξιν τῶν ἀγαθῶν τοῖς ἀξίοις δωρούμενος ἄτρεπτον.

71   Ὁ μὲν τοῦ Θεοῦ καὶ Πατρὸς Θεὸς Λόγος ἑκάστῃ μυστικῶς ἐνυπάρχει τῶν οἰκείων ἐντολῶν· ὁ δὲ Θεὸς καὶ Πατὴρ ὅλος ἐστὶν ἀχώριστος ἐν ὅλῳ τῷ οἰκείῳ Λόγῳ φυσικῶς. Ὁ τοίνυν δεχόμενος θείαν ἐντολὴν καὶ ποιῶν αὐτήν, τὸν ἐν αὐτῇ τοῦ Θεοῦ δέχεται Λόγον. Ὁ δὲ τὸν Λόγον διὰ τῶν ἐντολῶν δεξάμενος, δι᾽ αὐτοῦ τὸν ἐν αὐτῷ φυσικῶς ὄντα συνεδέξατο Πατέρα καὶ τὸ ἐν αὐτῷ φυσικῶς ὂν συνεδέξατο Πνεῦμα. [1157] Ἀμὴν γάρ, φησι, λέγω ὑμῖν, ὁ λαμβάνων ὅν τινα πέμψω, ἐμὲ λαμβάνει· ὁ δὲ ἐμὲ λαμβάνων, λαμβάνει τὸν πέμψαντά με. Ὁ γοῦν ἐντολὴν δεξάμενος καὶ ποιήσας αὐτήν, λαβὼν ἔχει μυστικῶς τὴν ἁγίαν Τριάδα.

72   Δοξάζει τὸν Θεὸν ἐν ἑαυτῷ, οὐχ ὁ λόγοις μόνον γεραίρων τὸν Θεόν, ἀλλ᾽ ὁ διὰ τὸν Θεὸν ὑπὲρ ἀρετῆς τὰ τῶν πόνων ὑπομένων παθήματα· καὶ ἀντιδοξάζεται παρὰ Θεοῦ, τὴν ἐν τῷ Θεῷ δόξαν, οἷον ἀρετῆς ἔπαθον κατὰ μέθεξιν τὴν τῆς ἀπαθείας κομιζόμενος χάριν. Πᾶς γὰρ ὁ δοξάζων τὸν Θεὸν ἐν ἑαυτῷ διὰ τῶν κατὰ τὴν πρακτικὴν ὑπὲρ ἀρετῆς παθημάτων, καὶ αὐτὸς ἐν τῷ Θεῷ δοξάζεται

2.70 The Lord is called light,[283] life,[284] resurrection,[285] and truth.[286] Light both as enlightener of souls and as one who drives off the darkness of ignorance; also as illuminating the mind for the thought of ineffable things and showing mysteries visible only to the pure; life as granting suitable movement among divine things to the souls who love the Lord; resurrection as raising the mind from the lethal passionate attachment to material things, pure of every manner of corruption and state of death; and truth as bestowing upon the worthy an unchanging character state of good dispositions.

2.71 God the Word of God the Father mystically indwells each of his own commandments; and God the Father is whole and undivided in his own whole Word by nature. He, therefore, who receives a divine commandment and does it, receives the Word of God in it.[287] And he who has received the Word through the commandments, through him has simultaneously received the Father who is in him by nature, and has simultaneously received the Spirit who is by nature in him. "For truly," it says, "I tell you, he who receives him whom I will send, receives me; and he who receives me, receives him who has sent me."[288] In consequence, he who has received a commandment and has done it, by having received, has mystically the Holy Trinity.

2.72 He glorifies God in himself does not honor God with words alone, but he who for the sake of God <also> endures the toils of afflictions in pursuit of virtue; and conversely he is glorified by God relative to the glory in God, being granted the gift of dispassion through participation as if the laurels of virtue. For anyone who is glorifying God in himself through the sufferings corresponding to

---

[283]Cf. Jn 8:12.
[284]Cf. Jn 14:6.
[285]Cf. Jn 11:25.
[286]Cf. Jn 14:6.
[287]Cf. Jn 14:21.
[288]Jn 13:20.

διὰ τῆς κατὰ τὴν θεωρίαν ἀπαθοῦς τῶν θείων ἐλλάμψεως. Φησὶ γὰρ ὁ Κύριος ἐπὶ τὸ πάθος ἐρχόμενος· Νῦν ἐδοξάσθη ὁ Υἱὸς τοῦ ἀνθρώπου καὶ ὁ Θεὸς ἐδοξάσθη ἐν αὐτῷ. Εἰ ὁ Θεὸς ἐδοξάσθη ἐν αὐτῷ, καὶ ὁ Θεὸς δοξάσει αὐτὸν ἐν ἑαυτῷ, καὶ εὐθὺς δοξάσει αὐτόν. Ὡς ἐντεῦθεν εἶναι δῆλον ὅτι τοῖς ὑπέρ ἀρετῆς παθήμασιν ἐπακολουθοῦσι τὰ θεῖα χαρίσματα.

73 Ἕως τὸν ἐν τῷ ῥητῷ τῆς ἁγίας Γραφῆς ποικίλως διὰ τῶν αἰνιγμάτων σεσωματωμένον ὁρῶμεν τὸν τοῦ Θεοῦ Λόγον, οὔπω τὸν ἀσώματον καὶ ἁπλοῦν καὶ ἐνιαῖον καὶ μόνον, ὡς ἐν ἀσωμάτῳ καὶ ἁπλῷ καὶ ἐνιαίῳ καὶ μόνῳ Υἱῷ νοητῶς τεθεάμεθα Πατέρα, κατὰ τό· Ὁ ἑωρακὼς ἐμὲ ἑώρακε τὸν Πατέρα. Καί· Ἐγὼ ἐν τῷ Πατρὶ καὶ ὁ Πατὴρ ἐν ἐμοί. Πολλῆς οὖν χρεία τῆς ἐπιστήμης, ὥστε διαδύντας πρότερον τὰ περὶ τὸν Λόγον τῶν ῥημάτων καλύμματα, οὕτω γυμνῷ τῷ νοῖ καθαρὸν αὐτὸν ἐφ᾽ ἑαυτὸν ἑστῶτα θεάσασθαι τὸν Λόγον, τὸν ἐν ἑαυτῷ σαφῶς ὡς ἐφικτὸν ἀνθρώποις τὸν Πατέρα δεικνύντα. Διόπερ ἀνάγκη τὸν εὐσεβῶς τὸν Θεὸν ἐπιζητοῦντα μηδενὶ κρατεῖσθαι ῥητῷ, ἵνα μή, ἀντὶ Θεοῦ, τὰ περὶ Θεὸν λάθῃ λαβών, τουτέστιν, ἀντὶ τοῦ Λόγου τὰ ῥητὰ στέργων ἐπισφαλῶς τῆς Γραφῆς, τοῦ Λόγου διαφυγόντος τὸν νοῦν ἐκ τῶν περιβλημάτων κρατεῖν δοκοῦντα τὸν ἀσώματον Λόγον· κατά γε τὴν Αἰγυπτίαν, τὴν μὴ τοῦ Ἰωσήφ, ἀλλὰ τῶν αὐτοῦ ἐπιλαβομένην ἱματίων· καὶ τοὺς παλαιοὺς ἀνθρώπους, οἱ μόνῃ τῇ εὐπρεπείᾳ τῶν ὁρωμένων ἐναπομείναντες, ἔλαθον τῇ κτίσει λατρεύοντες παρὰ τὸν κτίσαντα.

74 Ὁ τῆς ἁγίας Γραφῆς λόγος, κατὰ μέρος τοῖς [1160] ὑψηλοτέροις νοήμασι τὴν τῶν ἐπ᾽ αὐτῷ σωματικῶς διαπεπλασμένων ῥητῶν

the practical life in pursuit of virtue, such a one, too, is glorified in God through the dispassionate illumination of divine things corresponding to contemplation. For the Lord says about the impending passion: "Now the Son of Man is glorified, and God is glorified in him. If God is glorified in him, also God will glorify him in himself; and he will glorify him immediately."[289] It is clear from this that divine gifts follow upon sufferings in pursuit of virtue.

2.73 As long as we are seeing the Word of God embodied in the letter of the holy Scripture in various ways through enigmas, we have not yet mentally seen the bodiless, simple, unique, and only Father as he is in the bodiless, simple, unique, and only Son, according to the passage: "He who has seen me has seen the Father" and "I am in the Father, and the Father in me."[290] There is, therefore, a need for much science, so that, being immersed first in the veils of the phrases about the Word, in this way we might with a denuded mind see the pure Word himself standing by himself—as much as is possible for humans—clearly indicating the Father in himself. In consequence, it is necessary for him who seeks God piously not to latch on to a phrase, lest, instead of God, he unknowingly receive things about God;[291] that is, because he is dangerously devoted to the wording of Scripture instead of to the Word, the Word flees the mind which thought it had taken hold of the bodiless Word by his garments, indeed, much like the Egyptian woman who did not take hold of Joseph, but of his clothes instead;[292] or the humans of old, who remaining with only the comeliness of visible things, unknowingly worshipped the creation instead of the Creator.[293]

2.74 The sense of the holy Scripture, which by loftier thoughts is gradually stripped from the contrivance that results from taking

[289]Jn 13:31–32.
[290]Jn 14:9–10.
[291]Cf Jn 5:39–40.
[292]Cf. Gen 39:7–13. Cf. *Ambig.* prol. 3.
[293]Cf. Gen 39:12, Rom 1:25.

ἐκδυσάμενος σύνθεσιν, ὡς ἐν φωνῇ αὔρας λεπτῆς ὑπάρχων δείκνυται τῷ διορατικωτέρῳ νοΐ· τῷ διὰ τὴν ἄκραν ἀπόλειψιν τῶν κατὰ φύσιν ἐνεργειῶν, αἴσθησιν μόνον δυνηθέντι λαβεῖν τῆς τὸν Λόγον ποσῶς μηνυούσης ἁπλότητος κατὰ τὸν μέγα Ἠλίαν τὸν ἐν τῷ σπηλαίῳ Χωρὴβ ταύτης ἀξιωθέντα τῆς ὄψεως. Χωρὴβ γὰρ ἑρμηνεύεται νέωμα, ὅπερ ἐστὶν ἡ ἐν τῷ καινῷ Πνεύματι τῆς χάριτος ἕξις τῶν ἀρετῶν. Τὸ δὲ σπήλαιον ἡ τῆς σοφίας ἐστὶ κατὰ νοῦν κρυφιότης, ἐν ᾗ ὁ γενόμενος τῆς ὑπὲρ αἴσθησιν μυστικῶς αἰσθήσεται γνώσεως ἐν ᾗ λέγεται τυγχάνειν ὁ Θεός. Πᾶς οὖν κατὰ τὸν μέγαν Ἠλίαν ζητῶν ἀληθῶς τὸν Θεόν, οὐ μόνον ἐν Χωρὴβ γενήσεται, τουτέστιν, ὡς πρακτικὸς ἐν τῇ ἕξει τῶν ἀρετῶν, ἀλλὰ καὶ ἐν τῷ σπηλαίῳ τῷ ἐν Χωρήβ, τουτέστιν, ὡς θεωρητικὸς ἐν τῇ κρυφιότητι τῆς σοφίας τῇ ἐν μόνῃ τυγχανούσῃ τῇ ἕξει τῶν ἀρετῶν.

75 Ὅταν ὁ νοῦς τὰς ἐπικειμένας αὐτῷ πολλὰς περὶ τῶν ὄντων ἐκτινάξηται δόξας, τότε σαφὴς αὐτῷ τῆς ἀληθείας ὁ λόγος ἀναφαίνεται, διδοὺς αὐτῷ τῆς ὄντως γνώσεως τὰς ὑποθήκας καὶ τὰς πρώην ἐπ᾽ αὐτῷ προλήψεις ὡσεὶ λεπίδας τῶν ὀπτικῶν δυνάμεων ἀπωθούμενος, κατὰ τὸν θεσπέσιον καὶ μέγαν Ἀπόστολον Παῦλον. Λεπίδες γὰρ εἰσιν, ὡς ἀληθῶς, ἐπικείμεναι τῷ διορατικῷ τῆς ψυχῆς καὶ ἀπείργουσαι τὴν πρὸς τὸν ἀκραιφνῆ τῆς ἀληθείας λόγον διάβασιν, αἵ τε πρὸς τὸ ῥητὸν μόνον τῆς Γραφῆς ὑπολήψεις καὶ τῶν ὁρωμένων αἱ κατ᾽ αἴσθησιν προσπαθεῖς θεωρίαι.

76 Ὁ μὲν θεῖος Ἀπόστολος Παῦλος τὴν τοῦ Λόγου γνῶσιν ἐκ μέρους ἔφη γινώσκειν. Ὁ δὲ μέγας εὐαγγελιστὴς Ἰωάννης τεθεᾶσθαι λέγει τὴν αὐτοῦ δόξαν. Ἐθεασάμεθα γάρ, φησίν, τὴν δόξαν αὐτοῦ, δόξαν ὡς Μονογενοῦς παρὰ Πατρός, πλήρης χάριτος καὶ ἀληθείας.

literally the phrases in it, is shown to be in the more discerning mind as in the voice of a gentle breeze;[294] by the highest abandonment of natural activities—which are able only to apprehend sensory perception, when simplicity qualifiedly discloses the Word—it is made worthy of this vision, like the great Elijah in the cave of Horeb.[295] For Horeb interpreted means "ploughed land," which is precisely the character state of the virtues in the new Spirit of grace. And the cave is the hiddenness of wisdom in the mind; he who comes to be in it, perceives mystically that knowledge beyond sensory perception, in which it is said God is encountered. Everyone, therefore, who like the great Elijah seeks God truly, does come to be not only in Horeb; that is, as a man engaged in the practical life in the character state of the virtues; but also in the cave of Horeb; that is, as a contemplative in the hiddenness of that wisdom encountered only in the character state of the virtues.

2.75 When the mind shakes off the many opinions concerning beings that lie upon it, then the principle of truth shines clearly in it, giving it suppositions of real knowledge, and it puts off its former preconceptions as scales from the faculty of sight, like the most divine and great apostle Paul. For the interpretations of the Scripture only on the literal level and the impassioned contemplations of visible things through sensory perception are in truth scales,[296] accruing onto the discerning faculty of the soul and hindering advance toward the pure principle of truth.

2.76 The divine apostle Paul said he knew the knowledge of the Word "in part."[297] And the great evangelist John said he had seen his glory. "For we have seen," he says, "his glory, glory as of the Only-begotten by the Father, full of grace and truth."[298] And perhaps the

[294] 1/3 Kgs 19:12.
[295] 1/3 Kgs 19:12.
[296] Acts 9:18.
[297] 1 Cor 13:9.
[298] Jn 1:14.

Καὶ μήποτε ὁ μὲν ἅγιος Παῦλος τὴν ὡς Θεοῦ Λόγου γνῶσιν ἐκ μέρους ἔφη γινώσκειν· ἐκ γὰρ τῶν ἐνεργειῶν, ποσῶς, μόνον γινώσκεται. Ἡ γὰρ ἐπ᾽ αὐτῷ κατ᾽ οὐσίαν τε καὶ ὑπόστασιν γνῶσις, ὁμοίως πᾶσιν ἀγγέλοις τε καὶ ἀνθρώποις, καθέστηκεν ἄβατος, κατ᾽ οὐδὲν οὐδενὶ γινωσκομένη. Ὁ δὲ ἅγιος Ἰωάννης, τέλειον ὡς ἐν ἀνθρώποις, τὸν τῆς ἐνανθρωπήσεως τοῦ Λόγου μυηθεὶς λόγον, τὴν ὡς σάρκα Λόγον δόξαν ἔφη τεθεᾶσθαι· τουτέστι, τὸν λόγον, ἤγουν, τὸν σκοπόν, καθ᾽ ὅν ὁ Θεὸς γέγονεν ἄνθρωπος, πλήρη χάριτος ἐθεάσατο καὶ ἀληθείας. Οὐ γὰρ καθ᾽ ὅ κατ᾽ οὐσίαν Θεός, καὶ τῷ Θεῷ Πατρί ὁμοούσιος ὁ Μονογενὴς κεχαρίτωται, ἀλλὰ καθ᾽ ὅ φύσει κατ᾽ οἰκονομίαν γέγονεν, ἄνθρωπος καὶ ἡμῖν ὁμοούσιος, δι᾽ ἡμᾶς κεχαρίτωται τοὺς χρήζοντας χάριτος· καὶ ἐκ τοῦ πληρώματος αὐτοῦ διαπαντὸς κατὰ πᾶσαν ἡμῶν προκοπὴν τὴν ἀναλογοῦσαν δεχομένους χάριν. Ὥστε ὁ τὸν λόγον [1161] τέλειον ἐν ἑαυτῷ φυλάξας, ἀβέβηλον τοῦ δι᾽ ἡμᾶς σαρκωθέντος Θεοῦ Λόγου, τὴν πλήρη χάριτος καὶ ἀληθείας κομίσεται δόξαν, τοῦ δι᾽ ἡμᾶς ἑαυτὸν καθ᾽ ἡμᾶς δοξάσαντός τε καὶ ἁγιάσαντος κατὰ τὴν αὐτοῦ παρουσίαν. Ὅταν γάρ, φησίν, ἐκεῖνος φανερωθῇ, ὅμοιοι αὐτῷ ἐσόμεθα.

77   Ἕως ἡ ψυχή, τήν· ἀπὸ δυνάμεως εἰς δύναμιν, καί· ἀπὸ δόξης εἰς δόξαν ποιεῖται μετάβασιν, τουτέστι, τὴν ἀπὸ ἀρετῆς εἰς ἀρετὴν μείζονα προκοπὴν καὶ τὴν ἀπὸ γνώσεως εἰς γνῶσιν ὑψηλοτέραν ἀνάβασιν οὐκ ἐπαύσατο παροικοῦσα, κατὰ τὸ εἰρημένον· Πολλὰ παρῴκησεν ἡ ψυχή μου. Πολὺ γάρ ἐστι τὸ διάστημα καὶ τὸ πλῆθος τῶν ὀφειλουσῶν παρ᾽ αὐτῆς διαβαθῆναι γνώσεων, μέχρις οὗ διελεύσεται ἐν τόπῳ σκηνῆς θαυμαστῆς, ἕως τοῦ οἴκου τοῦ Θεοῦ· ἐν φωνῇ ἀγαλλιάσεως καὶ ἐξομολογήσεως, ἤχου ἑορτάζοντος·

holy Paul said he knew the knowledge of the Word of God in part, for he is only known to a limited degree on the basis of his activities. For knowledge concerning his substance and person in himself is to everyone alike, both to angels and humans, inaccessible, since it is known to no one in any way. And the holy John, being as perfect as possible among humans, having disclosed the rationale for the hominization of the Word, said he had seen the glory of the Word as flesh;[299] that is, he saw the rationale, or rather, the object in accordance with which God has become a human, full of grace and truth. For the Only-begotten, consubstantial with God the Father, has not given himself in accordance with what God is by substance, but rather in accordance with what he has become by nature economically, a human also consubstantial with us; he has given himself for the sake of us who need grace, who by our every progress are always receiving commensurate grace from his fullness. So, he who is keeping this rationale perfect in himself and the incarnation of God the Word for our sake undefiled, preserves full of grace and truth the glory of him who for our sake glorified and sanctified himself among us at the time of his presence. "For when," it says, "he is made manifest, we will be similar to him."[300]

2.77 So long as the soul makes a transition "from capacity to capacity"[301] and "from glory to glory,"[302] that is, a progress from virtue to greater virtue, and the ascent from knowledge to loftier knowledge, it does not cease from "being a sojourner," according to what was said: "Long has my soul been a sojourner."[303] For there is a great distance and an abundance of necessary knowledge to be traversed by it before it reaches "the place of the wondrous tabernacle, the very house of God, with a voice of rejoicing and praise, and the sound of

---

[299]Cf. Jn 1:14.
[300]1 Jn 3:2.
[301]Ps 83/84:7.
[302]2 Cor 3:18.
[303]Ps 119/120:6.

ἀεὶ φωναῖς, φωνήν (νοεραῖς, νοεράν) προστιθεῖσα τῇ προκοπῇ τῶν θείων θεωρημάτων, μετὰ τῆς κατὰ νοῦν ἐπὶ τοῖς θεωρηθεῖσιν ἀγαλλιάσεως, ἤγουν, χαρᾶς, καὶ τῆς ἀναλογούσης εὐχαριστίας. Τοιαύτας γὰρ ἑορτάζουσι πάντες οἱ τὸ Πνεῦμα τῆς χάριτος εἰληφότες ἐν ταῖς καρδίαις αὐτῶν κράζων· Ἀββᾶ, ὁ Πατήρ.

78   Ὁ τῆς θαυμαστῆς σκηνῆς τόπος καὶ ἀπαθής ἐστι καὶ ἀπήμων ἕξις τῶν ἀρετῶν· καθ᾽ ἥν ὁ τοῦ Θεοῦ γινόμενος Λόγος, διαφόροις ἀρετῶν κάλλεσι κατακοσμεῖ καθάπερ σκηνὴν τὴν ψυχήν. Ὁ δὲ οἶκος τοῦ Θεοῦ, ἡ ἐκ πολλῶν καὶ διαφόρων συγκειμένη θεωρημάτων γνῶσις ἐστί, καθ᾽ ἥν ἐνδημῶν τῇ ψυχῇ ὁ Θεός, τοῦ τῆς σοφίας κρατῆρος ἐμπίμπλησιν. Ἡ δὲ φωνὴ τῆς ἀγαλλιάσεώς ἐστι τὸ ἐπὶ τῷ πλούτῳ τῶν ἀρετῶν τῆς ψυχῆς σκίρτημα. Ἡ δὲ τῆς ἐξομολογήσεως ἡ ἐπὶ τῇ δόξῃ τῆς κατὰ τὴν σοφίαν εὐωχίας ἐστὶν εὐχαριστία. Ὁ δὲ ἦχος ἡ ἐξ ἀμφοῖν, ἀγαλλιάσεώς, φημι, καὶ ἐξομολογήσεως, κατὰ σύγκρασιν γινομένη διηνεκὴς μυστικὴ δοξολογία.

79   Ὁ γενναίως καταπαλαίσας τὰ πάθη τοῦ σώματος καὶ τοῖς ἀκαθάρτοις πνεύμασιν ἱκανῶς πολεμήσας, καὶ τῆς ἑαυτοῦ κατὰ ψυχὴν χώρας ἐξελάσας αὐτῶν τὰ νοήματα· καρδίαν εὐχέσθω καθαρὰν αὐτῷ δοθῆναι καί· πνεῦμα εὐθὲς ἐν τοῖς ἐγκάτοις ἐγκαινισθῆναι, τουτέστι, τελείως τῶν μὲν φαύλων κενωθῆναι λογισμῶν, τῶν δὲ θείων ἐννοιῶν πληρωθῆναι διὰ τῆς χάριτος ἵνα γένηται κόσμος Θεοῦ νοητῶς λαμπρός τε καὶ μέγας, ἐξ ἠθικῶν καὶ φυσικῶν καὶ θεολογικῶν συνεστὼς θεωρημάτων.

80   Ὁ τὴν καρδίαν καθαρὰν ἐργασάμενος, οὐ μόνον τῶν ὑποβεβηκότων καὶ μετὰ Θεὸν γνώσεται τοὺς λόγους, ἀλλὰ καὶ

celebrating,"[304] always adding a voice to voices (that is, an intellectual voice to intellectual voices) by progress in divine contemplations, with rejoicing in the mind over what is contemplated, that is, with joy, and with a commensurate thanksgiving. For all those who have received the Spirit of grace celebrate such things, calling out in their hearts: "Abba, Father."[305]

2.78   "The place of the wondrous tabernacle"[306] is the character state of the virtues, which is both dispassionate and untroubled, in accordance with which the Word of God, being present, adorns the soul like a tabernacle with the diverse beauties of the virtues. "The house of God" is the knowledge consisting in many and diverse contemplations, in accordance with which God, indwelling the soul, fills up the cup of wisdom. And "the voice of rejoicing" is frolicking because of the wealth of the virtues of the soul. And the voice of praise is thanksgiving for the glory of feasting in wisdom. And "the sound" is the unceasing mystical doxology that comes about from the combination of both, I mean, of rejoicing and praise.

2.79   Let him who has genuinely overthrown the passions of the body and has combatted admirably against the impure spirits, and who has driven out their thoughts from the realm of his soul, pray for him to be given a clean heart and for "a steady spirit" to be renewed "in his innermost parts;"[307] that is, to be perfectly emptied from vicious thought processes and to be filled through grace with divine insights, that he might become a bright and great world of God intelligibly, consisting of ethical, natural, and theological contemplations.

2.80   He who has wrought a clean heart, will know not only the *logoi* of things subordinated to and after God, but will even look upon

[304]Ps 41/42:4.
[305]Gal 4:6.
[306]Continuing from the previous chapter: Ps 41/42:4.
[307]Cf. Ps 50/51:10.

αὐτῷ—ποσῶς—μετὰ τὴν τῶν ὅλων διάβασιν ἐνορᾷ· ὅπερ ἐστὶν ἀκρότατον τέλος τῶν ἀγαθῶν, ἐν ᾗ γενόμενος ὁ Θεός, ἀξιοῖ τὰ ἴδια γράμματα διὰ τοῦ πνεύματος ἐγχαράττειν, καθάπερ τισὶ [1164] πλαξὶ Μωσαϊκαῖς· τοσοῦτον, ὅσον ἑαυτὴν διὰ πράξεως ἐπιδέδωκε καὶ θεωρίας, κατὰ τὴν τό· Αὔξανου, μυστικῶς κελεύουσαν ἐντολήν.

81 Καρδία καθαρὰ τάχα ἐκείνη λέγεται ἡ μηδεμίαν ἔχουσα φυσικὴν καθ᾽ οἱονδήποτε τρόπον πρὸς ὁτιοῦν κίνησιν· ἐν ᾗ καθάπερ πτυχίῳ καλῶς λειανθέντι διὰ τὴν ἄκραν ἁπλότητα γινόμενος ὁ Θεός, τοὺς ἰδίους νόμους ἐγγράφει.

82 Καρδία ἐστὶ καθαρὰ ἡ παντάπασιν ἀνείδεον τῷ Θεῷ καὶ ἀμόρφωτον παραστήσασα τὴν μνήμην· καὶ μόνοις τοῖς αὐτοῦ ἕτοιμον ἐνσημανθῆναι τύποις, δι᾽ ὧν ἐμφανὴς πέφυκε γίνεσθαι.

83 Ὁ τοῦ Χριστοῦ νοῦς, ὅν λαμβάνουσιν οἱ ἅγιοι κατὰ τὸν φάμενον· Ἡμεῖς δὲ νοῦν Χριστοῦ ἔχομεν, οὐ κατὰ στέρησιν τῆς ἐν ἡμῖν νοερᾶς δυνάμεως ἐπιγίνεται οὐδὲ ὡς συμπληρωτικὸς τοῦ ἡμετέρου νοὸς οὐδ᾽ ὡς μεταβαίνων οὐσιωδῶς καθ᾽ ὑπόστασιν εἰς τὸν ἡμέτερον νοῦν, ἀλλ᾽ ὡς τῇ οἰκείᾳ ποιότητι τὴν τοῦ ἡμετέρου νοὸς λαμπρύνων δύναμιν καὶ πρὸς τὴν αὐτὴν αὐτῷ φέρων ἐνέργειαν. Νοῦν γὰρ ἔχειν Χριστοῦ, ἔγωγέ φημι, τὸν κατ᾽ αὐτὸν νοοῦντα καὶ διὰ πάντων αὐτὸν νοοῦντα.

him—to a limited degree—after his transcendence of all things; this is the highest end of good things; when God comes to be inside the heart, he deems it fitting to engrave his own letters through the Spirit, just as on the tablets of Moses,[308] to the degree that the heart has devoted itself, through praxis and contemplation,[309] in accordance with the commandment that mystically enjoins: "Grow."[310]

2.81 Perchance that is called a "pure heart"[311] that has absolutely no natural motion toward anything at all; when God comes to be in it, he inscribes his own laws as if on a tablet beautifully polished by supreme simplicity.

2.82 A "heart" is "pure"[312] that represents its recollections as altogether formless and shapeless before God and stands ready to be imprinted with his characteristics alone, through which he naturally becomes manifest.

2.83 The mind of Christ, which the saints receive, according to what was spoken: "And we have the mind of Christ,"[313] comes about not by virtue of a privation of the intellectual faculty in us, nor as completing an essential part of our mind, nor as passing over in substance and in person into our mind;[314] but rather, as enlightening by his own quality the faculty of our mind and taking it toward the same activity that is in him.[315] For what "having the mind of Christ" means, I personally think, is to think like him and to think him through all things.

[308]Cf. Ex 31:18.
[309]Cf. Gregory of Nyssa, *V. Mos.* 2.152.
[310]Gen 35:11.
[311]Ps 50/51:10.
[312]Ps 50/51:10.
[313]1 Cor 2:16.
[314]Cf. Gregory of Nazianzus, *Or.* 39.8, Maximus, *Ambig.* 7.12 and 41.5–11.
[315]This was a particular linchpin of Maximus' theology expressed clearly in *Ambig.* 7.12, called into question after the outbreak of the Monenergistic heresy and clarified and defended by the Confessor in one of his last works, the *Opusc.* 1, PG 91.33B.

84. Σῶμα Χριστοῦ εἶναι λεγόμεθα, κατὰ τό· Ἡμεῖς δὲ σῶμα Χριστοῦ ἐσμεν, καὶ μέλη ἐκ μέρους, οὐ κατὰ στέρησιν τῶν ἡμετέρων σωμάτων, ἐκείνου τὸ σῶμα γινόμενοι· οὐδ' αὖ πάλιν ἐκείνου καθ' ὑπόστασιν εἰς ἡμᾶς μεταβαίνοντος ἢ μεληδὸν διατεμνομένου, ἀλλὰ τῷ καθ' ὁμοιότητα τῆς τοῦ Κυρίου σαρκὸς τὴν φθορὰν ἀποσείεσθαι τῆς ἁμαρτίας. Ὡς γὰρ ὁ Χριστὸς κατὰ φύσιν σαρκί τε καὶ ψυχῇ καθ' ὅ νοεῖται ἄνθρωπος ἀναμάρτητος ἦν, οὕτω καὶ ἡμεῖς, οἱ πεπιστευκότες αὐτῷ καὶ διὰ Πνεύματος αὐτὸν ἐνδυσάμενοι, κατὰ προαίρεσιν ἐν αὐτῷ χωρὶς ἁμαρτίας εἶναι δυνάμεθα.

85 Εἰσὶ παρὰ τῇ Γραφῇ καὶ χρονικοὶ αἰῶνες καὶ ἄλλων αἰώνων συντέλειαν περιέχοντες, κατὰ τό· Νυνὶ δὲ ἅπαξ ἐπὶ συντελείᾳ τῶν αἰώνων, καὶ τά ἑξῆς. Καὶ ἕτεροι πάλιν χρονικῆς ἐλεύθεροι φύσεως αἰῶνες, μετὰ τὸν ἐνεστῶτα τοῦτον χρόνον, αἰῶνα τὸν ἐπὶ συντελείᾳ τῶν αἰώνων, κατὰ τό·Ἵνα ἐνδείξηται ἐν τοῖς αἰῶσι τοῖς ἐπερχομένοις τὸν ὑπερβάλλοντα πλοῦτον, καὶ τὰ ἑξῆς. Εὑρίσκομεν δὲ παρὰ τῇ Γραφῇ καὶ πλῆθος αἰώνων, παρελθόντων τε καὶ ἐνεστώτων καὶ μελλόντων· καὶ αἰῶνας αἰώνων εἶναί τινας αἰῶνας καὶ αἰῶνος αἰῶνα καὶ χρόνους αἰωνίους καὶ γενεὰς συνημμένας αἰῶσι. Καὶ ἵνα μὴ νῦν, τὶ μεν διὰ τῶν χρονικῶν αἰώνων, τί δὲ διὰ τῶν αἰωνίων χρόνων καὶ [1165] γενεῶν βούλεται δηλοῦν ὁ λόγος, λέγοντες· τινὲς δὲ πάλιν ἁπλῶς οἱ αἰῶνες τῶν αἰώνων, τίς τε ὁ ἁπλοῦς αἰὼν καὶ ὁ αἰὼν τοῦ αἰῶνος, πολὺν παρὰ τὴν ὑπόθεσιν ἐκτείνωμεν λόγον τὰ περὶ τούτων τοῖς φιλομαθέσι σκοπεῖν ἐάσαντες, πρὸς τὸν σκοπόν, δι' ὅν ταῦτα προηγάγομεν, ἐπανέλθωμεν.

2.84 We are said to be the body of Christ according to the passage, "And we are the body of Christ, and an individual limb;"[316] not by virtue of a privation of our bodies do we become his body, nor, furthermore, as if he passed over in person into us, or were cut limb from limb; but rather, by the corruption of sin being shaken off by way of likeness to the flesh of the Lord. For as Christ by nature was sinless[317] in flesh and soul—from which things the human is thought to consist—so also we who have believed in him, and have put him on through the Spirit, are able, in him, to be without sin by choice.

2.85 In the Scripture there are both temporal ages that circumscribe the consummation of ages, according to the passage, "And now, once and for all, at the consummation of the ages . . . "[318] and so on, and also different ages that are free of temporal nature, beyond this time at hand, an age at the end of the ages, according to the passage, "That in the coming ages the overflowing riches he might show . . ."[319] and so on. And we find in the Scripture an abundance of ages, past, present, and future; and there are also certain kinds of ages: the ages of ages,[320] and an age of an age,[321] and temporal ages,[322] and generations joined by ages.[323] But lest we now prolong the treatise greatly and away from the subject in stating what the text wishes to signify through temporal ages, and what through the eternal times and generations, and again what are simply the ages of ages, and what is the age in the singular, and the age of the age, let us get back to the objective for which introduced these terms, leaving it to eager learners to investigate the matters concerning such topics.[324]

[316] 1 Cor 12:27.
[317] Cf. Heb 4:15.
[318] Heb 9:26.
[319] Eph 2:7.
[320] Cf. Ps 83/84:4.
[321] Cf. Ps 111/112:3.
[322] Cf. 2 Tim 1:9.
[323] Cf. Gen 9:12.
[324] Cf. Origen, *De princ.* 2.3.5 and *Qu. Thal.* 22, CCSG 7, pp. 137–143.

86 Οἴδαμεν τι κατὰ τὴν Γραφὴν ὑπεραιώνιον· ὅπερ ὅτι μὲν ἔστιν, ἐσήμανε· τί δὲ τοῦτό ἐστιν, οὐκ ὠνόμασε, κατὰ τό· Κύριος βασιλεύων τὸν αἰῶνα καὶ ἐπ᾽ αἰῶνα καὶ ἔτι. Οὐκοῦν ἔστι τι πρᾶγμα ὑπὲρ αἰῶνας ἡ ἀκραιφνὴς τοῦ Θεοῦ βασιλεία. Οὐ γὰρ δὴ θέμις εἰπεῖν ἦρχθαι ἢ φθάνεσθαι ὑπὸ αἰώνων ἢ χρόνων τὴν τοῦ Θεοῦ βασιλείαν. Ταύτην δὲ πιστεύομεν εἶναι τῶν σωζομένων κληρονομίαν, καὶ μονὴν καὶ τόπον, καθὼς ὁ ἀληθὴς παραδίδωσι λόγος· ὡς τέλος τῶν δι᾽ ἐφέσεως πρὸς τὸ ἔσχατον ὀρεκτὸν κινουμένων· ἐν ᾧ γινόμενοι, πάσης τῆς ὁποιασοῦν δέχονται παῦλαν κινήσεως· ὡς μηκέτι χρόνου τινὸς ὄντος αὐτῶν ἢ αἰῶνος τοῦ διαβαθῆναι ὀφείλοντος, οἷα δὴ μετὰ πάντα καταντήσασιν εἰς τὸν Θεόν, τὸν πρὸ πάντων ὄντα τῶν αἰώνων καὶ ὅν φθάνειν αἰώνων φύσις οὐ πέφυκεν.

87 Ἐφ᾽ ὅσον χρόνον τίς ἐστιν ἐν τῇ ζωῇ ταύτῃ, κἂν τέλειός ἐστι κατὰ τὴν ἐνθάδε κατάστασιν, καὶ πράξει καὶ θεωρίᾳ, τὴν ἐκ μέρους ἔχει καὶ γνῶσιν καὶ προφητείαν καὶ ἀρραβῶνα Πνεύματος ἁγίου, ἀλλ᾽ οὐκ αὐτὸ τὸ πλήρωμα· ἐλευσόμενός ποτε μετὰ τὴν τῶν αἰώνων περαίωσιν εἰς τὴν τελείαν λῆξιν, τὴν πρόσωπον πρὸς πρόσωπον τοῖς ἀξίοις δεικνῦσαν αὐτὴν ἐφ᾽ ἑαυτῆς ἑστῶσαν τὴν ἀλήθειαν, ὡς μηκέτι ἐκ τοῦ πληρώματος μέρος ἔχειν, ἀλλ᾽ αὐτὸ τὸ πλήρωμα τῆς χάριτος κατὰ μέθεξιν ὅλον κομίζεσθαι· καταντήσεσθαι γάρ, φησίν ὁ Ἀπόστολος, πάντας (δηλονότι τοὺς σωζομένους) εἰς ἄνδρα τέλειον, εἰς μέτρον ἡλικίας τοῦ πληρώματος τοῦ Χριστοῦ, ἐν ᾧ εἰσιν οἱ θησαυροὶ τῆς σοφίας καὶ τῆς γνώσεως ἀπόκρυφοι· ἧς φαινομένης, τὸ ἐκ μέρους καταργηθήσεται.

2.86 We know by the Scripture that there is something beyond the age; it points out that this very thing exists, but it does not name what it is, according to the passage: "The Lord is ruling eternally, both beyond the age and forever."[325] Therefore, there is a certain reality beyond the ages: the pure rulership of God. For it is impermissible to say the rulership of God was begun, or that it was preceded by ages or times. We believe this to be the inheritance of the saved, and their abode and place, as the true word has transmitted, as being the end of those being moved by their impulse toward the ultimately desirable;[326] coming to be in which, they receive rest from any kind of motion whatsoever, since there is no longer any time or age necessary for them to go through, because indeed after all things they will have arrived into God, who is before all ages and whom the nature of the ages inherently cannot precede.[327]

2.87 For the time that someone is in this life, although he be perfect in his condition here below, both by practice and contemplation, he has knowledge, prophecy, and the pledge of the Holy Spirit in part, but that is not the fullness; when he has come to the perfect standstill beyond the traversing of the ages, the standstill itself shows the truth as it is in itself, standing "face to face" with the worthy, since no longer having a part of the fullness, by participation he recovers the whole fullness of grace itself; for, the Apostle says, all (that is, the saved) will turn "into the perfect man, by the measure of the stature of the fullness of Christ,"[328] in whom the treasures of wisdom and knowledge are hidden[329] and "what is in part will be abolished" when they appear.[330]

[325] Ex 15:18.
[326] Cf. *Ambig.* 7.5.
[327] By way of critique of Origen's theory of motion and time, more extensively refuted in *Ambig.* 7.2–14. Also see Gregory of Nyssa, *In Ps.* 6, GNO 6, pp. 188–189.
[328] Eph 4:13.
[329] Cf. Col 2:3.
[330] 1 Cor 13:10.

88   Ζητοῦσὶ τινες, πῶς ἔσται τῶν ἀξιουμένων τῆς ἐν τῇ βασιλείᾳ
τοῦ Θεοῦ τελειότητος ἡ κατάστασις· πότερον κατὰ προκοπὴν καὶ
μετάβασιν ἤ κατὰ τὴν ἐν στάσει ταυτότητα· πῶς τε τὰ σώματα καὶ τὰς
ψυχὰς εἶναι χρεὼν ὑπολαμβάνειν. Πρὸς δὴ τοῦτο στοχαστικῶς ἐρεῖ
τις ὅτι καθάπερ ἐπὶ τῆς σωματικῆς ζωῆς διττὸς ἐστιν ὁ τῆς τροφῆς
λόγος· ὁ μὲν πρὸς αὔξησιν, ὁ δὲ πρὸς συντήρησιν τῶν τρεφομένων,
μέχρις οὗ φθάσωμεν τὸ τέλειον τῆς σωματικῆς ἡλικίας, τρεφόμεθα
πρὸς αὔξησιν· ἐπειδὰν δὲ τὸ σῶμα στῇ τῆς εἰς μέγεθος ἐπιδόσεως,
οὐκέτι τρέφεται πρὸς αὔξησιν, ἀλλὰ πρὸς συντήρησιν. Οὕτως καὶ ἐπὶ
τῆς ψυχῆς διττὸς ὁ τῆς τροφῆς λόγος. Τρέφεται γὰρ προκόπτουσα
ταῖς ἀρεταῖς καὶ [1168] τοῖς θεωρήμασι, μέχρις οὗ διαβᾶσα τὰ
ὄντα πάντα φθάσῃ τὸ μέτρον τῆς ἡλικίας τοῦ πληρώματος τοῦ
Χριστοῦ, ἐν ᾧ γινομένη, πάσης τῆς πρὸς ἐπίδοσίν τε καὶ αὔξησιν διὰ
τῶν μέσων ἵσταται προκοπῆς· ἀμέσως τρεφομένη τὸ ὑπὲρ νόησιν
(καὶ διὰ τοῦτο τυχὸν ὑπὲρ αὔξησιν) τῆς ἀφθάρτου τροφῆς εἶδος,
πρὸς συντήρησιν τῆς δοθείσης αὐτῇ θεοειδοῦς τελειότητος καὶ
ἔκφανσιν τῶν τῆς τροφῆς ἐκείνης ἀπείρων ἀγλαϊῶν, καθ᾽ ἥν τὸ ἀεὶ
εὖ ὡσαύτως εἶναι ἐνδημῆσαν αὐτῇ δεχομένη, γίνεται θεὸς τῇ μεθέξει
τῆς θεϊκῆς χάριτος, πασῶν τῶν κατὰ νοῦν καὶ αἴσθησιν ἐνεργειῶν
αὐτή τε παυσαμένη καὶ ἑαυτῇ τὰς τοῦ σώματος συναναπαύσασα
φυσικὰς ἐνεργείας, συνθεωθέντος αὐτῇ κατὰ τὴν ἀναλογοῦσαν
αὐτῷ μέθεξιν τῆς θεώσεως. Ὥστε μόνον τὸν Θεὸν διά τε τῆς ψυχῆς
καὶ τοῦ σώματος φαίνεσθαι, νικηθέντων αὐτῶν τῇ ὑπερβολῇ τῆς
δόξης τῶν φυσικῶν γνωρισμάτων.

89   Ζητοῦσί τινες τῶν φιλομαθῶν, κατὰ ποῖον ἔσται τρόπον ἡ
τῶν αἰωνίων μονῶν τε καὶ ἐπαγγελιῶν διαφορά· πότερον καθ᾽

2.88 Some inquire what the quality of the condition of those made worthy of perfection in the kingdom of God will be: whether it will accord with progress and change, or with the sameness of rest; also how one is to take existence relative to how bodies and souls will be. One might say speculatively to this that just as in bodily life the principle of nutrition is twofold—the one for growth and the other for sustenance of those being nourished (until we arrive at the perfection of bodily stature, we are nourished for growth, but when the body ceases from its increase in size, it is no longer nourished for growth, but for sustenance)—so also in the case of the soul the principle of nutrition is twofold. For it is nourished progressing by the virtues and contemplations, until, having transcended all beings, it arrives at the " . . . measure of the stature of the fullness of Christ;"[331] having come to be in it, the soul ceases from every progress toward increase and from growth through intermediaries, being fed directly, in a way beyond thought (and thus likely beyond growth), the form of the incorruptible nourishment for the sustenance of the God-like perfection it has been given and the manifestation of the boundless splendors of that nourishment, in accordance with which, also receiving well-being as abiding in it, it becomes God by participation of divine grace, itself resting from all its intellectual and sensory activities, and along with itself also arresting the natural activities of the body, that along with the soul is being deified by a participation of deification proper to itself. The result is that God alone shines through both soul and body, when their natural identifying marks are overcome by the excess of glory.[332]

2.89 Some of the eager learners inquire of what quality the mode of difference between the eternal abodes and the promises will be:[333]

[331]Eph 4:13.

[332]Maximus has carefully taken pieces from a text strongly reminiscent of *De princ.* 2.11.7 and with it restructured the Origenistic theory of human motion, growth, and stability. Cf. *Qu. Thal.* 25 CCSG 7, p. 163.9–10, 59, CCSG 22, pp. 53.128–131, and 65, pp. 283.522–285.549, and *Ambig.* 67.10.

[333]Cf. Jn 14:2; Heb 11:33.

ὑπόστασιν τοπικὴν ἢ κατ' ἐπίνοιαν τῆς ἰδιαζούσης καθ' ἑκάστην μορφὴν πνευματικῆς ποιότητός τε καὶ ποσότητος. Καὶ τοῖς μὲν δοκεῖ τὸ πρῶτον· τοῖς δὲ τὸ δεύτερον· ὁ δὲ γνούς, τί τό· Ἡ βασιλεία τοῦ Θεοῦ ἐντὸς ὑμῶν ἐστι, καὶ τί τό· Πολλαὶ μοναὶ παρὰ τῷ Πατρί, τοῦ δευτέρου μᾶλλον γενήσεται.

90 Ζητοῦσί τινες, ποίαν διαφορὰν ἔχει πρὸς τὴν τοῦ Θεοῦ βασιλείαν ἡ τῶν οὐρανῶν βασιλεία· πότερον καθ' ὑπόστασιν διαφέρουσιν ἀλλήλων ἢ κατ' ἐπίνοιαν. Πρὸς οὓς ῥητέον ὅτι διαφέρουσι μέν, οὐ καθ' ὑπόστασιν, δέ. Μία γὰρ καθ' ὑπόστασιν ἄμφω, ἀλλὰ κατ' ἐπίνοιαν· ἡ μὲν γὰρ βασιλεία τῶν οὐρανῶν τῆς τῶν ὄντων ἀκραιφνοῦς κατὰ τοὺς ἑαυτῶν λόγους ἐν τῷ Θεῷ προαιωνίου γνώσεώς ἐστι κατάληψις, ἡ δὲ τοῦ Θεοῦ βασιλεία τῶν προσόντων τῷ Θεῷ φυσικῶς ἀγαθῶν κατὰ χάριν ἐστὶ μετάδοσις· καὶ ἡ μὲν κατὰ τὸ τέλος τῶν ὄντων, ἡ δὲ κατ' ἐπίνοιαν μετὰ τὸ τέλος τῶν ὄντων ἐστί.

91 Τό· Ἤγγικεν ἡ βασιλεία τῶν οὐρανῶν οὐκ ἔστιν, ὡς οἶμαι, χρονικῆς συστολῆς, οὐ γὰρ ἔρχεται μετὰ παρατηρήσεως· οὔτε ἐροῦσιν· Ἰδοὺ ὧδε, ἰδοὺ ἐκεῖ, ἀλλὰ τῆς πρὸς αὐτῶν τῶν ἀξίων [1169] αὐτῆς κατὰ διάθεσιν σχέσεώς ἐστιν· Ἡ γὰρ βασιλεία τοῦ Θεοῦ, φησίν, ἐντὸς ὑμῶν ἐστιν.

92 Ἡ τοῦ Θεοῦ καὶ Πατρὸς βασιλεία δυνάμει μὲν ἐν πᾶσί ἐστιν τοῖς πιστεύουσιν, ἐνεργείᾳ δὲ ἐν τοῖς ἀποθεμένοις διόλου διαθέσεως πᾶσαν τὴν κατὰ φύσιν ψυχῆς τε καὶ σώματος ζωήν, καὶ μόνην

whether it is about a substantial place or about a particular concept of spiritual quality and quantity applicable to each image. And to some it seems it is the first, whereas to others the second; but he who knows what it means that "The kingdom of God is within you"[334] and that "With my Father there are many abodes"[335] will side, rather, with the second.

2.90 Some inquire what qualitative difference the kingdom of heaven[336] represents vis-à-vis the kingdom of God:[337] whether they differ substantially or conceptually from each other. To them it must be said that they differ, not substantially, however, for both are one substantially, although different conceptually, for the one, the kingdom of heaven, is the apprehension of the pure pre-eternal knowledge of beings according to their own *logoi* in God; the other, the kingdom of God, is the impartation by grace of the goods by nature preexisting in God; moreover, the one is at the end of beings, the other is conceptually beyond the end of beings.[338]

2.91 The passage, "The kingdom of heaven has drawn near,"[339] does not mean, as I take it, the contraction of time: For it "does not come with warning, nor will they say: Look it is here, look it is there!"[340] Rather, it is about the dispositional relationship with those worthy of it: "For the kingdom of God," it says, "is within you."[341]

2.92 The kingdom of God the Father is in potentiality in all those who believe, but in actuality in those who have altogether thrust away from their disposition all life of soul and body according to

[334]Luke 17:21.
[335]Cf. Jn 14:2.
[336]Cf. Mt 3:2, 4:17, etc.
[337]Cf. Lk 17:20, etc.
[338]Cf. Evagrius, *Pra.* 2–3.
[339]Mt 3:2, 4:17.
[340]Lk 17:21–22.
[341]Lk 17:21.

κτησαμένοις τὴν τοῦ πνεύματος καὶ δυναμένοις λέγειν· Ζῶ δὲ οὐκέτι ἐγώ, ζῇ δὲ ἐν ἐμοὶ Χριστός.

93   Τήν βασιλείαν τῶν οὐρανῶν εἶναί, τινες λέγουσι, τὴν ἐν οὐρανοῖς τῶν ἀξίων διαγωγήν, ἕτεροι δὲ τὴν ὁμοίαν τοῖς ἀγγέλοις τῶν σωζομένων κατάστασιν, ἄλλοι δὲ τὸ εἶδος αὐτὸ τῆς θεϊκῆς ὡραιότητος τῶν φορεσάντων τὴν εἰκόνα τοῦ Ἐπουρανίου. Συνάδουσι δὲ τῇ ἀληθείᾳ, κατὰ τὸ ἐμοὶ δοκοῦν, καὶ αἱ τρεῖς περὶ τούτου δόξαι. Πᾶσι γὰρ κατὰ τὴν ἀναλογίαν τῆς ἐν αὐτοῖς κατὰ ποιόν τε καὶ ποσὸν δικαιοσύνης, ἡ μέλλουσα δίδοται χάρις.

94   Ἕως ὅτου κατὰ τὴν πρακτικὴν φιλοσοφίαν ἀνδρικῶς τοὺς θείους διεξέρχεταί τις ἀγῶνας, τὸν διὰ τῶν ἐντολῶν ἐξελθόντα παρὰ τοῦ Πατρὸς εἰς τὸν κόσμον παρ᾽ ἑαυτῷ κατέχει Λόγον. Ἐπειδὰν δὲ τῶν κατὰ τὴν πρᾶξιν πρὸς τὰ πάθη παλαισμάτων ἀφιέμενος, ὡς νικητὴς παθῶν καὶ δαιμόνων ἀποφανθείς, πρὸς τὴν διὰ θεωρίας γνωστικὴν μετέλθη φιλοσοφίαν, συγχωρεῖ τῷ Λόγῳ μυστικῶς ἀφεῖναι πάλιν τὸν κόσμον, καὶ πορευθῆναι πρὸς τὸν Πατέρα. Διὸ φησιν ὁ Κύριος τοῖς μαθηταῖς· ὅτι Ὑμεῖς ἐμὲ πεφιλήκατε καὶ πεπιστεύκατε ὅτι ἐγὼ παρὰ τοῦ Θεοῦ ἐξῆλθον. Ἐξῆλθον παρὰ τοῦ Πατρὸς καὶ ἐλήλυθα εἰς τὸν κόσμον· πάλιν ἀφίημι τὸν κόσμον, καὶ πορεύομαι πρὸς τὸν Πατέρα· κόσμον εἰπών, τυχὸν τὴν κατὰ τὴν πρᾶξιν τῶν ἀρετῶν ἐπίπονον ἐργασίαν, Πατέρα δέ, τὴν κατὰ νοῦν ὑπερκόσμιον καὶ παντὸς ἐλευθέραν ὑλικοῦ φρονήματος κατάστασιν, καθ᾽ ἥν ἐν ἡμῖν ὁ τοῦ Θεοῦ γίνεται Λόγος, τῆς πρὸς τὰ πάθη καὶ τοὺς δαίμονας μάχης παυόμενος.

95   Ὁ δυνηθεὶς νεκρῶσαι διὰ πράξεως τὰ μέλη τὰ ἐπὶ τῆς γῆς καὶ νικῆσαι διὰ τοῦ λόγου τῶν ἐντολῶν τὸν ἐν αὐτῷ τῶν παθῶν κόσμον, οὐδεμίαν ἕξει λοιπὸν θλίψιν· τὸν κόσμον ἐάσας ἤδη καὶ ἐν Χριστῷ γεγενημένος, τῷ τὸν κόσμον νικήσαντι τῶν παθῶν

nature and attain only the life of the spirit, those able to say, "And I no longer live, but Christ lives in me."[342]

2.93   Some say that the kingdom of heaven is the transferal of the worthy to the heavens; others, a condition of the saved similar to that of the angels; yet others, the form itself of the divine beauty of those who carry the image of the heavenly man.[343] And the three opinions concerning this matter harmonize with the truth, as it seems to me. For the future grace is given to all in proportion to the justice—its quality and quantity—that is in them.

2.94   For as long as someone courageously goes through the divine contests by way of practical philosophy, he clutches the Word to himself, who through the commandments went out from the Father into the world. And when he is released from wrestling with the passions through the practical life, as having been declared victor over passions and demons, he passes over to gnostic philosophy through contemplation, mystically makes way for the Word to leave the world again, and go to the Father. Therefore the Lord says to the disciples, "You have loved me, and have believed that I came from God. I came from the Father and have come into the world; again I leave the world and go to the Father,"[344] by "world" possibly meaning the accomplishment of the virtues through toilsome practice; by "Father" the supramundane condition in the mind also free from every material thought, by virtue of which the Word of God comes to be in us, resting from the fight with the passions and demons.

2.95   He who has been able to mortify his earthly members[345] through the practical life and to vanquish the world of the passions within him through the word of the commandments, will have no remaining affliction; he has already left the world and has come to

[342]Gal 2:20.
[343]Cf. 1 Cor 15:49.
[344]Jn 16:27–28.
[345]Cf. Col 3:5.

καὶ πάσης εἰρήνης χορηγῷ. Ὁ γὰρ τὴν προσπάθειαν τῶν ὑλικῶν μὴ ἀφείς, διὰ παντὸς θλίψιν ἕξει, τοῖς κατὰ φύσιν ἀλλοιουμένοις τὴν γνώμην συναλλοιούμενος. Ὁ δὲ γενόμενος ἐν Χριστῷ κατ᾽ οὐδένα λόγον αἰσθήσεται τῆς οἱασοῦν ὑλικῆς μεταπτώσεως. Διὸ φησιν ὁ Κύριος· Ταῦτα λελάληκα ὑμῖν, ἵνα ἐν ἐμοὶ εἰρήνην ἔχητε. Ἐν τῷ κόσμῳ θλίψιν ἕξετε, ἀλλὰ θαρσεῖτε, ἐγὼ νενίκηκα τὸν κόσμον. Τουτέστιν· ἐν ἐμοὶ τῷ Λόγῳ τῆς ἀρετῆς εἰρήνην ἔχετε· ἀπηλλαγμένοι τῆς τῶν ὑλικῶν παθῶν τε καὶ πραγμάτων στροβώσεώς τε καὶ ταραχῆς· ἐν δὲ τῷ κόσμῳ, τουτέστι ἐν τῇ προσπαθείᾳ τῶν ὑλικῶν, θλίψιν, διὰ τὴν αὐτῶν ἀλλεπάλληλον μετάπτωσιν. [1172] Θλίψιν γὰρ ἔχουσι ἀμφότεροι, καὶ ὁ πράττων τὴν ἀρετήν, διὰ τὸν αὐτῇ συνημμένον πόνον· καὶ ὁ τὸν κόσμον ἀγαπῶν, διὰ τὴν τῶν ὑλικῶν ἀποτυχίαν· ἀλλ᾽ ὁ μὲν θλίψιν σωτήριον, ὁ δὲ φθαρτικὴν καὶ ὀλέθριον. Ἀμφοτέρων δὲ ἐστιν ὁ Κύριος ἄνεσις· τοῦ μὲν καταπαύων ἐν ἑαυτῷ κατὰ τὴν θεωρίαν δι᾽ ἀπαθείας τοὺς πόνους τῶν ἀρετῶν, τοῦ δὲ τὴν πρὸς τὰ φθειρόμενα σχετικὴν προσπάθειαν διὰ τῆς μετανοίας ἀφαιρούμενος.

96 Ἡ ἐν τῷ τίτλῳ προγραφὴ τῆς τοῦ Σωτῆρος αἰτίας, πρακτικῆς καὶ φυσικῆς καὶ θεολογικῆς φιλοσοφίας ὄντα Βασιλέα τὸν σταυρωθέντα σαφῶς καὶ Κύριον ἔδειξε. Ῥωμαϊστὶ γὰρ καὶ Ἑλληνιστὶ καὶ Ἑβραϊστὶ φησιν ἀναγεγράφθαι τὸ λόγιον. Νοῶ δὲ διὰ μὲν τοῦ Ῥωμαϊστὶ τὴν πρακτικήν, ὡς τῆς Ῥωμαίων βασιλείας κατὰ τὸν Δανιὴλ ὁρισθείσης εἶναι πασῶν ἀνδρικωτέρας τῶν ἐπὶ γῆς βασιλειῶν· πρακτικῆς δὲ ἴδιον, εἴπερ τι ἄλλο, ἡ ἀνδρεία. Διὰ δὲ τοῦ Ἑλληνιστί, τὴν φυσικὴν θεωρίαν, ὡς μᾶλλον τοῦ Ἑλλήνων ἔθνους παρὰ τοὺς λοιποὺς ἀνθρώπους, τῇ φυσικῇ σχολάσαντος φιλοσοφίᾳ.

be in Christ, who has conquered the world of the passions, and is bestower of all peace. He who has not left the passionate attachment to material things, will constantly have affliction, since he changes his mentality along with things that are changeable by nature. He who has come to be in Christ in no way will have sensory perception of any material change whatsoever. Therefore the Lord says, "I have said these things to you, so that in me you might have peace. In the world you will have affliction, but be courageous: I have overcome the world."[346] That is, in me, the Word of virtue, "you have peace," being delivered from both the whirlwind and disorder of material passions and realities; "In the world," that is, in the passionate attachment to material things, "you will have affliction," on account of their successive change. For both have affliction: he who practices virtue, due to the toil involved in it, and he who loves the world, because of the disappointment of material things. But the former has salvific affliction, the latter corrupting and destructive affliction. The Lord is the abatement of both; of the former, by stopping in himself the toils of the virtues by contemplation through dispassion; of the latter by removing through repentance the relational passionate attachment to corruptible things.

2.96 The public warning in the inscription about the Savior's crime clearly showed the crucified man to be King and Lord of practical, natural, and theological philosophy. For they say the inscription had been written in Latin, Greek, and Hebrew.[347] And by Latin I understand practical philosophy, since according to Daniel[348] the kingdom of the Romans had been appointed to be more courageous than all the other kingdoms on the earth; since a property of practical philosophy, among other things, is courage; and by Greek I understand natural contemplation, since the nation of the Greeks has dedicated itself to natural philosophy more than the rest of

[346]Jn 16:33.
[347]Cf. Jn 19:20.
[348]Cf. Dn 2:40.

Διὰ δὲ τοῦ Ἑβραϊστί, τὴν θεολογικὴν μυσταγωγίαν, ὡς τοῦ ἔθνους τούτου προδήλως ἀνέκαθεν τῷ Θεῷ τοὺς πατέρας ἀνατεθέντος.

97 Δεῖ μὴ μόνον ἡμᾶς εἶναι παθῶν σωματικῶν φονευτάς, ἀλλὰ καὶ τῶν κατὰ ψυχὴν ἐμπαθῶν λογισμῶν ὀλετῆρας, κατὰ τὸν λέγοντα ἅγιον· Εἰς τὰς πρωΐας ἀπέκτενον πάντας τοὺς ἁμαρτωλοὺς τῆς γῆς τοῦ ἐξολοθρεῦσαι ἐκ πόλεως Κυρίου πάντας τοὺς ἐργαζομένους τὴν ἀνομίαν, τουτέστι, τὰ τοῦ σώματος πάθη, καὶ τῆς ψυχῆς τοὺς ἀνομοῦντας λογισμούς.

98 Ὁ τὴν ὁδὸν τῶν ἀρετῶν χωρὶς τῆς ἐφ᾽ ἑκάτερα ῥοπῆς μετ᾽ εὐσεβοῦς καὶ ὀρθῆς γνώσεως συντηρήσας ἀλώβητον εἴσεται τὴν γινομένην πρὸς αὐτὸν τοῦ Θεοῦ διὰ τῆς ἀπαθείας παρουσίαν. Ψαλῶ γὰρ καὶ συνήσω ἐν ὁδῷ ἀμώμῳ πότε ἥξεις πρός με. Ὁ γὰρ ψαλμὸς τὴν ἐνάρετον πρᾶξιν δηλοῖ· ἡ δὲ σύνεσις τὴν ἐπ᾽ ἀρετῇ γνωστικὴν ἐπιστήμην, καθ᾽ ἥν τῆς θείας αἰσθάνεται παρουσίας, ὁ δι᾽ ἀγρυπνίας τῶν ἀρετῶν προσδεχόμενος τὸν Κύριον αὐτοῦ.

99 Οὐ δεῖ τὸν εἰσαγόμενον εἰς εὐσέβειαν, διὰ μόνης ἄγεσθαι χρηστότητος πρὸς τὴν πρᾶξιν τῶν ἐντολῶν, ἀλλὰ μὴν καὶ τῇ μνήμῃ τῶν θείων δικαιωμάτων, δι᾽ ἀποτομίας συχνότερον αὐτὸν ἀγωνίσασθαι, ἐφ᾽ ᾧ μὴ μόνον πόθῳ τῶν θείων ἐρᾶν, ἀλλὰ καὶ φόβῳ τῆς κακίας ἀπέχεσθαι· Ἔλεον γὰρ καὶ κρίσιν ᾄσομαί σοι, Κύριε, ἵνα καὶ αὐδῇ τῷ Θεῷ κατὰ πόθον τερπόμενος καὶ εὐτονῇ πρὸς τὸ ᾆσμα, τῷ φόβῳ στομούμενος.

100 Ὁ δι᾽ ἀρετῆς καὶ γνώσεως ἁρμοσάμενος τὸ [1173] σῶμα πρὸς τὴν ψυχήν, γέγονε κιθάρα Θεοῦ καὶ αὐλὸς καὶ ναός. Κιθάρα μὲν ὡς καλῶς φυλάξας τὴν τῶν ἀρετῶν ἁρμονίαν, αὐλὸς δὲ ὡς διὰ τῶν

humanity. And by Hebrew I understand theological initiation, since this nation was clearly set up by God from above as the forbearers.

2.97 It is necessary for us to be not only murderers of bodily passions, but also eradicators of impassioned thoughts in the soul, according to the holy man who said, "At dawn I killed all the sinners of the earth in order to eradicate from the city of the Lord all who commit lawlessness,"[349] that is, the passions of the body and the lawless thoughts of the soul.

2.98 He who with pious and right knowledge preserves unblemished the way of the virtues without turning to either side, will know through dispassion God's presence taking place in him. "For I will sing a psalm, and I will be sagacious in a blameless way when you are with me."[350] Now, the psalm indicates the virtuous practical life; the sagacity, scientific knowledge founded upon virtue, by which he who receives his Lord through indefatigable attention to the virtues has a perception of the divine presence.

2.99 It is not necessary for him who is being inducted into piety to be led to the practice of the commandments by kindness alone, but also, in fact, for him to contend more often with rigor by the reminder of the divine retributions, for him not only to love divine things with desire, but also for him to abstain from vice with fear: For "I will sing to you, oh Lord, about mercy and judgment,"[351] that he might sing to God delighted by desire, and have strength for the song, hardened by fear.

2.100 He, who through virtue and knowledge has adapted the body to the soul, has become a lyre of God, a flute, and a temple. A lyre, as having beautifully kept the harmony of the virtues, a flute,

[349] Ps 100/101:8.
[350] Ps 100/101:1–2.
[351] Ps 100/101:1. Cf. *Carit.* 1.81–82.

θείων θεωρημάτων εἰσδεχόμενος τὴν τοῦ Πνεύματος ἔμπνευσιν, ναὸς δὲ ὡς διὰ τὴν κατὰ νοῦν καθαρότητα τοῦ Λόγου γεγονὼς κατοικητήριον.

as receiving through divine contemplations the insufflation of the Spirit, and a temple, as having become by purity in mind the dwelling place of the Word.[352]

---

[352]Cf. Eph 2:22.

Bibliography

Primary Sources by Editor

Baehrens, W.A. *Origenes Werke. Homiliae in Genesim.* GCS 29. Leipzig: Teubner, 1920.

Boor, C. de. *Theophanis chronographia*, vol. 1. Hildesheim: Olms, 1963.

Brock, Sebastian P. *An Early Syriac Life of Maximus the Confessor.* In *Analecta Bollandiana*, 91 (1973), pp. 299–346.

Cantarella, R. S. *Massimo Confessore. La mistagogia ed altri scritti.* Florence: Testi Cristiani, 1931.

Ceresa-Gastaldo, Aldo. *Massimo Confessore: Capitoli sulla carità.* VS 3. Rome: Editrice Studium: Rome, 1963.

Combefis, Franciscus. *Sancti Maximi Confessoris, Graecorum theologi eximiique philosophi; Operum tomum primus.* Paris: 1675.

Constas, Nicolas. *On Difficulties in the Church Fathers: The Ambigua, Volumes 1 and 2.* DOML 28, 29. Cambridge, MA: Harvard University Press, 2014.

Cooke, H.P. and Hugh Tredennick. *Aristotle: Categories, On Interpretation, Prior Analytics.* LCL 325. Cambridge, MA: Harvard University Press, 1938.

Daniélou, Jean. *Grégoire de Nysse. La vie de Moïse*, 3rd ed. SC 1. Paris: Éditions du cerf, 1968.

Declerck, J.H. *Maximi Confessoris quaestiones et dubia.* CCSG 10. Turnhout: Brepols, 1982.

Dodds, E.R. *Proclus. The Elements of Theology*, 2nd ed. Oxford: Clarendon Press, 1977.

Gallay, Paul. *Grégoire de Nazianze. Discours 27–31.* SC 250. Paris: Éditions du cerf, 1978.

Guillaoumont A. and C. Guillaumont. *Évagre le Pontique. Traité pratique ou le moine*, vol. 2. SC 171. Paris: Éditions du cerf, 1971.

Görgemanns, H. and H. Karpp. *Origenes vier Bücher von den Prinzipien.* Darmstadt: Wissenschatfliche Buchgesellschaft, 1976.

Hett, W.S. *Aristotle: On the Soul, Parva Naturalia, On Breath.* LCL 288. Cambridge, MA: Harvard University Press, 1936.

Heil, G. and A. M. Ritter. *Corpus Dionysiacum ii: Pseudo-Dionysius Areopagita. De coelesti hierarchia, de ecclesiastica hierarchia, de mystica theologia, epistulae.* PTS 36. Berlin: De Gruyter, 1991.

Jäger, Werner. *Gregorii Nyseni Opera.* Leiden: Brill, 1960ff.

Laga, Carl and Carlos Steel. *Maximi Confessoris Quaestiones ad Thalassium,* vols. 1 and 2. CCSG 7, 22. Turnhout: Brepols, 1980, 1990.

_____. *Maxime le Confesseur: Questions à Thalassios, Tome 1 (Questions 1 à 40).* SC 529. Paris: Cerf, 2010.

Migne, J.P. ed. *Patrologia Cursus Completus: Patrologia Graeca.* Vols. 14, 17, 79, 90, 91, 103. Turnhout: Brepols, 1979.

Rauer, M. *Origenes Werke,* vol. 9, 2nd ed. GCS 49 (35). Berlin: Akademie Verlag, 1959.

Sinkewicz, R.E. *Saint Gregory Palamas, The One Hundred and Fifty Chapters.* ST 83. Toronto: Pontifical Institute of Medieval Studies, 1988.

Suchla, B.R. *Corpus Dionysiacum i: Pseudo-Dionysius Areopagita. De divinibus nominibus.* PTS 33. Berlin: De Gruyter, 1990.

Tredennick, H. *Aristotle: The Metaphysics, Books I–IX.* LCL 271. Cambridge, MA: Harvard University Press, 1975.

_____. *Aristotle: The Metaphysics, Books X–XIV.* LCL 287. Cambridge, MA: Harvard University Press, 1969.

Wendland, P. *Philonis Alexandrini opera quae supersunt,* vols. 1–5. Berlin: Reimer, 1897–1906.

Secondary Sources

Bathrellos, Demetrios. *The Byzantine Christ.* Oxford: Oxford University Press, 2004.

Bury, J.B. *History of the Later Roman Empire,* vol 2. New York: Dover, 1958.

Cooper, Adam. *Holy Flesh, Wholly Deified.* Oxford: Oxford University Press, 2005.

De Angelis, Bernardo. *Natura, persona, libertà: L'antropologia di Massimo il Confessore.* Rome: Armando Editore, 2002.

Garrigues, Juan Miguel. *Maxime le Confesseur: La charité: Avenir divine de l'homme.* Paris: Beauchesne, 1976.

Gersh, Stephen. *From Iamblichus to Eriugena*. Leiden: Brill, 1978.

Karayiannis, Vasilios. *Maxime le Confesseur: Essence et énergies de Dieu*. Paris: Beauchesne, 1993.

Kulakovskij, Julian. "K kritike izvestij Feofana o poslednem gode pravlenija Foki." *Vizantijskij Vremenik* 21, (1914).

Larchet, *La divinisation de l'homme selon saint Maxime le Confesseur*. Paris: Éditions du cerf, 1996.

Lackner, W. "Der Amtstitel Maximos des Bekenners." *Jahrbuch der Österreichischen Byzantinistik* 20 (1971), 63–65.

Levčenko, M. "Venety i prasiny v Vizantii v V–VII vv," *Vizantijskij Vremenik* 26 (1947).

Louth, Andrew. *Maximus the Confessor*. New York: Routledge, 1999.

Michaud, E. "S. Maxime le confesseur et l'Apocataste." *Revue Internationale de Théologie* 10, 1902.

Mondin, Battista. *L'uomo secondo il disegno di Dio: trattato di antropologia teologica*. Bologna: Edizioni Studio Domenicano, 1992.

Ostrogorsky, George. *History of the Byzantine State*. Translated: Joan Hussey. New Brunswick, NJ: Rutgers University Press, 1969.

Pareti, Luigi. "Verdi e azzurri ai tempi di Foca," *Studi Italiani di Filologia Classica*, 19 (1912), 305–315.

Perl, Eric. "Methexis: Creation, Incarnation, Deification in St. Maximus Confessor." Yale University, Ph.D. Dissertation, 1991.

Riou, Alain. *Le monde et l'église selon Maxime le Confesseur*. Paris: University of Paris Press, 1973.

Sherwood, Polycarp. *An Annotated Date-List of the Works of Maximus the Confessor*. Rome: Herder, 1952.

_____. *The Earlier Ambigua of St. Maximus the Confessor*. Rome: Orbis Catholicus, 1955.

Thunberg, Lars. *Microcosm and Mediator: The Theological Anthropology of St. Maximus the Confessor*. 2nd ed. Chicago: Open Court Publishing Company, 1995.

Tollefsen, Torstein. *The Christocentric Cosmology of St. Maximus the Confessor*. Oxford: Oxford University Press, 2008.

Von Balthasar, Hans Urs. *Kosmische Liturgie*. 2nd ed. Einsiedeln: Johannes Verlag, 1961.

POPULAR PATRISTICS SERIES

ST VLADIMIR'S SEMINARY PRESS
1-800-204-2665 • www.svspress.com